Chris Scott's first big walking adventure took him along the Pennine Way in the hot summer of 1976. It's all been downhill since then, but he did manage to update previous editions of Trailblazer's *Coast to Coast* and *Pennine Way* guides. He also writes about the Sahara, vehicle overlanding and packboats.

Author

Glyndŵr's Way
First edition: 2024

Publisher: Trailblazer Publications (⌨ trailblazer-guides.com)
The Old Manse, Tower Rd, Hindhead, Surrey, GU26 6SU, UK

British Library Cataloguing in Publication Data
A catalogue record for this book is available from the British Library

ISBN 978-1-912716-32-6

© **Trailblazer** 2024: text and maps

Series Editor: Anna Jacomb-Hood **Editor**: Nicky Slade **Cartography**: Nick Hill
Proofreading: Bryn Thomas & Jane Thomas **Layout**: Nicky Slade **Index**: Jane Thomas
Illustrations: © Nick Hill (pp68-71) **Photographs** (flora): © Bryn Thomas
All other photographs: © Chris Scott (unless otherwise indicated)

The maps in this guide were prepared from out-of-Crown-
copyright Ordnance Survey maps amended and updated by Trailblazer.

Acknowledgements
Thanks, as ever, to all at Trailblazer: Nicky Slade for editing, Nick Hill for maps, Jane
Thomas for proofreading and index. Thanks, too, to Nick S for lodgings and lifts, Angela
W for late night taxi services, Jason for last-minute poly-tunnel camping, and modelling
services from Barry and Richard. Dave McGlade at the Offa's Dyke Association was very
helpful in pointing the way towards the obscure origins of this trail, greatly helped by Jo
Hindes's additional research at the Natural Resources Wales in Bangor, as well as
Amanda at Powys CC Archives in Llandrindod Wells.

A request
The author and publisher have tried to ensure that this guide is as accurate and up to date
as possible. Nevertheless, things do change. If you notice any changes or omissions for
the next edition, please contact us at Trailblazer (⌨ info@trailblazer-guides.com). A free
copy of the next edition will be sent to persons making a significant contribution.

Warning: hill walking can be dangerous
Please read the notes on when to go (pp14-16) and health and safety (pp76-82 & p173).
Every effort has been made by the author and publisher to ensure that the information
contained herein is as accurate and up to date as possible. However, they are unable to
accept responsibility for any inconvenience, loss or injury sustained by anyone as a result
of the advice and information given in this guide.

Updated information on: ⌨ trailblazer-guides.com

Photos – Front cover and this page: Below Foel Fadian,
near the highest point on the walk (505m, Map 27)
Previous page: Clywedog Reservoir, from the trail on the way to Hafren Forest (Map 23)
Overleaf: On the Pumlumon (Plynlimon) Fawr Horseshoe (see pp173-80)

Printed in Malaysia through D'Print Pte Ltd

Glyndŵr's
WAY

62 large-scale maps & guides to 20 towns and villages
PLANNING – PLACES TO STAY – PLACES TO EAT
KNIGHTON–WELSHPOOL–KNIGHTON

CHRIS SCOTT

TRAILBLAZER PUBLICATIONS

Contents

INTRODUCTION

PART 1: PLANNING YOUR WALK

Practical information for the walker

Itineraries

What to take

Getting to and from the Glyndŵr's Way

PART 2: HISTORY, ENVIRONMENT AND NATURE

History of the Welsh rebellion

The environment and nature

Flora and fauna

PART 3: MINIMUM IMPACT WALKING & OUTDOOR SAFETY

Minimum impact walking

Health and outdoor safety

PART 4: ROUTE GUIDE AND MAPS

Using this guide 83

↖ = walking clockwise ↙ = walking anti-clockwise

APPENDICES

Contents

ABOUT THIS BOOK

This guidebook contains all the information you need to undertake all or parts of the Glyndŵr's Way so you can plan your trip without having to consult numerous websites and other books and maps. When you're ready to go, there's comprehensive public transport information to get you to and from the trail and detailed maps (1:20,000) to help you find your way along it.

● Reviews of campsites, hostels, B&Bs, guesthouses and hotels
● Walking companies if you want an organised tour or your luggage carried
● Itineraries for all levels of walkers
● Answers to all your questions: when is the best time to walk, how hard is it, what to pack and the approximate cost of the trip
● Walking times and how to use GPS tracklogs as a back-up to navigation
● Cafés, pubs, tea-shops, restaurants, and shops/supermarkets along the route
● Rail, bus and taxi information for the towns and villages on or near the Way
● Street maps of the main towns and villages
● Historical, cultural and geographical background information

Note that this edition of the guide is liable to more change than usual. Some of the B&Bs, hotels, pubs, restaurants and tourist attractions may not survive the hardships caused by rising fuel prices, inflation and staff shortages. Do forgive us where your experience on the ground contradicts what is written in the book; please email us – info@trailblazer-guides.com so we can add your information to the updates page on the website.

❏ **MINIMUM IMPACT FOR MAXIMUM INSIGHT**

Nature's peace will flow into you as the sunshine flows into trees. The winds will blow their freshness into you and storms their energy, while cares will drop off like autumn leaves. **John Muir** (one of the world's first and most influential environmentalists, born in 1838)

Why is walking in wild and solitary places so satisfying? Partly it is the sheer physical pleasure: sometimes pitting one's strength against the elements and the lie of the land. The beauty and wonder of the natural world and the fresh air restore our sense of proportion and the stresses and strains of everyday life slip away. Whatever the character of the countryside, walking in it benefits us mentally and physically, inducing a sense of well-being, an enrichment of life and an enhanced awareness of what lies around us. All this the countryside gives us and the least we can do is to safeguard it by supporting rural economies, local businesses, and low-impact methods of farming and land-management, and by using environmentally sensitive forms of transport – walking being pre-eminent.

About this book

INTRODUCTION

The 'Hidden Heartland of Wales' is how National Trail promotional postcards describe the Glyndŵr's Way, and they're not wrong. Looping off Offa's Dyke for **134.5 miles (216.5km)** across the width of Powys and back to the English border at Welshpool, 'the Forgotten Path' might be another name for this overlooked National Trail. The walk

> The trail threads a tenuous link between places associated with Glyndŵr's 15th century rebellion against the English

straddles a sparsely populated 'No-Man's Land' between the some-times over-run tourist enclaves of Snowdonia and the Brecon Beacons. Once on the walk, if you do meet another soul, it's more likely to be a working local than a fellow hiker.

Some mystery surrounds the founding of the walk in the mid-1970s (see p10) which commemorates **Owain Glyndŵr**, a 15th-century Welsh 'Braveheart' little known beyond Wales. The trail threads a tenuous link between places associated with Glyndŵr's rebellion against the English, though once you're underway there's little evidence of his deeds which spanned the entire country. None of that detracts from your ramble across the eerie moors, upland sheep pastures, old droving roads, river valleys, woodlands and forests of mid-Wales.

Obviously you can walk Glyndŵr's Way in

Owain Glyndŵr statue, Corwen

INTRODUCTION

The Way sometimes follows ancient Roman tracks which evolved into drove roads.

❏ TRAIL FACTS

Today's Glyndŵr's Way has barely a level mile with, according to our GPS data, an **average daily climb of 2500 feet** (773m) over a typical 15-mile day (24km) and usually with a very similar descent. Stages 6 and 7 are over 3000ft (900m plus), with the last two stages both under 1900ft (570m), though you may not think so by then. Factor in bad weather or nagging injuries and a fair number of walkers don't complete the trail in one sweep.

Though it doesn't feel like it, **just over a quarter** of the walk (about 36 miles) is on asphalt, almost all **deserted country lanes**. Take heart that the original 1970s route was nearly twice that. But remarkably, the trail crosses busier A roads just half a dozen times and on the one occasion outside a town's high street it *follows* an A road (Map 34), there's a wide verge.

At any other time you're walking along a wide, surfaced track along which you could slowly drive a car – as in the forestry sections. Elsewhere, tracks possibly dating back to Roman times are covered in turf – the best surface to walk on and which may have become **droving** byways that never evolved into modern roads. Tracks then narrow into paths until they're no wider than a sheep's gait, or diffuse into a barely discernible line across a grassy field. Lacking an accurately aligned fingerpost, this is where our maps or a GPS tracklog (see p19) can help you know where to aim for.

In the interests of privacy as well as not getting run over by a reversing threshing

machine, you'll often see the path make a dogleg around a farmyard or property. It can feel a little odd or even intimidating marching through a working farmyard which can also set off a chorus of furious barking from some (hopefully well-tethered) dogs.

In high summer upland patches of **Access Land** (England and Wales' version of 'right to roam', see p75) may be almost completely obscured by thick, shoulder-high **bracken** which often also obscures the knee-high waymarking posts (**photo left**) sometimes used. At this time of year you'll also encounter fields of tall thistles, some of which can resemble **marker posts** (see p17) from afar and briefly lead you astray.

Down on the rolling pastures you're often walking alongside a **boundary line** which can be a wire fence, a hedgerow of hawthorns, rowan or other small trees which can become an avenue. Elsewhere you parallel a gnarled line of deformed trees that were once coppiced and laid over to make a multi-trunked fence line with stones or thorny stuffing filling the gaps. At other times you'll pass the edge of an old-growth woodland copse or a conifer plantation, and only south of Llanbadarn and around Machynlleth will you notice a few hundred yards of dry-stone slate walls or their remnants.

either direction or start in the middle and walk backwards, but most tackle the trail in the intended, **clockwise** sweep from Knighton to Welshpool. As the route is a horseshoe rather than linear, you end up in the same locale on the once much-fought-over English border, with Welshpool having the better transport links. Wherever you finish up, you can then close a loop by walking a further two days and 28 miles (45km) along Offa's Dyke to either terminus.

South of Machynlleth the energetic might also take a day out to bag the 2467-foot (752m) summit of **Pumlumon Fawr**, the highest point in mid-Wales. Our new cross-country route to and from the summit passes close to the site of Glyndŵr's first big victory over the English at Mynydd Hyddgen.

Then we have **gates and stiles** and National Trails have overseen a whole lot of work replacing stiles with gates. Stiles effectively exclude rogue motorbikers, but owners of big dogs don't like them and neither will you feel safe on them when they've been unmaintained for decades (**photo right**).

According to 🖳 en.powys.gov.uk (search 'footpaths'), the '*landowner is responsible for making sure that any stiles and gates are kept in a good state of repair. We have a duty to make sure that landowners do this and to offer a grant of 25% towards repairing or replacing gates and stiles*'. This task can be assisted by your feedback to officials at Powys County Council or National Trails, even if it may not always generate a response. Having said that, long overdue action was taken in 2022 to repair the decrepit flight of steps below 'The Warren' woods just north of Llwydiarth/Pont Llogel (Map 46), with the nearby stiles possibly becoming gates too. In other places, one or two landowners have insisted on fitting solid new timber stiles without adjacent gates, while one, mile-long section out of Llangadfan has half-a-dozen wobbly stiles. All in all, there were only about **a dozen stiles** on the Glyndŵr's Way when we passed through.

That leaves a whole lot of **gates**; we estimate up to 500 with, for example, about 70 between Machynlleth and Llanbrynmair alone. Compare that to the Pennine Way which is twice as long and is said to have nearly 300 gates but with many more miles of drystone walls and about 450 stone- or wooden stiles.

In most cases these gates are handy points to mount National Trail waymarking roundels to avoid confusion with other nearby gates. Some are full-width galvanised field gates which swing open at the lightest touch before swinging back unaided onto self-locking latches. Nearly all narrower, walker-sized bridle gates are self-locking too. Elsewhere, older field gates have collapsed from their hinges and rest on stiff slide bolts which not everyone will have the strength to lift and operate. A few are tied up with knotted nylon twine or use a less annoying twine loop to lasso the post when the original latch has failed. One thing we did find was that in high summer more field gates are **left open**, presumably to allow animals to wander from field to field.

Covering the entire route twice between March and August, we barely found any **boggy** or muddy sections compared to the notorious mires of northern England and the Highlands. But our March walk followed a dry winter and the August one was in the middle of a record-breaking hot summer, so all that could change. What mud you do encounter is most often caused by trampling by rarely-seen lowland cattle rather than leg-swallowing peat. The moorland wastes of our Pumlumon Fawr horseshoe side trip (see p173) are an exception.

Looking down on Machynlleth, near the halfway point, a perfect place to break your walk.

On our maps you'll also find out-of-town **benches** for a bit of a sit down, as well as indications where **short-cuts** along backroads might shorten your walk at either end of the day if you're running late or have had enough.

Machynlleth is one of only two towns along the actual route, the site of Owain Glyndŵr's short-lived 1404 parliament and crowning as the last native Prince of Wales. The other is Llanidloes. With Welshpool and Knighton at either end, they are referred to as the 'four towns'.

Origins of the Glyndŵr's Way trail

A lack of places of refreshment is more than compensated for by the splendid isolation of central Wales and there can be but few paths where in fairly regular Saturday [day] walks, no other walkers were met… **Peter Weetman**, ODA Newsletter, 1983

The idea for a 'Glyndŵr's Way' was proposed by an as-yet unidentified individual as a Powys County Council (PCC) initiative. According to a 1983 walker's report for the Offa's Dyke Association (ODA; quoted above), a long-distance path signposted as 'Glyndŵr's Way' existed as early as 1978. At this time both the Pembrokeshire Coast Path and Offa's Dyke Path had been National Trails since 1970 and 1971 respectively, so there may have been a momentum to establish more such trails in Wales.

The project made use of the Manpower Services Commission, a training and job creation scheme established by the government in 1973 to tackle unemployment,

Left: The Market Hall, Llanidloes (see p111) dates from the early 1600s.

INTRODUCTION

Owain Glyndŵr's Parliament House in Machynlleth (see p129).

though how this translated into trailblazing a long-distance path is unclear. The trail was presumably intended as a prestige project for newly formed Powys CC, amalgamated in 1974 from counties including Radnorshire and Montgomeryshire through which today's walk passes. Glyndŵr's armies actually roamed far and wide across the four corners of Wales, but keeping the project in one administrative authority greatly simplified its management. This may explain why, for example, Sycharth, Owain Glyndŵr's ancestral estate and possible birthplace just 10 miles off the path, is excluded – it wasn't in Powys in 1974.

By the summer of 1977, 16 illustrated leaflets describing history and folklore along the 132-mile walk were published by the PCC Planning Information Service; the basic maps being revised over the years until the walk gained National Trail status in 2002. The original route was compromised by a scarcity of contiguous footpaths so ended up following country roads because PCC had no authority to create new Rights of Way – a power limited to the then Countryside Council for Wales. All these things had to be addressed before the National Trail could give their stamp of approval many years later.

While the walk has a historical rather than geographical theme, its start and end were sensibly based on rail access at Knighton and Welshpool. These are among Powys' half dozen largest towns which goes to show what a sparsely populated county it is – Canterbury has a larger population. Both termini being on the Offa's Dyke Path also enabled closing the loop with a two-day walk back to the start point. Machynlleth, also on the the rail network and the self-styled 'ancient capital of Wales', was always going to be the walk's focal point.

Right: Ruins of the Bryntail lead mine below Clywedog dam wall (see p122). In the 1870s Wales was the world's top lead producer.

Above and below: Lake Vyrnwy with its stone dam wall and iconic tower was built in the 1880s to supply Liverpool with clean water.

By 1990 plans were afoot to upgrade the route to a National Trail, with PCC appointing a Glyndŵr's Way Project Officer in 1993. The plan was duly approved and public funds were allocated to upgrade the path to the required standards, which included a somewhat subjective 'scenic' rating that's been successfully achieved. When you think of the decades it took for the Pennine Way (Britain's first National Trail), or even Alfred Wainwright's more popular Coast to Coast (due 2025) to be similarly beatified by the hallowed acorn icon, the ascent of Glyndŵr's Way occurred in record time.

In 1995 the Glyndŵr's Way Project Report was submitted to the Countryside Council for Wales (today: Natural Resources Wales, see p57), the latest body which was funding the route. It stressed the need for environmental sustainability as well as tangible economic benefits to local communities. Subsequently, further route refinements were negotiated with relevant parties and landowners; today's sometimes tortuous routing may be a result of those delicate negotiations, rightly driven by the wish to avoid tarmac roads. Some landowners may have been uncomfortable with new footpaths cutting across their land, as well as the projected '3000 walkers per year' – about the number who walk Offa's Dyke Path or the Pennine Way which have had to tackle localised path erosion. The 'nimbys' needn't have worried; it's doubtful if annual usage has ever exceeded a few hundred, even after the first independent guidebook by Richard Sale was published in 1985.

The turn of the millennium coincided with the 600th anniversary of Owain Glyndŵr's rebellion and just two years after the founding of a devolved Welsh Assembly (now known as the *Senedd Cymru* or Welsh Parliament). That year a much improved and officially '135-mile' (217km) **Glyndŵr's Way** (*Llwybr Glyndŵr*) **National Trail** was announced but officially

opened in Machynlleth in 2002 with dignitaries including cricketer, Ian Botham who was setting off to Cardiff on one of his many charity walks. Despite this auspicious start, today Glyndŵr's Way remains the National Trail you're most likely to have all to yourself, while being as satisfying as any other long walk in the remoter corners of the beautiful British countryside.

How difficult is Glyndŵr's Way?

Ideally Glyndŵr's Way won't be the very first time you set out to walk for days cross-country. So as well as being reasonably fit and for the moment, injury-free, it's important that you also have a feel for route finding, handling yourself in the wilds and a good understanding of the equipment you'll need to achieve that.

The difficulty in walking the Glyndŵr's Way is not so much in the terrain or prolonged, back breaking gradients – there are few of the latter. The **challenge** will be in establishing an itinerary that strikes an achievable balance between your **stamina** and **somewhere to rest your head for the night for several consecutive days**. This book divides the walk into the **nine stages** that end with the best availability of places to stay, which means sustaining a **15-mile average** to reach each night's necessarily **booked accommodation**. This is what puts you under pressure if you're having a rough time, because even then, some of the stages end with barely two lodging options to rub together. And should you reach a road midway through the day and want to bail out early, there are **few**

The church at Abbeycwmhir with its neo-Byzantine tower. The ruins of the Cistercian abbey (see p104) are also in the village.

Several of the 1865 slate county boundary stones that marked the border between Powys and Dyfed can still be seen on the Pumlumon Fawr Horseshoe side trip (see pp173-80).

transport links, or indeed much traffic at all along country lanes. Some villages list one bus a week so you're very much **on your own**.

If you're unsure you can manage 15 miles day for well over a week, consider shorter daily averages (see boxes pp34-5), although this then creates further challenges with reaching your accommodation. A much better idea is to **break the walk** at Machynlleth more or less halfway, where you might take a day off or head home to return at leisure. Otherwise, walking at least 134 miles nonstop in nine days may put you at risk of injury or drop you into a spell of miserable weather because you had to book your lodgings weeks or months ago and can't get off the ride. And remember that these days, bad weather for walking might include exceedingly hot days. In July 2022 Machynlleth hit a record 35°C, at which point some locals swear they saw the long-dormant town clock twitch for a few magical seconds.

How long do you need?

The established timeframe to walk Glyndŵr's Way is **nine days**, in clearly defined stages which occasionally feel as though they meander around the countryside until they reach a place with lodgings. This book adopts that well-proven staging but also suggests alternatives for **longer** and **shorter** durations (see boxes pp34-7). However, unlike other long-distance walks in the UK, note that these alternative schedules can end some distance from the scant lodging options, which requires either back-up transport or wild camping (see p22). Though most aspire to walk the whole Glyndŵr's Way in one go, you don't

See p34-7 for some suggested itineraries covering different walking speeds

Opposite: On the trail between Llanidloes and Dylife.

have to do it like this and, as already suggested, you may well have a more enjoyable time if you tackle it in sections on separate occasions.

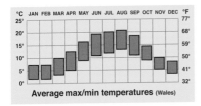

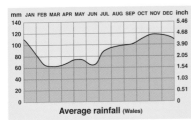

Average max/min temperatures (Wales)

Average rainfall (Wales)

When to go

SEASONS

Not surprisingly, the months when the weather is less likely to be inclement are May to September. With the odd freezing night, April and October often bring bright and breezy days when the surroundings can be at their best, particularly in autumn. Note the elevation profiles on the colour maps (pp195-204) as the first half of the walk puts you above 1300ft (400m) every day.

Spring April can be warm and sunny on odd days but seldom for sustained periods. Conditions are more likely to be changeable, with blustery showers, freezing nights and a bleakness reminding you that winter has only just passed. On the other hand, less rain falls on average in spring than at any other time of the year. We did our initial pass in mid-March catching a two-day 'heatwave' around Dylife, followed by just one brief battering of hail in early April. The milder weather of May and June

makes it one of the best times to tackle the trail. There's also something to be said for the trail not being overgrown, as it can be in high summer.

Summer July and August are the busier holiday months and though the conditions are usually ideal for walking, with a greater likelihood of long periods of warm settled weather and many hours of daylight, the popularity of mid-Wales means accommodation options may be lean, even if the chance of meeting fellow walkers on the actual trail is still rare.

Autumn Late September and October are a good time to be on the trail to appreciate the full benefit of the autumn colours in the woodland. Although the air temperature can remain relatively mild, October can see the first frosts, and rain is an ever-present misery, intensifying as the year draws to its close. Nevertheless, many connoisseurs consider autumn the best time of year for walking.

Winter Even though they're becoming milder and snow is now rare, only the hardiest of souls will attempt the walk in winter. **Short days** mean you'll want to be at your day's end by 4-5pm. Colder days, wind and driving rain will make conditions tough although you can hit lulls when the sun comes out.

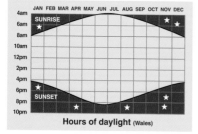

Hours of daylight (Wales)

DAYLIGHT HOURS

If walking in autumn, winter and early spring, you must take account of how far you can walk in the available daylight. The table (left) gives the sunrise and sunset times (Greenwich Mean Time) for the middle of each month at latitude 52.5° North which runs through Hafren Forest (Map 24), giving a reasonably accurate picture of daylight hours. Depending on the weather, you should get a further 30-45 minutes of usable light before sunrise and after sunset.

Below: It's well worth taking the Pumlumon Fawr Horseshoe side trip (see pp173-80).

Practical information for the walker

ROUTE FINDING

Once you get in tune with where to look and what to expect, you'll find the trail very well way-marked. A typical marker post may have a thick plastic yellow cap and up to **three roundels**: the white-on-black National Trail **acorn icon**; the gold-on-white '**Llwybr Glyndŵr**' Welsh dragon roundel (Owain Glyndŵr's battle standard), although the gold fill is often faded, leaving only the red dragon's outline; and most of the time a **yellow-on-black arrow** with a boot-print showing the way ahead. Often it's **blue-on-yellow** with a horse-shoe, indicating a cycleable bridleway (see pp181-2). These arrows indicating the direction of the trail ahead aren't always well aligned.

Without referring to this book's maps for orientation, **posts** are often the only way of knowing where to go. They can be full height and topped with the yellow plastic cap, but for some reason **knee-high posts** are also used which can disappear into in full summer bloom. Tall or short, a few of these have fallen down over the years – we re-erected a couple where possible but otherwise where this has happened, crossing a pathless field or hillside can be a shot in the dark. Time to refer to your compass alongside our maps or a GPS

❏ **ANNUAL EVENTS**

The following events may need to be considered when planning your walk as accommodation in the area is often booked up months in advance.

● **Machynlleth Comedy Festival** (🖳 machcomedyfest.co.uk) Around the first weekend in May; live comedy in interesting performance spaces.

● **Llanidloes Carnival** (**fb**) Second Saturday of July; bands, proces-sions, a children's workshop and floats and more.

● **Welshpool Country & Western Show** (🖳 countrywestern.org.uk). In mid-July.

● **Guilsfield Show** (🖳 guilsfieldshow.com) Second weekend in August; a community-run event including horses, dogs, horticulture, cookery, photography, floristry, arts and crafts and much more.

● **Knighton Show** (🖳 knightontc.wales/knighton-carnival, **fb**) Last Saturday in Aug; horticultural exhibitions, old cars, food stalls and dogs.

● **Gŵyl Machynlleth Festival** (🖳 moma.cymru/en/about/festival) End of August; a celebration of Welsh and international music and culture.

tracklog on your electronic device. Gadgets not your style? Even if you decide to simply blunder on in a likely direction, chances are you'll soon pick up the next post or waymarked gate. These posts are supplemented with weather-gnarled **finger posts.** Alongside a clear trail they may feel redundant but occasionally they do point with the precision of a Welsh archer over the brow of trackless field to a small gate hidden in the brush. Aided by the waymarking and following the trail maps in this book, the alert walker is unlikely to lose their orientation for more than a few minutes and will soon get a feel for where and how frequently a waymark ought to appear.

ELECTRONIC NAVIGATION AIDS AND MAPPING APPS

GPS on your smartphone

These days individuals who don't routinely clutch a **smartphone** every waking hour are regarded as eccentric. But not all devoted users appreciate that a modern mobile can receive a **GPS** signal from space as well as estimate your position often as accurately using **mobile data** signals from hilltop masts. These signals are two different things: GPS comes free from American, Russian or European satellites and is everywhere all the time but works best outdoors. Much stronger 4- or 5G mobile signals (some say too strong!) beam off towers up 40 miles away and are what you pay the phone company for.

Accessing an online map with mobile data (internet via your phone signal, not wi-fi), your position can be pinpointed with great accuracy, but only if you have a good signal, which is not the case in most of mid-Wales. Locals suggest '3' or EE are the least bad, but even some villages lack a mobile signal.

Unless you happen to own one with a decent-sized colour screen, there's little benefit in buying a **handheld GPS** device except that *with decent maps*

❏ WAYWARD WAYMARKERS: A MYSTERY

'Why are farmers purposely ripping out direction stickers [sic]. *Let's get lost around their farms!'*

This was the irate Sharpie message scrawled across the yellow cap on a post near Dylife. Chatting with a couple at the Clywedog café earlier that day, we'd been warned that the often-useful yellow arrow post roundels had been prised off or even unscrewed, leaving only the NT acorn and red Llwybr Glyndŵr dragon roundels. After being caught out and blundering across pathless fields, initially we too assumed a hacked-off farmer had sabotaged the posts, but to what benefit? Why would they want you staggering around their land, upsetting the ewes?

Next morning walking back up to join the trail from Dylife, we chatted with a local sheep farmer and son coming down the track on a quad. He explained that he'd long since given up trying to fathom the minds and actions of some walkers, and we concluded it must be some kind of targeted vandalism by persons unknown. Later visits revealed arrow roundels missing from just a mile out of Llanidloes which supports this theory – it was not a single farmer. Reporting the phenomenon and locations went unacknowledged, and returning a few months later roundels were still missing and some useful posts had fallen over too. This can be one occasion where having a tracklog (see opposite) on your device is helpful.

installed, you can be certain of establishing your location against a map anytime, any place, anywhere.

Mapping apps: paid vs free

The best way to use your mobile as a bombproof navigation aid is to **download a mapping app plus maps covering the Glyndŵr's Way**. That will work with GPS where there is no phone signal. The online map which shows the Glyndŵr's Way most accurately and consistently is the well-known **OS 1:50k Landranger and 1:25k Explorer series**. Pre-digital era hikers won't need persuading of OS maps' readability and reliability. On a Landranger, National Trails are marked as three red dashes then a red diamond, plus a 'Glyndŵr's Way' every once in a while. Zoom in to the 1:25k Explorer and it's the same pattern of dashes and diamonds, but in green. Ideally, your on-screen location dot is pulsing right on that track. Currently, the OS Maps app (🖥 shop.ord nancesurvey.co.uk/apps/os-maps-subscriptions) costs just £4.99 for a month – less than a single used OS paper map. By the year it's much cheaper.

Although there are free online maps and mapping apps, they don't have the same reliability. Younger users more familiar with Google Maps will find the path's orientation often incorrect, while free, user-editable OpenStreetMap (OSM) used by various platforms including 🖥 garmin.opentopomap.org/#great_britain, proved to be mostly hit, but occasionally miss, with the path disappearing in places. Other free phone mapping apps (search something like: 'Top 10 GPS navigation apps') might have adverts, or full functionality disabled until you cough up some money. The popular Maps.me app is targeted towards urban users and drivers, not hill walkers who benefit from OS levels of detail. On the current version Glyndŵr's Way is shown but very rarely identified alongside other adjacent paths and tracks, and so downloading a tracklog and our waypoints (see p20) may clarify the way ahead.

Download a free tracklog

The best way to secure free backup navigation in your digital gadget is to download a **tracklog**: a continuous, winding line marking the walk from end to end. It can be traced with a mouse off a digital map (as National Trails seem to have done off an OS), or recorded live using a GPS enabled device (as we did and Wikiloc contributors do; see below). When recorded live, tracklogs are actually hundreds of pinged waypoints separated by intervals of either time or more usefully distance (say, around 10 metres). Some smartphones or mapping apps can't display a tracklog with over 500 points so they get truncated into fewer straight lines like the NT version, resulting in some loss in precision.

Anyone can record or trace a tracklog, which can include errors or extraneous data. The most accurate we've found is on the user-generated **Wikiloc** global trail resource. First, download the free app from 🖥 wikiloc.com/outdoor-navigation-app, then the Glyndŵr's Way tracklog at 🖥 wikiloc.com/hiking-trails/glyndwrs-way-61276255. Recorded by a diligent Wikilocs contributor in 2020, we have verified this tracklog and, apart from an easily spotted glitch near the top of Gorn Road (our Map 19) and a couple of unedited return excursions to overnight lodgings (which prove it was recorded live, not traced off an online map), it follows the actual waymarked route precisely.

You can view the route on Wikilocs with various Open Source background maps, including high-resolution Esri satellite view, as used by the 'Maps' app included free with Apple OS, as well as the 'Aerial' layer in 🖳 bing.com/maps. In almost all cases Esri **satellite imagery** is clearer and newer than anything on Google, and 🖳 bing.com/maps also include OS Landranger/Explorer mapping as a layer; a very useful resource when combined with the 'Aerial' view, though the former may not be bang up to date.

As mentioned, National Trails have a free tracklog at 🖳 nationaltrail.co .uk/en_GB/trails/glyndwrs-way/trail-information – look for 'GPX downloads'. There is no NT associated mapping app, and at the time of research the NT tracklog was simplified and marginally less accurate than the Wikiloc example above. However, the only time it strayed up to 200m off the waymarked trail was on our maps 39 and 41, where it copied a rare example of inaccurate OS mapping. This suggests the NT tracklog is merely a tracing off an OS map – something anyone can do at home with a mapping app – and was not recorded by an actual walker. The best thing on the NT map page is being able to view the tracklog online over **zoomable OS mapping**, along with interactive features like some lodgings and shops.

Waypoints and what3words

Besides those navigation options, this book offers an additional one. The maps in the book all feature at least one numbered **waypoint**, marked directly onto the map. It corresponds with the list on pp181-3 which gives the position in **decimal degrees** (d.d.) as well as **what3words**, eg: 52.590562, -3.853296 ///betray ing.processes.vesting – alongside a description: 'Machynlleth town clock'. D.d. is the format common to mobile phones and the least error-prone. The ° (degree) symbol is not needed, but both the **comma** and the following **dash** must be used. The former signifies a waypoint, not a phone number or calculation; the latter dash means west of the Greenwich meridian. Dropping the dash signifies a longitude *east* of the meridian, so Machynlleth gets mirrored somewhere in the North Sea near Amsterdam.

You can either manually key the nearest presumed waypoint from the list at the back of this book into your phone/GPS (a process prone to user errors), or just download the list for free at 🖳 trailblazer-guides.com/gps-waypoints and take it from there. There are versions in both .kml and .gpx format; one will work on your phone or mapping app.

In summary

To recap: online versions of excellent OS maps (identical to their latest paper editions or maybe even more up-to-date) depict the Glyndŵr's Way with 99.9% accuracy, while the Wikilocs tracklog shows an accurate route which will display on any digital map or mapping app on your smartphone. Having the phone on standby and minimal other apps working will maximise your battery life, but obviously carrying a back-up power bank makes sense.

Stepping back a bit, we're on the Glyndŵr's Way, not the Tibetan plateau, so in clear conditions you'll rarely need to refer to your digital gadget for navigation. By and large the waymarking is crystal clear; often so is the track below your feet, and this book's hand-drawn maps show what lies ahead. 'Big picture' paper maps will help too (see p42). Without a phone and tracklog, aligning our maps with a magnetic compass will identify a bearing to take across pathless fields until the next gate or post becomes visible (usually a minute or two).

Whatever your navigation method, it does pay to **regularly keep track of your position** so when you go wrong you can tell where you've veered off. You're most likely to make a mistake due to fallen or otherwise obscured posts or waymarkers, or while chatting away. Backtracking usually solves that.

ACCOMMODATION

The Covid pandemic and subsequent crises have shaken up the range of lodgings along the Glyndŵr's Way. Traditional, retiree-run B&Bs and some pubs fell by the wayside. Of those that remain, some now require **two-night minimum** bookings, or have switched to self-catering by the week, all making less work between changeovers.

For the one-night wayfarer this leaves scant options away from the four towns; often a choice of just a couple of places which might add up to less than half a dozen beds. A comprehensive selection of places to stay along the full length of the trail is given in each section of the route guide, Part 4.

Although the interactive map on the National Trails Glyndŵr's page (▢ nationaltrail.co.uk/en_GB/trails/glyndwrs-way/trail-information) lists lodgings, these appear to be user-generated with no verification and are often hopelessly out-of-date. The LDWA (see box p43) offers a similar database but results seem even sketchier. To save you hours of internet searching and trawling through room-booking websites, we've done it all for you and more besides, so our list starting from p85 is as complete and up-to-date as could be at the time of going to press. Campsites apart, **wi-fi** is now ubiquitous so is only highlighted when it's not available.

Sifting though the options may choke your finely honed spirit of spontaneity because, outside of the cooler months you'll have to **book your accommodation** weeks ahead to secure a *full run* of lodgings for the entire ten nights in one sweep. Route finding being relatively straightforward, this is the primary challenge in the planning stage. At any time you'll be juggling ever-shrinking availability with a weather forecast or your own free time. One solution is to carry **lightweight camping gear** to fill the gaps; a tent, mat and sleeping bag fit for a cold night can weigh as little as 3.5kg (7.7lbs), and if it's just for a couple of nights, you can send it to a village post office or the previous night's planned lodgings for collection, then send it onward or back home from the next one.

Camping

On the Glyndŵr's Way, depending on your schedule, you'll find places to pitch your tent on most nights. These range from full-on campsites with ablution blocks and a trampoline, to a basic farmer's field with a tap on the end of a hose. **Costs** are from £5 for the latter and up to £25 for the former. By the time you get to campsite-free Abbeycwmhir, Dylife and Llanbrynmair you may welcome a break from your silnylon sarcophagus, or may have summoned up the nerve to camp wild (see p22).

Upmarket 'glamping' ranges from designer wooden sheds with a mattress, to quaintly decorated shepherd's huts and has become a big thing in mid-Wales. Often attached to a hot tub, the latter can be more of a B&B, but many of these 'lifestyle' places usually require a minimum booking of two nights. Even so, it's worth asking; some places make exceptions for Glyndŵrists or may have a one-night gap between longer bookings, but you need to call ahead to confirm this.

Attractive as the savings and vagabond's romance may be, not all of us can face the thought of camping every night for a week or more, especially if uncomfortable with wild camping. One good way of breaking things up is to factor in lodgings every second or third night, if for no other reason than to recharge your gadgets. Another way of reducing the effort and weight associated with cooking for yourself each evening is to eat in a pub or similar, while camping, wild or otherwise.

Campers will need to plan carefully to make sure they carry breakfast and lunch for two days on some stretches, as food outlets are few and far between outside the main towns. The longest *overnight* stage with no shops, pubs or cafés are the 23 miles (37km) from the Caffi Clywedog (Map 22) to Machynlleth, although near Dylife, Staylittle is just a mile off the route (Map 24).

Wild camping

Wild camping in England and Wales is only legal with the permission of the landowner. That said, we can offer some practical advice on wild camping along Glyndŵr's Way, whether out of necessity or preference, since the chances of running into or knowing how to contact the landowner are slim. A couple of farmers we asked at random said they'd ignore a lone tent on their land, while expecting it to be gone without trace next morning.

As the idea suggests, aim to do so in the wilds and out of sight of occupied properties. This will usually mean stopping a bit before or after the end of the stages given in this book. And if you're likely to be seen from afar (and the weather allows), consider not putting up your tent until dusk and aim to be gone early. A good way to do this is to identify a suitable spot, go and get a meal in a village pub or similar (where possible) then head back out into the dusk. Luckily, getting going on the trail early is one of the big advantages of wild camping.

Woodland, however scant, is well suited to stealth camping, but doing so alongside running water far from anywhere is a rare luxury, so anticipate your overnight needs and **fill up a water bag** from a stream or a tap. And even if there's wood all around, do not make open fires.

While offering little cover, the lofty expanses of the commons and moorland (more prevalent on the walk's southern arm) are also unlikely to raise anyone's ire and will offer some superb settings. Read between the lines of our route descriptions and maps identifying barns and isolated copses, while cross-referencing likely spots in advance using satellite imagery (the Esri platform is best; see p19). Other than that, carry and use a backpackers **trowel** to 'park the breakfast' so the only trace of your overnight visit is something that would require a dedicated CSI team to detect. In short, pitch late, move on early and leave nothing but some flattened foliage.

Bunkhouses

There are three bunkhouses all on- or within easy reach of the trail, coincidentally one night after the other at Llanidloes, Staylittle (Dylife) and Machynlleth costing from £20 in a dorm. All have self-catering facilities and Staylittle offers evening meals. 'Llani' and Staylittle are modern, purpose-built lodges catering for outdoors groups and are well worth a visit. The Machynlleth bunkhouse is one end of a converted attic in an old barn evoking the good old days.

B&B-style accommodation

Whether your accommodation calls itself a bed & breakfast (B&B), pub, inn, hotel or guesthouse, that won't necessarily indicate what to expect in terms of facilities or even price range, so check carefully before booking. See also p84.

● **Rates** Proprietors quote rates on a per-room or a per-person basis. Usually it's for a room so the capacity is limited by the number of beds. In this guide we quote rates on **a per person (pp) basis based on two sharing a room**; a typical B&B will range in price from £30pp for a nice room (in other words £60 for a room) and from £40pp for a room with en suite facilities. Pubs and guesthouses will charge £35-45pp and hotels are likely to charge £40pp or more. Bear in mind that hotel rates don't always include breakfast so check in advance.

Lone walkers occupying a twin or double room will pay the full room price unless there's a **single room rate** offered; rarely less than 70% of the full rate. It is often necessary to pay a deposit when making your booking online; this may be refunded if you cancel well in advance but is more commonly non-refundable unless you have a good story. Check the cancellation terms.

● **B&B** Usually a room in the owner's own home, the attraction lies in getting insight into the locality. Most rooms will have tea- and coffee-making facilities, a TV, wi-fi and an en suite, private or shared bathroom and the rate includes breakfast.

An en suite room attracts a premium even if it's just an elbow-bashing shower cubicle squeezed in a corner. So don't automatically turn your nose up at a bathroom across the corridor, which may have a deep, inviting **bath** to ease away the aches with a long hot soak.

Finding sustenance in the four towns is not a problem. The more isolated B&Bs will usually offer an **evening meal**, though you should always pre-book this. Where possible, ring ahead if you've been delayed on the trail since meals may be served at a set time. Alternatively hosts may drive you to the nearest pub if it's too far to walk.

● **Guesthouses** It's said guesthouses lack the personal touch of a good B&B but on Glyndŵr's Way you're unlikely to notice any difference, including price. The best guesthouses are those that 'cater for walkers', which means they understand the needs of a weary pilgrim clad in muddy boots and sodden water-proofs. They may have a **sitting room** (lounge) exclusively for guest use, a real bonus at the end of a day when retiring to your room instead of relaxing in a comfy chair can seem something of an anti-climax. It also gives you the opportunity to chat with the host or other guests.

● **Pubs and inns** Although you won't have far to hobble from your room downstairs to the restaurant, or have to risk the eccentricities of B&B hosts, bear in mind that a room above the bar on a Friday or Saturday night might be quite noisy. So unless you're getting stuck into the footie-loving melée, on these nights ask for a quiet room if possible.

● **Hotels** Some walkers are reluctant to pay hotel prices and have an outdated belief that grubby walkers aren't welcome in the genteel surroundings. The Lake Vyrnwy Hotel (see p156) might be an exception, but this is mid-Wales, not Portofino, and in the four towns the hotels are mostly pubs rather than spa retreats, with prices that compare well with other options. Check whether the rate includes breakfast.

Airbnb

Airbnb (🖳 airbnb.co.uk) has arrived in mid-Wales and it's always worth checking the website; you might find a gem or a £25 bargain unlisted elsewhere. Because contact details and even locations are hidden and property details are vague, we rarely include them in this guide, though many of the lodgings we do list are also on Airbnb. However, we have checked to see what's generally available for the one-nighters at given points.

Airbnb was originally intended to offer 'unique stays and experiences' for guests to connect with locals and communities, envisaged as a bed for the night in the host's private home and breakfast in the morning. While this is still the case for some listings, you might also find anything from luxury self-catering apartments, with no local host in sight, to rooms in a pub (such as the *Whistling Badger* in Llanidloes) and rates may or may not include breakfast.

Remember that Airbnbs aren't all officially registered or accredited so standards (and prices) may vary widely. The best are indistinguishable from a regular B&B and will offer evening meals as well as packed lunches for the day ahead. The key to success is to read the listing details carefully so you are clear what is on offer and to message the property owner before booking if you need to clarify anything.

FOOD AND DRINK

Breakfast and lunch

A fry-up of bacon, eggs and sausages used to be considered a normal breakfast by many walkers, but remember when in Wales ask for a 'full Welsh' rather than a 'full English' if you're to avoid a punch in the face. (The main difference is laverbread, see box opposite). If the novelty of a fat-laden fry-up wears off, something lighter will almost always be available. Literally or metaphorically, once you spice it up, porridge is a healthier way of filling up each morning.

You'll need to plan what to do for lunch as chances are it'll be taken perched on a gate. If you can't buy something somewhere, just about all B&B hosts in shopless locations will provide a **packed lunch** for around £8. If you don't fancy breakfast or want an early start, the canny walker will ask to trade it for a packed lunch.

Better still, plan to buy day snacks at the **dozen village shops** along the path or just off it (see table p32-3), thus helping support the local economy. Note, though, that they are not evenly spread, and some stretches are devoid of any kind of shop. Take a careful note of **opening hours** and recheck them at the last minute; times will vary with the season and demand, if not the greater economic situation. In any event, you should always carry some back-up rations (see p79).

Evening meals

While the four towns will ensure you go to bed well fed, elsewhere it can mean a walk to the pub in the next village or nothing at all. That being the case, as mentioned, your local lodgings usually address that need by offering evening meals if booked in advance. Expect to pay from £10-15.

Dietary requirements

Vegetarians, vegans and others with special dietary requirements will be used to planning carefully or expect to carry hefty loads. The four towns and village shops will ease the challenge while **Machynlleth** is uniquely well catered with veg and vegan outlets. One delighted vegan camper we met spent five days there!

Though expensive, there's something to be said for carrying a couple of lightweight, high-calorie freeze-dried backpackers' meals along with the means to boil water or a flask filled up that morning. A flask may not be such a bad idea as the only place that sells **butane gas** canisters (as well as meths) is The Store (see p134) on New St, behind Parliament House in Machynlleth.

PLANNING YOUR WALK

☐ **WELSH SPECIALITIES**

● **Laverbread** Seaweed with oatmeal fried in bacon fat and served for breakfast. Even supermarkets stock it now.

● **Bara brith** A dense fruit loaf made with marmalade, mixed fruit, spices, egg and flour, similar to Irish barmbrack.

● **Welsh cakes** Tasty cakes full of currants and sultanas, similar to scones but thinner and cooked on a griddle. Found in supermarkets and in most tea shops and cafés.

● **Welsh rarebit** Melted cheese with a hint of mustard laid over buttered toast, though recipes vary.

● **Leek and parsley broth** (*Cawl cennin a phersli*) Broth made from beef and lamb with root vegetables, herbs and leeks.

● **Tregaron granny's broth** (*Cawl mamgu Tregaron*) Another soup full of vegetables with beef and bacon.

● **Wyau mon** Eggs in cheese sauce with potatoes and leeks.

● **Miner's delight** (*Gorfoledd y glowyr*) A rabbit casserole.

● **Oggy** The Welsh equivalent of the Cornish pasty containing beef, leeks, potato, onions and gravy in a thick pastry crust; originally the standard lunch for miners. If you order three expect the reply 'Oi! oi! oi!'.

Drinking water

On a typical 15-mile day you want to drink at least **two litres of water**; much more on a hot day. Two litres is quite a weight to carry, but many walkers are reticent about drinking from natural streams or springs, not least because of the recent pollution scandal on the not-too-distant Wye (as well as many southern English rivers). Just remember, the hills along the Glyndŵr's Way are a far cry from the algae-choked, lowland Wye, and the intensive farming along its banks. While you might not want to top-up alongside a muck-splattered sheep shed, using your instincts you can safely collect water from any tap or at higher elevations without any purification palaver. The tannin which stains hill water brown is not at all toxic in the quantities you'll ingest – just think of it as flat 'Coca Cola water'! At other times it's highly unlikely a remote rural dwelling will turn you away, sweaty browed and empty bottle in hand.

MONEY

The pandemic saw the old-guard – both vendor and customer – plunge headfirst into **cashless transactions** so that these days a B&B can be paid via PayPal on the spot. But there's still a place for cash, so bring about £200 and load up or replenish from supermarket **ATMs** in the four towns. As elsewhere, banks have gone the way of Owain Glyndŵr's battalions, but cash can also be drawn at **village post offices** with a debit card. For further details see 🖥 postoffice.co.uk (Products & Services; then Branch & banking services).

For budgeting, see box opposite.

WI-FI AND PUBLIC PHONES

Most campsites apart, pretty much everywhere offers free wi-fi to visitors, even if a phone signal might be weak or non-existent. Pubs will usually have a **wi-fi** connection too. You won't be surprised to hear that **public phones** are thin on the ground in mid-Wales. While the familiar red telephone boxes may remain, in most cases they now house the village defibrillator or some flowers alongside a selection of used paperbacks.

❏ OPENING DAYS/HOURS

The opening days and hours for the pubs, restaurants and cafés mentioned in Part 4 are as accurate as possible. However, the pressures caused by shortage of staff and increasing energy costs – let alone if the weather is bad, or if there is no demand – mean that places may close early or not open at all, so it is essential to check in advance, particularly if it involves a detour off the route and there are few other food options. Where businesses have a Facebook page (denoted by **fb**) these are worth checking as they tend to be kept more up to date with changes in opening hours than main websites.

❏ **BUDGETING**

Your budget will depend largely on the type of accommodation you use and your eating habits as well as your travel costs to and from your walk.

See **Accommodation** (pp21-24) for details of campsite charges and room rates.

Your next biggest outlay will be for food. If you camp and cook your own meals you'll keep costs to a minimum. These escalate as you go up the lodging and dining scales but broadly speaking, a cooked breakfast is £7-9pp, a packed lunch prepared by your B&B around £8pp, and a main dish in a pub starts from around £12pp (plus drinks), although you could get a takeaway (in towns) for less.

In summary, including accommodation, per person per day as a **minimum**:

Camping (self catering)	£15-25
Camping (eating out)	£25-40
Bunkhouse/Pod (self catering)	£30-35
Bunkhouse/Pod (eating out)	£35-50
B&B/Guesthouse	£65-80
Pub/Hotel	£75-90

Don't forget to also set aside some money for bus fares, taxis, baggage transfer, beer, teas and coffees, snacks, ice cream, laundry and, rather more crucially, any changes of plan.

WALKING COMPANIES

For walkers wanting to make their holiday as easy as possible there are several outfits offering a range of services from 'route planning' to baggage carrying and/or accommodation booking for self-guided tours. Because of the scarcity of lodgings at many points, some of these itineraries will include a taxi collection either from a road-accessible point somewhere along a stage, or at the end of a stage, possibly back to your previous night's lodgings.

Baggage transfer

It might only weigh a few kilos, but the thought of carrying a backpack puts a lot of people off walking long-distance trails, even if they're not camping. Let the purists scoff; a baggage-carrying service can deliver your bags to your night's accommodation leaving you free to walk unencumbered. The costs are obviously much lower if walking in a group.

Note that unlike elsewhere in Britain, in just about all cases the companies on p30 simply **hire local taxis** with whom they've struck a deal, rather than run their own fleet of vans. You might try to do the same. If you're having problems carrying your bags for a day or two some of your B&B hosts may also be happy to do the transporting for a small charge. Likewise some of the taxi firms listed (see Part 4) can provide a similar service within a local area. Prices vary, depending on the mileage involved and the individual concerned, but for the most part you can expect to pay a minimum of £15.

PLANNING YOUR WALK

Accommodation booking

Although all the contact details are provided in the book, the companies on p30 can book your accommodation for a fee. Just make sure you leave them enough time; when the handful of beds in a village are gone, they're gone. Welshpool Tourist Information Centre (see p168; ☎ 01938 552043, 🖳 welshpooltown

❑ INFORMATION FOR FOREIGN VISITORS

• **Currency** The British pound (£) comes in notes of £50, £20, £10 and £5, and coins of £2 and £1. The pound is divided into 100 pence (usually referred to as 'p', pronounced 'pee') which come in 'silver' coins of 50p, 20p, 10p and 5p, and 'copper' coins of 2p and 1p. Cash is the most welcome form of payment though debit/credit cards are accepted in some places. Up-to-date currency **exchange rates** can be found on 🖳 www.xe.com, at some post offices, and at most banks and travel agents.

• **Business hours** Most **village shops** are open Monday to Friday 9am-5pm and Saturday 9am-12.30pm, though some open as early as 7.30/8am; many also open on Sundays but not usually for the whole day. Occasionally you'll come across a local shop that closes at lunchtime on one day during the week, usually a Wednesday or Thursday; this is a throwback to the days when all towns and villages had an 'early closing day'. **Supermarkets** are open Monday to Saturday 8am-8pm (sometimes longer) and on Sunday from about 9am to 5 or 6pm, though main branches of supermarkets generally open 10am-4pm or 11am-5pm.

Main **post offices** generally open Monday to Friday 9am-5pm and Saturday 9am-12.30pm; **banks** typically open at 9.30/10am Monday to Friday and close at 3.30/4pm, though in some places both post offices and banks may open only two or three days a week and/or in the morning, or limited hours, only. **ATMs (cash machines)** located outside a bank, shop, post office or petrol station are open all the time, but any that are inside will be accessible only when that place is open. However, ones that charge, such as Link machines, may not accept foreign-issued cards.

Pub hours are less predictable as each pub may have different opening hours, especially in rural areas. However, most pubs in towns open daily 11am-11pm (some close at 10.30pm on Sunday) but **some close in the afternoon**. The last entry time to most **museums and galleries** is usually half an hour, or an hour, before the official closing time.

• **Public (bank) holidays** Most businesses are shut on 1 January, Good Friday (March/April), Easter Monday (March/April), the first and last Monday in May, the last Monday in August, 25 December and 26 December.

• **School holidays** School holiday periods in Wales are generally: a one-week break late October, two weeks around Christmas/New Year, a week in mid February, two weeks around Easter, a week in late May/early June (to coincide with the bank holiday on the last Monday in May), and six weeks from late July to early September. Private-school holidays fall at the same time, but tend to be slightly longer.

• **EHICs and travel insurance** Although Britain's National Health Service (NHS) is free at the point of use, that is only the case for residents. All visitors to Britain should be properly insured, including comprehensive health coverage. Though Britain has left the EU, the European Health Insurance Card (EHIC) does still entitle EU nationals (on production of the EHIC, so ensure you bring it with you) to necessary medical treatment under the NHS while on a temporary visit here. To make sure

council.gov.uk/services/tourist-office) also offer an accommodation booking service with booking fees.

Self-guided holidays

The following companies provide customised packages for walkers which usually include itineraries, maps and guidebooks, accommodation booking, daily

this is still the case when you visit, however, contact your national social security institution. Also note that the EHIC is not a substitute for proper medical cover on your travel insurance for unforeseen bills and for getting you home should that be necessary. Also consider cover for loss and theft of personal belongings, especially if you are camping or staying in bunkhouses, as there may be times when you'll have to leave your luggage unattended.

● **Weights and measures** Milk in Britain is still sometimes sold in pints (1 pint = 568ml), as is beer in pubs, though most other **liquids** including petrol (gasoline) and diesel are sold in litres. Road **distances** are given in miles (1 mile = 1.6km) rather than kilometres, and yards (1yd = 0.9m) rather than metres. The population remains divided between those who still use inches (1 inch = 2.5cm) and feet (1ft = 0.3m) and those who are happy with centimetres and millimetres; you'll often be told that 'it's only a hundred yards or so' to somewhere, rather than a hundred metres or so.

Most **food** is sold in metric weights (g and kg) but the imperial weights of pounds (lb: 1lb = 453g) and ounces (oz: 1oz = 28g) are often displayed too. The **weather** – a frequent topic of conversation – is also an issue: while most forecasts predict temperatures in °C, some people continue to think in terms of °F (see temperature chart on p15 for conversions).

● **Time** During the winter the whole of Britain is on Greenwich Mean Time (GMT). The clocks move one hour forward on the last Sunday in March, remaining on British Summer Time (BST) until the last Sunday in October.

● **Smoking & vaping** Smoking in enclosed public places is against the law. The ban relates not only to pubs and restaurants, but also to B&Bs, bunkhouses and hotels. These latter have the right to designate one or more bedrooms where the occupants can smoke, but the ban is in force in all enclosed areas open to the public – even in a private home such as a B&B. Should you be foolhardy enough to light up in a no-smoking area, which includes pretty well any indoor public place and even some outdoor ones, such as public playgrounds, you could be fined £50, but it's the owners of the premises who suffer most if they fail to stop you, with a potential fine of £2500.

Although the ban does not apply to vaping, premises can and do impose their own restrictions on the use of e-cigarettes indoors.

● **Telephones** The international access code for Britain is ☎ 44, followed by the area code minus the first 0, and then the number you require. Within the UK, to call a number with the same code as the landline phone you are calling from, the code can be omitted: dial the number only. It is cheaper to ring at weekends (from midnight on Friday till midnight on Sunday), and after 7pm and before 7am on weekdays. If you're using a **mobile (cell) phone** that is registered overseas, consider buying a local SIM card to keep costs down.

● **Emergency services** For police, ambulance, fire and mountain rescue dial ☎ 999, or the EU standard number ☎ 112.

PLANNING YOUR WALK

baggage transfer as well as transport at the start, end and maybe during your walk, and extra nights along the way. Just about all of them can tailor their options to meet your requirements.

● **Byways Breaks** (☎ 0151-722 8050, 🖥 byways-breaks.co.uk; Liverpool) Provide a flexible accommodation booking and luggage service, along the whole path or any section of it, and in either direction.

● **Celtic Trails** (☎ 01291-689774, 🖥 celtictrailswalkingholidays.co.uk; Tintern) Family-owned, Wales-based walking company with over 25 years of experience offering various self-guided itineraries, with lodgings booked and baggage transferred.

● **Contours Holidays** (☎ 01629-821900, 🖥 contours.co.uk; Matlock) From short breaks to the full walk and bring-a-dog option.

● **Drover Holidays** (☎ 01497-821134, 🖥 droverholidays.co.uk; Hay-on-Wye) Self-guided itineraries for the whole or part of the Way, in dog-friendly accommodation.

● **Exploring Mid Wales** (☎ 0791 426 5654, 🖥 exploringmidwales.co.uk; Brecon) Offers self-guided itineraries both for the whole path and in parts.

● **Great British Walks** (☎ 01600-713008, 🖥 great-british-walks.com; Monmouth) Self-guided itineraries from 5-8 nights to Machynlleth; 4-6 days from Machynlleth to Welshpool and the whole walk from 9 to 14 days.

● **Let's Go Walking** (☎ 01837-880075, 🖥 letsgowalking.co.uk; Devon) The full walk over 11 nights or 17 nights, to Machynlleth over 10 nights (7-11 miles a day) and Machynlleth to Welshpool over 8 nights (same daily distances).

● **Wales Walking Holidays** (☎ 07483 229606, 🖥 waleswalkingholidays.com; Anglesey) Can customise itineraries according to the customer's requirements.

Guided/group walking tours

If you don't trust your map-reading skills or simply prefer the company of other walkers as well as an experienced guide, there are a couple of companies that can help you. Packages usually include meals, accommodation, transport arrangements and baggage transfer but you should check carefully before booking.

● **Drover Holidays** (see above) Offers tailor-made guided walking tours for the whole or part of the Way, with dog-friendly accommodation.

● **Exploring Mid Wales** (see above) Offer fully guided itineraries both for the whole path and in parts.

WALKING WITH A DOG

Judging by the warnings and even threats including reported dog shootings on several sheep farm gate posts, an unleashed dog is about as welcome on the Glyndŵr's Way as another dose of Mad Cow Disease. Furthermore, few lodgings want the risk of dealing with dirty, ill-trained or unpredictable mutts.

People do walk the trail with dogs (one couple we met resorted to shuttling a motorhome and a car, day by day) but it's extremely important that dogs and their owners **behave in a responsible manner**, the exact meaning of which seems to vary among individuals. Dogs should always be **kept on leads** while on the footpath to avoid disturbing wildlife, livestock and other walkers. With that in mind, you and your dog may wonder what's the point of being out in the open countryside if they can't run around freely?

Like you, your dog also needs to be pretty fit to complete this walk while being unaware of what lies ahead. You may not believe it as you watch it haring around the fields but like you, dogs have a finite amount of energy, so consider whether yours really is up to walking 15 miles a day. It would be embarrassing to have to call in mountain rescue to retrieve your prematurely pooped pooch, as happened near the summit of Ben Nevis in 2022. See also pp183-4 for more on long-distance walking with a canine companion.

DISABLED ACCESS

It's the same old story: just about the only parts of the trail which are accessible to wheelchair and scooter users are sections where the path follows roads and country lanes. For more on access for the disabled, contact the Disabled Ramblers (🖳 disabledramblers.co.uk).

Itineraries

PLANNING

Some walkers like to walk non-stop. Others amble along, stopping to admire the vistas or catalogue the flowers (see p62-4). You may want to walk Glyndŵr's Way in one go, tackle it in a series of long weekends, or use the trail for a series of linear day walks. All is possible but this guide has been divided up into the nine well-established stages between settlements on roads with lodgings. All stages include at least one point during the day which is accessible by road.

The planning map opposite the inside back cover and table of village and town facilities on pp32-3 summarise the essential information for you to make a plan. Look for suggestions on p35-8 for how to experience the best of the Way over a day or a weekend.

Having made a rough plan, turn to Part 4 where you'll find summaries of the route, full descriptions of lodgings, places to eat and other services in each town and village, along with detailed trail maps.

VILLAGE AND TOWN FACILITIES
◀WELSHPOOL Knighton to Welshpool – Walking Clockwise

PLACE*	DISTANCE* MILES	KM	PO/ ATM	EATING PLACE*	FOOD SHOP	PUB	CAMP SITE	BUNK/ POD	B&B/ HOTEL
Knighton	0	0	✔	✔✔	✔	✔✔	✔		✔✔
Llangunllo	6¼	10				✔(DO)			
t/o (Beguildy)	7½	12(+1½/2.4)	✔		✔	✔			✔
Felindre	1½	2.5				✔(DO)	✔	✔P	✔
Llanbadarn Fyn	7	11.4		✔	✔				
Abbeycwmhir	8½	13.5				✔(DO)	✔(U)		✔
Llanidloes	15¼	24.7	✔	✔✔	✔✔	✔✔	✔	✔B	✔✔
Clywedog Dam	6	9.5		✔			✔(U)		✔
Hafren Forest	5	8.1						✔B	
t/o (Staylittle)	2	3 (+1/1.6)	✔		✔			✔B	
t/o (Dylife)	1½	2.5 (+½/0.8)						✔H	✔
Machynlleth	14	22.7	✔	✔✔	✔	✔✔		✔B	✔✔
Penegoes	2¼	3.8					✔	✔B/P	
Glantwymyn	6½	10.3	(✔)		(✔)				✔
Llanbrynmair	7	11.1		✔✔	✔	✔			✔
Llangadfan	11¼	18.2	✔	✔	✔	✔	✔		✔
Lake Vyrnwy	7½	12.1		✔	✔	✔	✔✔		✔
Llwydiarth	2¾	4.5	✔		✔				
Pontrobert	8	12.9	(✔)		(✔)	✔(DO)			
Meifod	3½	5.5	✔		✔	✔	✔		✔
Welshpool	11¼	18.2	✔	✔✔	✔✔	✔✔	✔†	✔P†	✔✔

TOTAL DISTANCE 134½ miles/*216.5km*

NOTES

*PLACE & DISTANCE Places in **bold** are on the path; places in brackets and not in bold – eg (Beguildy) – are a short walk off the path. **DISTANCE** is given from the place above. Distances are between **places on the route** or to the **main turnoff (t/o)** to places in brackets. For example the distance from Llangunllo to the **turnoff** for Beguildy is 7½ miles. Bracketed distances eg (+1) show the additional distance off the route – eg Beguildy is 1½ miles/2.4km off Glyndŵr's Way.

PLANNING YOUR WALK

WHICH DIRECTION?

With only 28 miles or good transport connections separating Welshpool from Knighton, it's largely a matter of personal choice which direction you choose to walk, though most start at Knighton and walk towards Welshpool (ie: clockwise), as we did.

If you're up for a challenge, walking anti-clockwise from Welshpool to Knighton does mean you will tick off the biggest daily ascent figure (3799ft /1158m) of the whole walk as you climb from near sea level at Machynlleth up and over Foel Fadian to Dylife.

VILLAGE AND TOWN FACILITIES
Welshpool to Knighton – Walking Anticlockwise `KNIGHTON ▷`

PLACE*	DISTANCE* MILES	KM	PO/ ATM	EATING PLACE*	FOOD SHOP	PUB	CAMP SITE	BUNK/ POD	B&B/ HOTEL
Welshpool	0	0	✔	✔✔✔	✔✔✔	✔✔✔	✔†	✔P†	✔✔✔
Meifod	11¼	18.2	✔		✔	✔	✔		✔✔
Pontrobert	3½	5.5	(✔)		(✔)	✔(DO)			
Llwydiarth	8	12.9	✔		✔				
Lake Vyrnwy	2¾	4.5		✔	✔	✔	✔✔		✔✔
Llangadfan	7½	12.1	✔	✔	✔	✔	✔		✔
Llanbrynmair	11¼	18.2		✔✔	✔	✔			✔✔
Glantwymyn	7	11.1	(✔)		(✔)				✔✔
Penegoes	6½	10.3					✔	✔B/P	✔
Machynlleth	2¼	3.8	✔	✔✔✔	✔✔	✔✔✔		✔B	✔✔✔
t/o (Dylife)	14	22.7 (+½/0.8)						✔H	✔
t/o (Staylittle)	1½	2.5 (+1/1.6) ✔				✔			✔B	
Hafren Forest	2	3						✔B	
Clywedog Dam	5	8.1		✔			✔(U)		✔
Llanidloes	6	9.5	✔	✔✔✔	✔✔✔	✔✔✔	✔	✔B	✔✔✔
Abbeycwmhir	15¼	24.7				✔(DO)	✔(U)		✔✔
Llanbadarn Fyn	8½	13.5		✔	✔				
Felindre	7	11.4				✔(DO)	✔	✔P	✔
t/o (Beguildy)	1½	2.5(+1½/2.4) ✔				✔	✔			✔
Llangunllo	7½	12				✔(DO)			
Knighton	6¼	10	✔	✔✔✔	✔✔	✔✔✔	✔		✔✔✔

TOURIST INFO	The only TICs are in **Knighton** & **Welshpool**
EATING PLACE	✔ = one place ✔✔ = two ✔✔✔ = three or more
PUB	(DO) = drinks only, no food
FOOD SHOP	(✔) = limited opening hours
CAMPING	(U) = no official campsite though can camp nearby; ask locally
	† = 2 miles/3.2km north-east of Welshpool at Buttington
BUNK/HOSTEL	H = independent hostel B = bunkhouse P = camping pod or static caravan
B&B/HOTEL	✔ = one place ✔✔ = two ✔✔✔ = three or more

PLANNING YOUR WALK

The route guides and maps in Part 4 give an overview and timings for both directions. As route-finding instructions are written onto the maps rather than in the text, you'll easily be able to follow this guidebook in either direction. In the text and maps look for the **Welshpool direction arrow symbol** `◀ WELSHPOOL` which indicates information for those walking **north/clockwise from Knighton to Welshpool** and the Knighton direction arrow symbol `KNIGHTON ▷` with shaded text (also on the maps) for those walking **south/anti-clockwise from Welshpool to Knighton**.

Terrain wise, the southern half to Machynlleth involves **higher elevations**, but every day, not least the last 12 miles into Welshpool, has its ups and downs. The colour maps at the back of the book include elevation profiles.

SUGGESTED ITINERARIES – SEE BOXES pp34-7

All the itineraries are suggestions only and could be adapted to suit your own requirements. This book divides the Glyndŵr's Way into nine stages as this offers the best choice of accommodation at the end of each day. This means walking a distance of 11¼-15½ miles (18.2-25.2km) a day with one longer day of 18¾ miles (30.3km), although this could be divided into two shorter days of 11¼ miles (18.1km) and 7½ miles (12.1km) with an extra night at Llangadfan. The itineraries on the following pages offer alternatives for longer or shorter daily distances. Note that, unless you are wild camping (see p22), for alternative itineraries it may be necessary to walk further or arrange transport to reach your accommodation for the night (and back to your start point the next morning). An end point with vehicle access may not have a reliable mobile phone signal so taxis or collections will have to be booked in advance for a fixed time.

PLANNING YOUR WALK

KNIGHTON TO WELSHPOOL (CLOCKWISE) – SEE ALSO p36

ITINERARY WITH SHORT DAILY DISTANCES

A daily average of just under 10 miles (16km), but with only six of thirteen days **ending at lodgings**. However, if you have transport back to the nearest accommodation you could spend more than one night in several locations, which may open up your options for a bed in places with a two-night minimum booking policy.

Day	Daily schedule	Miles (approx)	km	Nearest accommodation
1	Knighton to Beacon Hill crossroads*, Map 4	9½	15.3	Knighton, Beguildy
2	Beacon Hill crossroads* Map 4 to Llanbadarn Ffynydd	12¾	20.5	Beguildy, Abbeycwmhir
3	Llanbadarn Ffynydd to Abbeycwmhir	8½	13.7	**Abbeycwmhir**
4	Abbeycwmhir to junction nr Pen y Lan, Map 18	10¼	16.5	Llanidloes
5	Pen y Lan to Ty Capel B&B, Map 22	11¾	19	**Ty Capel B&B**
6	Ty Capel B&B to 'Small parking space', Map 26	11	17.6	Dylife, Pennant
7	'Small parking space' Map 26 to Machynlleth	12¼	19.7	**Machynlleth**, Penegoes
8	Machynlleth to Glantwymyn	8½	13.7	Penegoes, **Glantwymyn**
9	Glantwymyn to 'Cattle grid & gate', Map 39	12¾	20.5	Llanbrynmair, Llangadfan
10	Cattle grid & gate to Lake Vyrnwy	12½	20	**Lake Vyrnwy**
11	Lake Vyrnwy to Pontrobert	10½	17	Meifod
12	Pontrobert to B4392, Map 51	8	13	Welshpool
13	B4392, Map 51 to Welshpool	7½	12	**Welshpool**

* **Note**: The track from the south-east may not be accessible by vehicle. If not, it's a 15-20 minute walk to a road near Llancoch farm (and only another 10-15 mins to Llangynllo/Llangunllo station).

THE BEST DAY AND WEEKEND WALKS

As always, returning to your starting point will be an issue on these short linear walks. Don't count on buses apart from Llanbrynmair on a main road, although given the meandering nature of Glyndŵr's Way, the road distance back to your starting point is sometimes much less, making taxis a less costly option than you might imagine.

Additionally, all of the day walks listed below will make very agreeable **there-and back overnighters**, so returning you to your parked vehicle.

Day walks

● **Knighton to Felindre** (Maps 1-7; 15¼ miles/24.5km; 8 hrs) A satisfying day out ending with an afternoon's romp across the borderland moors and great pub in nearby Beguildy. Felindre is just 10 miles by road back to Knighton. See also pp88-96.

WELSHPOOL TO KNIGHTON (ANTI-CLOCKWISE) – SEE ALSO p37

ITINERARY WITH SHORT DAILY DISTANCES

A daily average of just under 10 miles (16km), but with only six of thirteen days **ending at lodgings**. However, if you have transport back to the nearest accommodation you could spend more than one night in several locations, which may open up your options for a bed in places with a two-night minimum booking policy.

Day	Daily schedule	Miles/km (approx)	Nearest accommodation
1	Welshpool to B4392, Map 51	7½ 12	Welshpool
2	B4392, Map 51 to Pontrobert	8 13	Meifod, Welshpool
3	Pontrobert to Lake Vyrnwy	10½ 17	**Lake Vyrnwy**
4	Lake Vyrnwy to 'Cattle grid & gate', Map 39	12½ 20	Llangadfan
5	'Cattle grid & gate' to Glantwymyn	12¾ 20.5	**Glantwymyn**
6	Glantwymyn to Machynlleth	8½ 13.7	**Machynlleth**
7	Machynlleth to 'Small parking space', Map 26	12¼ 19.7	Dylife, Pennant
8	'Small parking space' Map 26 to Ty Capel B&B	11 17.6	**Ty Capel B&B**
9	Ty Capel B&B to junction nr Pen y Lan, Map 18	11¾ 19	Llanidloes
10	Pen y Lan to Abbeycwmhir	10¼ 16.5	**Abbeycwmhir**
11	Abbeycwmhir to Llanbadarn Ffynydd	8½ 13.7	Abbeycwmhir, Beguildy
12	Llanbadarn Ffynydd to Beacon Hill crossroads*, Map 4	12¾ 20.5	Beguildy, Felindre
13	Beacon Hill crossroads* to Knighton	9½ 15.3	**Knighton**

* Note: The track from the south-east may not be accessible by vehicle. If not, it's a 15-20 minute walk to a road near Llancoch farm (and only another 10-15 mins to Llangynllo/Llangunllo station).

● **Felindre to Abbeycwmhir** (Maps 7-13; 15½ miles/24.9km; 8 hrs) Another one of the walk's best days, winding among sheep and wind turbines and with a handy shop halfway. It's 15 miles/24.2km back to Felindre along backroads. See also pp97-103.

● **Dylife to Machynlleth** (Maps 25-31; 15¼ miles/24.7km; 7-8hrs) Many walkers' favourite day on the trail, dropping from the Cambrian heights to Machynlleth, but not the effortless descent it might seem. With plentiful taxis in Mach, it's less than 10 miles/16km by road back up to Dylife. See also pp125-36.

● **Pumlumon horseshoe** (circular) (Maps 25-26 & A-E, 12 miles/19.3km + 3 miles/5km from/to parking space, total 15 miles/24.3km; 7-8 hrs) By GW stan-

---

KNIGHTON TO WELSHPOOL (CLOCKWISE) – SEE ALSO p34
ITINERARIES WITH LONG DAILY DISTANCES

7 DAYS

One week itinerary, walking 15-18 miles (24-29km) a day with three longer days of over 20 miles (32km). This is a tough pace with four days on the trail **ending close to lodgings**.

Day	Daily schedule	Miles/km	Nearest accommodation
1	Knighton to Llanbadarn Ffynydd	22¼/35.75	Felindre, Abbeycwmhir
2	Llanbadarn Ffynydd to Llanidloes	23¾/38.5	**Llanidloes**
3	Llanidloes to 'Small parking space',	17¼/27.5	Dylife, Machynlleth
	Map 26		
4	Small parking space to Glantwymyn	20¾/33.5	**Glantwymyn**, Llanbrynmair
5	Glantwymyn to Llangadfan	18/29	**Llangadfan**
6	Llangadfan to Pontrobert	18/29	Meifod
7	Pontrobert to Welshpool	15½/25	**Welshpool**, Buttington

9 DAYS

Nine days of walking 11-15½ miles (18-25km), with one longer day of 18¾ miles (30.25km)* as per the stages of this book. This schedule offers the best choice of **accommodation options** at the end of each day.

Day	Daily schedule	Miles/km	Nearest accommodation
1	Knighton to Felindre	15¼/24.5	**Felindre**, Beguildy
2	Felindre to Abbeycwmhir	15½/25	**Abbeycwmhir**
3	Abbeycwmhir to Llanidloes	15¼/24.5	**Llanidloes**
4	Llanidloes to Dylife	13¼/21.5	Staylittle, **Dylife**
5	Dylife to Machynlleth	15¼/24.5	**Machynlleth**, Penegoes
6	Machynlleth to Llanbrynmair	15½/25	Glantwymyn, **Llanbrynmair**
7	Llanbrynmair to Lake Vyrnwy*	18¾/30.25	**Lake Vyrnwy**
8	Lake Vyrnwy to Meifod	14¼/22.75	**Meifod**
9	Meifod to Welshpool	11¼/18.25	**Welshpool**, Buttington

* or divide this stage into two days with a night at **Llangadfan**, 11½ miles/18.5km from Llanbrynmair

dards, a tough moorland slog that gets you out into the wilds, onto the peaks and then right back to a roadside parking space by a gate. Probably best done as a one off than incorporated into the full walk. See also pp173-80.

● **Machynlleth to Llanbrynmair** (Maps 31-37; 15½ miles/25.2km; 7½ hrs) A full day out with the potential for stirring hilltop views along the Dovey Valley followed by an 11-mile bus ride back to Mach if you're quick (see p48). See also pp137-44.

● **Llanbrynmair to Llangadfan** (Maps 37-43; 11.3 miles/18.2km; 5-6 hrs) A paltry 11 miles along forestry tracks and moorland gorse, ending at a fine pub and a heavenly drive or cycle back to Llanbrynmair via the Nant yr Eira valley. See also pp146-50.

WELSHPOOL TO KNIGHTON (ANTI-CLOCKWISE) – SEE ALSO p35
ITINERARIES WITH LONG DAILY DISTANCES

7 DAYS

One week itinerary, walking 15-18 miles (24-29km) a day with three longer days of over 20 miles (32km). This is a tough pace with four days on the trail **ending close to lodgings**.

Day	Daily schedule	Miles/km	Nearest accommodation
1	Welshpool to Pontrobert	15½/25	Meifod
2	Pontrobert to Llangadfan	18/29	**Llangadfan**
3	Llangadfan to Glantwymyn	18/29	**Glantwymyn**
4	Glantwymyn to 'Small parking space', Map 26	20¾/33.5	Machynlleth, Dylife
5	'Small parking space' to Llanidloes	17¼/27.5	Clywedog Dam, **Llanidloes**
6	Llanidloes to Llanbadarn Ffynydd	23¾/38.5	Abbeycwmhir
7	Llanbadarn Ffynydd to Knighton	22¼/35.75	Felindre, **Knighton**

9 DAYS

Nine days of walking 11-15½ miles (18-25km), with one longer day of 18¾ miles (30.25km)* as per the stages of this book. This schedule offers the best choice of **accommodation options** at the end of each day.

Day	Daily schedule	Miles/km	Nearest accommodation
1	Welshpool to Meifod	11¼/18.25	**Meifod**
2	Meifod to Lake Vyrnwy	14¼/22.75	**Lake Vyrnwy**
3	Lake Vrnwy to Llanbrynmair*	18¾/30.25	**Llanbrynmair**
4	Llanbrynmair to Machynlleth	15½/25	**Machynlleth**, Penegoes
5	Machynlleth to Dylife	15¼/24.5	**Dylife**, Staylittle
6	Dylife to Llanidloes	13¼/21.5	**Llanidloes**
7	Llanidloes to Abbeycwmhir	15¼/24.5	**Abbeycwmhir**
8	Abbeycwmhir to Felindre	15½/25	**Felindre**, Beguildy
9	Felindre to Knighton	15¼/24.5	**Knighton**

* or divide this stage into two days with a night at **Llangadfan**, 7½ miles/12km from Lake Vyrnwy

PLANNING YOUR WALK

● **Lake Vyrnwy to Meifod** (Maps 45-50; 14¼ miles/22.9km; 7-8 hrs) Some say it's the last good day on the trail, as you leave the wilds of mid-Wales and follow the Vyrnwy river via pretty villages and pastures back to the tidy gardens of Meifod in the lowland Marches. See also pp157-64.

Weekend walks

● **Knighton to Abbeycwmhir** (Maps 1-13; 30¾ miles/49.4km) Two of the walk's best days lined up one after the other. A great taster for what lies ahead. To get back it's six miles south to Pen y Bont train station which is five stops from Knighton. See also pp88-103.

● **Felindre to Llanidloes** (Maps 7-20; 30¾ miles/49.6km) Chances are you'll see no other walkers on this 30-miler to Llani where good transport links reach back to the outside world. It's 24 miles by road back to Felindre. See also pp97-116.

● **Llanidloes to Machynlleth** (Maps 20-31, 28½ miles/46.1km) Another auspicious alignment of consecutive traildays up and over the Cambrian mountains. Less than 20 miles apart by road, this is a great weekender with relatively straightforward transport logistics. See also pp117-36.

● **Lake Vyrnwy to Welshpool** (Maps 45-54; 25½ miles/41.1km) From the dam wall follow the banks of the Vyrnwy river as it spills down towards the English border. By road it's about 20 miles. See also pp157-172.

What to take

Knowing what gear you'll need takes experience; the more you know the less you need. And the more money you spend wisely the lighter and more compact and durable your gear can all be. For those new to long-distance walking the suggestions below will help you strike a balance between comfort, expense and minimal weight.

KEEP YOUR LUGGAGE LIGHT

One of the pleasures of hiking is discovering how little we actually need to be comfortable on the trail, especially if we have overnight lodgings and meals taken care of. It's all too easy to pile things in 'just in case', then risk paying the price with a higher risk of injury, plain misery, or literally paying someone to transport your bags for you when you've had enough.

THE PACK ON YOUR BACK

If camping you'll need a pack of around **70 litres**. It's vital a pack this size has a **stiffened back system** (most do) so the weight is resting on a thickly padded hip belt, not hanging from your shoulders. An adjustable sternum or **chest strap** drawing the shoulder straps together ensures the load is pulled close to your back and makes a huge difference to a secure fitting, too. Don't get a big back-pack without one of these.

Play around with different ways of packing your gear and adjusting all those straps until you get it just right. You'll find that after a few days on the trail your system becomes optimised. Some even find clipping heavy items across the chest counteracts the inevitable stoop of a huge load on the back. All these straps can make getting to the pockets on your clothing tricky, so it helps if your hip belt has integrated pockets with additional pouches on the shoulder straps. Or wear a bum bag to carry your phone, guidebook, maps and other essentials.

If staying in bunkhouses you may need to carry a sleeping bag for which a 40- to 60-litre pack should be fine. If using B&Bs everything can fit into a pack **from 20-litres**, providing you're prepared to wash clothes once in a while. Either way, stash similar things in different coloured stuff sacks so they're easier to pull out of the dark recesses of your pack. Fit a **waterproof rucksack liner** or a tough plastic bin bags to guarantee protection from rain.

If you decide to circumvent the whole 'pack light' conundrum by using a baggage-transfer service (see p27) you can bring an elegant wheeled suitcase for your main bag, then you'll only need a small daypack for the day's walk.

CARRYING WATER

Unless you replenish from natural sources, taps and washrooms or by knocking on doors, the two litres of water you'll need a day are best carried in a large **hydration bladder** which usually slips in a dedicated sleeve or pocket in your pack. That done, it's not a bad idea to carry an additional 300ml reserve in a **bottle** as a back-up, as you can't easily tell how fast your hydrator is being used without pulling it out.

FOOTWEAR

Boots
Lifting your feet nearly half a million times between Knighton and Welshpool, you want the **lightest footwear** that's **durable** and ideally, **waterproof** while being as **comfortable** as your favourite slippers. That is quite a tall order seeing as most of us are unused to walking 15 miles a day, day after day. The success of your uninterrupted Glyndŵr's walk rests on footwear that's matched to your body weight and the load you're carrying. A great way to ensure this is to **not set off with untried footwear**.

Though they're far more durable and can be re-waxed as necessary rather than rely on wafer-thin membranes, for most walkers the days of needing to break-in one-piece leather boots are long gone. Today less rugged hiking footwear uses fabric, suede or soft leather uppers into which is bonded a magical breathable membrane – Gore-Tex being the best known. Boots like this may not last more than a couple of years, but they'll be more **reliably comfortable** for many more people. Comfort means avoiding blisters (see below) but also not ending the day with sore feet because the boot's sole is too thin to insulate your feet from the stony trail. Any boot you can bend like a plimsoll won't survive a day unless you're as dainty as Kylie Minogue in her prime, but anything too stiff will resemble wearing a pair of clogs which will lead to heel blisters. Some favour low-cut **trail shoes** but these are more suited to day hikes, not consecutive eight-hour days. Comfort also means not having your toes mashed together like a ballerina. The best boot makers offer models with **wide fittings**. You'll soon learn if you're in that category

Boots usually come with **removable insoles** which can be little more than a shaped piece of foam. Though expensive for what they are, we've found thermally folded insoles like the *Sole* brand can transform a boot's comfort. *Sole* also make fairly thick and stiff insoles which can better insulate your feet from stony terrain. For foot care and blister-avoidance advice see pp76-8.

Socks

It pays to start each day with a fresh and dry pair of socks so bring up to three pairs. Walking pros wear thin liner socks under a thicker merino wool sock. It makes sense as the close fitting liners become a second skin, separating any blister-causing friction from the outer sock or the boot's inner surface. Natural fibres makes them much more comfortable while wool wicks away moisture better than cotton.

An interesting idea are ArmaSkin socks: thin synthetic fibre inner socks with a clingy, silicon interior coating. These really do look like they form a stable second skin over your feet, transferring any rubbing to the shiny outer surface and the outer sock but, judging by online reviews, they'll probably not last more than 200 miles.

Extra footwear

Bring a light pair of compact spare shoes to wear when not on the trail as there'll be moments when you can't face spending another second in your boots.

CLOTHES

The huge reservoirs of mid-Wales weren't filled up by fairies carrying glitter-flake watering cans, so you'll need protection from pelting rain while not sweating like a cheese in a greenhouse.

Base layer

A thin lightweight **thermal top** made from synthetic material draws moisture away, keeping you dry. It will be cool if worn on its own in hot weather and warm when worn under other clothes in cooler conditions. A spare would be sensible as most synthetic fabrics get smelly, but washed in a hand basin then wrung out by being rolled up in a tightly twisted towel, they dry very quickly. That said, there's something to be said for the magical, odour-free properties of

merino wool as a base layer. On the trail avoid cotton which absorbs sweat or rain and will chill you rapidly when you stop moving.

Outer layer

Above all, invest in a **cagoule** or **waterproof shell** with a breathable membrane liner, a fitted hood, a two-way zip as well as under-arm vents and a few pockets so you can face a wet day with confidence. Adjustable zips can also help with **venting** so that it can also be worn to keep the wind off without feeling clammy.

Leg wear

Whatever you wear on your legs it should be **light**, **quick-drying** and not restricting; that rules out denim jeans. Many walkers find polyester tracksuit leggings do the job. Your legs actually generate and so lose little heat compared to your torso and head, so in fine weather or even light rain, a pair of **shorts** will be one less thing to wash.

Not everyone gets on with **waterproof overtrousers** which can soon make you heat up. If your main pair of trousers is reasonably windproof and quick-drying you may not need separate waterproof overtrousers. **Gaiters** aren't essential but can keep your boots and socks drier for longer in very wet and muddy conditions.

Underwear

Two or three changes of what you normally wear should suffice. Women may find a **sports bra** more comfortable because pack straps can cause bra straps to dig into your shoulders.

Headwear

Some form of **hat** is worth carrying at any time of the year, either to keep you warm, or to keep the sun or sweat out of your eyes.

TOILETRIES

A small bottle of **soap** can be useful to freshen up in a stream and can be used as shaving cream or laundry detergent. Add a small tube of **toothpaste** and a **toothbrush** and enough **toilet paper** to get you through to the next supply. Try to avoid doing so, but if you're planning to defecate outdoors, use a lightweight **trowel** to bury your output (see p73). Finally, a **razor, deodorant**, **suncream** and **tampons/sanitary towels** should cover your needs. You may also find some **insect repellent** useful.

FIRST-AID KIT

While there are pharmacies, health centres and even hospitals in the four towns, it's always a good idea to carry a small first-aid kit to cover common problems. A basic kit will contain **paracetamol/ibuprofen** for aches and pains; **sticking plasters** for minor cuts or more common blisters (for which Compeed is best known, though plain smooth tape pre-emptively applied also works well); a **bandage, antiseptic wipes/cream**; **safety pins**; **tweezers** and small **scissors**.

GENERAL ITEMS

Essential

Even if you rarely use one in your daily life, only a few diehards will deny the value of carrying a **smartphone** on the trail. Remember, you don't have to turn it on until you actually need it. Doing so is certainly a way of making the battery last for days with the help of charging cables and USB wall plugs. As mentioned, bring a float of **cash** too and a wristwatch means you don't have to use the phone.

Useful

The trail is well marked, so are our maps and you can estimate north from the sun's position and time of day, so won't need a **compass** very often, but on the occasions when it's cloudy and you're befuddled (and you don't have an electronic version at hand), it might be handy. Other items, some of which will hopefully not be needed, include a piercing emergency **whistle** to get attention; a **headtorch** in case you end up walking in the dark; **emergency snacks** which your body can quickly convert into energy (see p79); a small **penknife**; and bags for packing out any rubbish. If carrying heavy loads, **walking poles** or a longer staff reduce the impact on your knees on climbs and provide stability on descents (see p78).

CAMPING GEAR

Experience has proved the value of choosing a **tent** that can withstand wet and windy conditions, a three-season **sleeping bag** and above all, a thick **sleeping mat**. On top of that you'll need **cooking gear** (a stove and fuel; a pan and a lid, plus a mug, cutlery and a scrubber for washing up).

MAPS

As mentioned on p19, a **free GPS tracklog** allied with **digital mapping** from the OS subscription service will do you on the Glyndŵr's Way. It may not be the case in the remotest wilds of Britain, but providing you have back up battery power or turn them on as needed, smartphones and GPS devices with loaded maps can replace additional paper maps and a compass, because 98.4% of the time the waymarking combined with this book's mapping will be more than adequate. However, some walkers may feel more comfortable with some of the paper maps listed below.

Although our 1:20k maps (5cm=1km; 3⅛ inches=1 mile) in this book will confidently guide you along the trail, in the planning stage it's helpful to see the **big picture** away from the Glyndŵr's corridor which our colour maps, far less a smartphone or even a computer screen back home can't adequately manage. Most might assume the obvious candidates are **Ordnance Survey's** 1:50k Landrangers (2cm=1km; 1¼ inches=1 mile). Three sheets: 137 *Church Stretton & Ludlow*, 136 *Newtown & Llanidloes* and 125 *Bala & Lake Vyrnwy* cover 90% of the walk, plus a 14-mile sliver of sheet 135 *Aberystwyth & Machynlleth*, from near Aberhosan before Machynlleth to just before Abercegir, about 5 miles after Mach. Landrangers depict the walk's route with near 100% accuracy, though like all paper maps updated every few years, they can't always keep up with forest clearances or wind farm installations. Online versions may be more up to date.

It's hard to see the need for the six 1:25k Explorer OS maps which cover the walk when you have good mapping in this book already, but **A-Z** produce a handy *Glyndŵr's Way Adventure Atlas* booklet (2019; £8.95) using 1:25k OS mapping along the routes immediate corridor, should you prefer a reliable back-up to our mapping.

You'll get a much broader spread either side of the trail from **Harvey's** (⌨ harveymaps.co.uk) partly bilingual single-sided plastic map at 1:40k scale. It covers the walk in eight overlapping panels with an OS National Grid overlay

---

❏ SOURCES OF FURTHER INFORMATION

Trail information

● **The National Trail website** (⌨ nationaltrail.co.uk/glyndwrsway) The official website for the trail with ideas on planning your trip, an interactive map with a track-log to download, as well as a news page giving information on works or diversions on the trail, although not all sections are up to date. They're also on Facebook and Twitter.

● Also on Twitter are @glyndŵrsway who post or retweet nice pictures along the trail.

Tourist information and tourist boards

Tourist information centres (TICs) provide all manner of local information for visitors but are more aimed towards holidaymakers and day trippers looking for something to do. Some offer an accommodation-booking service (for which there is usually a fee) and also sell tickets for National Express coaches and trains. There are TICs in Knighton (see p86) and Welshpool (p168).

The **Mid Wales Tourist Board** (⌨ visit midwales.com) has a wide variety of useful information including details of local festivals and events and even the best 'dark skies' spots for stargazing.

Organisations for walkers

● **Backpackers Club** (⌨ backpackersclub.co.uk). Members receive a quarterly magazine, access to a comprehensive information service (including a library), discounts on maps and a farm-pitch directory. Annual membership costs £20 for an individual or £30 for a family.

● **The Long Distance Walkers' Association** (⌨ ldwa.org.uk). Membership includes a journal, *Strider*, published three times a year giving details of challenge events and local group walks as well as articles. Though they no longer produce their *UK Trailwalkers' Handbook*, their website has extensive and detailed information on all the UK long distance paths. Individual membership costs £18 a year (open from October) and family membership for two adults is £25.50.

● **Ramblers** (⌨ ramblers.org.uk) Looks after the interests of walkers throughout Britain. They publish a large amount of information including their quarterly *Walk* magazine (also available to non-members from newsagents). Membership costs £36.60/49 individual/joint.

plus background information. Published in 2014 and also costing £8.95, it would complement this guidebook, especially if using a bike and mixing routes up a bit. Harvey's also sell this map as a download for £20.49, but that rather misses the point of getting the bigger picture.

Enthusiastic map buyers can reduce the expense if they're members of the Backpackers Club (see box p43) who sell them at a significant discount. Public libraries may also have OS maps that can be borrowed free by members.

OS offers a custom-made map service where you choose the centre of the map and pick the scale and format and they print it up. You can even design the cover. This service costs over twice as much as their standard maps and the three Landrangers listed above manage to cover the Glyndŵr's Way nearly completely. 'For personal use' the remaining sliver of sheet 135 could be printed off from an online screenshot.

RECOMMENDED READING

Flora and fauna field guides

Any good guide will be fine; the range of field guides published by Collins is unfailingly practical.

- *Collins Bird Guide, 3rd edition* by Lars Svensson et al (Collins, 2023)
- *Collins Complete Guide to British Wild Flowers* by Paul Sterry (Collins, 2008) or *Collins Wild Flower Guide* by David Streeter et al (Collins 2016)
- *Collins Complete Guide to British Insects* by Michael Chinery (Collins, 2009)
- *The Mammals of Britain and Europe* by David Macdonald and Priscilla Barrett (Collins, 2005)
- *Collins British Tree Guide* by Owen Johnson (Collins 2015) or the much more user friendly *What's that Tree?* by Tony Russell with the RSPB (DK, 2013) which is available in Kindle format.

Also in the RSPB's series of *What's that* pocket guides for beginners are *What's That Bird?* (2012); *What's That Flower?* (2013) and *What's That Butterfly?* (2014) with useful visual comparisons.

There are also several field guide apps for smartphones, including those that can identify birds by their song and appearance. One to consider is 🖳 merlin.allaboutbirds.org.

A similar app for identifying trees will be found at the 🖳 woodlandtrust.org. Of course there is no app if you have no signal which is why a pocket book or e-book may be more useful on Glyndŵr's Way.

General reading

- *Owain Glyndŵr* by Glanmor Williams (University of Wales Press, 2005) Written by an eminent Welsh historian, this is said to be the definitive account of Wales' last native prince.
- *Wild Wales* by George Borrow (Bridge Books, 2009) Quirky, opinionated yet irrepressible account of the author's visit to Wales in the mid-19th century. Free download on Amazon Kindle.

● *A History of Wales* by John Davies (Penguin, 2007) Many consider this the definitive account of Welsh history from the Ice Age to the present, though at over 780 pages, you'd expect nothing less. Honest, objective and packed with detail, Chapter 5 (1282-1530) covers the rebellion over about 50 pages.

● *The Drovers' Roads of Wales* by Shirley Toulson (Wildwood House, 1977) Finely illustrated with photos by Fay Godwin, *Drovers' Roads* describes several walks along Wales' many ancient trade routes, including tracks between Machynlleth and Llandiloes, bringing cattle to the West Midlands via the Kerry Ridgeway northeast of Felindre (said to be the oldest road in Wales). Assisted by their energetic corgis, by the end of the 18th century, drovers led pigs, geese and turkeys as well as sheep and cattle. They played a key social and economic role as carriers of news and cash-free credit brokers between remote farms and the Welsh gentry and the livestock markets in Shrewsbury, Hereford and as far as London at a time when brigands still preyed on wayfarers. Now out of print but you may find it second-hand online.

● *A Short History of the World According to Sheep* by Sally Coulthard (Anima, 2021) You'll see your fair share of sheep along Glyndŵr's Way. High time then to acquaint yourself with the pivotal role your ovine escorts have played in the shaping of human history, not least Wales.

● *Understanding Welsh Place Names: What They Mean and How to Say Them* by Gwili Gog (Northern Eye, 2010) If you've ever wondered what all those vowel-starved combinations of place names mean, the answer is in this finely illustrated small book, with a lot more besides.

● *Owain Glyndŵr's Way* by Richard Sale (Hutchinson, 1985) This was the first independent guide to the original route and while not so good on mapping and routes (like the original PCC leaflets; see p11), it's valuable for its engaging and thoroughly researched history and folklore, and all delivered with a light touch over 144 pages. Used copies are available online, with the 1992 Constable edition expanding on the subject and in a more pocketable size. The last edition was in 2001.

● *On the Black Hill* by Bruce Chatwin (Vintage Classics, 1982) This family saga spans the latter 19th- and 20th century, describing the largely uninterrupted and self-imposed misery of farming the hills of south Radnorshire. Amos, a fanatically religious brute, marries 'class betraying' Mary resulting in Benjamin and Lewis, their repressed but emotionally conjoined twins. Made into a film in 1987.

PLANNING YOUR WALK

❏ **OWAIN GLYN DŴR SOCIETY**
Established in 1996 to raise awareness of this key figure in Welsh history, the Owain Glyn Dŵr Society's website (⌨ owain-glyndwr.wales) is one of the most detailed online sources into the life and times of the legendary Welsh prince. Visualising the sweep and dates of the historical events outlined on pp51-7 is a lot easier on the video map animation linked from the website, where you'll also find audio and video presentations as well as timelines and much more.

Getting to and from the Glyndŵr's Way

Both Knighton and Welshpool, at either end of the trail, are easily reached by train, bus or National Express coach and of course, road. You can even walk there along the Offa's Dyke. In addition, trains serve Machynlleth (the same line as Welshpool) and buses will reach down to Llanidloes. Elsewhere, away from trunk roads, local buses might come just once a week. If you're doing the walk in sections, it's easiest to plan breaks in Llanidloes and Machynlleth.

NATIONAL TRANSPORT

By rail

There are two rail routes which intersect with the walk. The **Heart of Wales Line** (🖳 heart-of-wales.co.uk), modestly comprising just two carriages, links Shrewsbury with Swansea and stops at **Knighton** (Trefyclo) and nearby

PLANNING YOUR WALK

❏ **GETTING TO BRITAIN**

● **By air** Most international airlines serve London Heathrow (🖳 heathrow.com) and London Gatwick (🖳 gatwickairport.com). A number of budget airlines fly from many of Europe's major cities to the other London terminals at Stansted (🖳 stanstedairport.com) and Luton (🖳 london-luton.co.uk).

There are also flights from Europe to **Bristol** (🖳 bristolairport.co.uk), **Cardiff** (🖳 cardiff-airport.com) and **Birmingham** (🖳 birminghamairport.co.uk) which are closer to Glyndŵr's Way than London. For details of airlines and destinations served visit the website for the relevant airport.

● **From Europe by train** Eurostar (🖳 eurostar.com) operates a high-speed passenger service between Paris, Brussels, Amsterdam (and some other cities) and London. In London trains arrive and depart from St Pancras International. St Pancras has connections to the London Underground and to all other main railway stations in London. For more information about rail services from Europe contact your national rail operator, or Railteam (🖳 railteam.eu).

● **From Europe by coach** Eurolines (🖳 eurolines.eu) works with a huge network of long-distance coach operators connecting many cities in mainland Europe with London, where it links in with the British National Express network (see opposite). Flixbus (🖳 flixbus.com) also provides services from destinations in mainland Europe to London.

● **From Europe by ferry** (with or without a car) Numerous ferry companies operate routes between the major North Sea and Channel ports of mainland Europe and the ports on Britain's eastern and southern coasts as well as from Ireland to both Wales and England. A useful website for further information is 🖳 directferries.com.

● **From Europe by car** LeShuttle (formerly Eurotunnel; 🖳 eurotunnel.com) operates a shuttle train service between Calais and Folkestone, taking one hour between the motorway in France and the motorway in Britain.

❏ **PUBLIC TRANSPORT – TRAIN SERVICES**
Note: not all stops are listed and only direct services are included.

Transport for Wales (TfW; 🖵 tfw.wales)
● Manchester Piccadilly to Cardiff via Crewe, Shrewsbury, Ludlow, Hereford, Abergavenny & Newport: daily at least 1/hr.
● Birmingham (International and/or New St) to Aberystwyth via Shrewsbury, **Welshpool** and **Machynlleth**: Mon-Sat up to 8/day, Sun 6/day.
● Holyhead/Bangor to Cardiff via Chester, Wrexham, Shrewsbury, Craven Arms, Ludlow, Hereford, Abergavenny & Newport : Mon-Sat from 9/day, Sun 2/day.
● Shrewsbury to Swansea via **Knighton**: Mon-Sat 4/day, Sun 2/day (Heart of Wales line).

Avanti (🖵 avantiwestcoast.co.uk)
● London Euston to Liverpool Lime St via Crewe, Mon-Sat 2/hr, Sun 1/hr
● London Euston to Glasgow Central via Crewe, Mon-Sat 2/hr, Sun 1/hr
● London Euston to Birmingham New St via Crewe, Mon-Sat 2/hr, Sun 1/hr
● Birmingham to Shrewsbury, Mon-Sat 1/hr (see TfW for Sunday service)

Llangunllo (Llangynllo station is 1.4 miles north of Llangunllo village, see Map 3). The busier **Cambrian Line** (🖵 thecambrianline.co.uk) runs from Birmingham via Shrewsbury and **Welshpool** to **Machynlleth** where it divides south for Aberystwyth or Pwllheli on the Llyn peninsula to the north. So for most visitors travelling by rail, **Shrewsbury** will be the key station to getting there and back as both the above lines meet here as do other routes to the cities of England, Wales and beyond.

National Rail Enquiries (🖵 nationalrail.co.uk) provides all timetable and fare information. Fares vary widely, but significant savings can be made by booking in advance and of course, using **rail cards**. You can buy tickets at larger railway stations in the UK or online through the relevant company or 🖵 thetrainline.com. For details of the main operators and general frequency of service see box above.

By coach

National Express (🖵 nationalexpress.com) is the principal long-distance coach operator in Britain. Travel by coach is usually cheaper than full-price trains but takes longer. The best fares are those bought at least a week in advance.

There is currently only one direct service of use to Glyndŵr's Way walkers: NX409 London to Aberystwyth via Birmingham, Shrewsbury, **Welshpool** & **Llanidloes** (1/day).

By car

Non-residential roadside or public car parks are not usually suited for stays of over a week, but provided you can arrange secure parking at either end (try the Offa's Dyke Centre in Knighton, see p86), a car frees you from juggling with transport schedules, especially if you live in an ill-served corner of the country. From Welshpool getting back to Knighton via Shrewsbury can be done in 3-4

PLANNING YOUR WALK

☐ PUBLIC TRANSPORT – BUS SERVICES

Notes The details below were correct at the time of writing but services and operators change so it is essential to check before travelling. Many of the services listed operate year-round; however, they may operate less frequently in the winter months (generally November to March/April). Services operate with the same frequency in the opposite direction. Note that **not all stops are listed.**

Bus Times (☐ bustimes.org) is a very useful website for finding bus stops.

Celtic Travel (☎ 01686-412231, ☐ celtic-travel.co.uk)
X47§ Llandrindod Wells to Aberystwyth via **Llanidloes**, Mon-Sat 2-3/day
X75 Llanidloes to Shrewsbury via Newtown & **Welshpool**, Mon-Sat 6/day.

Lloyds Coaches (☎ 01654-702100, ☐ lloydscoaches.com)
T2 Aberystwyth to Bangor via **Machynlleth** & Dolgellau, Mon-Sat 9/day, Sun 3-4/day (Change at Dolgellau for T3 to Wrexham)
T12 Machynlleth to Wrexham via Penegoes, **Glantwymyn/Cemmaes Rd**, **Llanbrynmair**, Newtown and **Welshpool**, Mon-Sat 6-7/day
X29 Machynlleth to Tywyn via Pennal & Aberdyfi, Mon-Sat 9/day, Sun 2-3/day
33/36§ Machynlleth to Dinas Mawddwy via **Penegoes & Glantwymyn/ Cemmaes Rd**, Mon-Sat 5/day (3/day continue to Dolgellau)

T36 Dyfi Valley BwcaBus *(Note: must be prebooked by calling ☎ 01654-702100 at least 2hrs ahead)*
Machynlleth to **Glantwymyn/Cemmaes Rd** via **Penegoes**, Mon-Fri 5/day

T37 Cadfarch BwcaBus *(Note: must be prebooked by calling ☎ 01654-702100 at least 2hrs ahead)*
Machynlleth to Aberhosan via **Penegoes & Abercegir**, Mon-Fri 2/day

Minsterley Motors (☎ 01743 791208, ☐ minsterleymotors.co.uk)
738/740 **Knighton** to Ludlow, Mon-Sat 4/day

Owen's Travelmaster (☎ 01691-652126, ☐ owenstravel.co.uk)
76A Dolanog to **Welshpool** via **Pontrobert** & Meifod, Mon only 1/day

Oswestry Community Action (Qube) ☐ qube-oca.org.uk/dial-a-ride *(Must be prebooked on ☎ 01691 671571 at least 2 hrs ahead)*
T82§ Lake Vyrnwy Dam to Oswestry via **Abertridwr** Garage, Wed only 1/day

Tanat Valley Coaches (☎ 01691-780212, ☐ tanat.co.uk)
76/76B Llanfyllin to **Welshpool** via Meifod, Mon-Sat 3-4/day

§ School/shopping bus so usually runs one way early morning with return journey mid/late afternoon.

Public Transport

Bus service — Train service

NOT TO SCALE

hours. That said, for a visit of a couple of days and with fuel costs shared, parking a car can work well, especially if the place you end at is reasonably well served with public transport. The crook of the walk at Machynlleth is where distances are close enough to make the cost of a shared taxi back to the car bearable. Most others find it's easier to use public transport; you can sit back and congratulate yourself on the twin moral victories of supporting rural transport services while reducing your carbon footprint.

LOCAL TRANSPORT

The map on p49 gives an overview of the most useful bus and train routes for walkers; for contact details and the approximate frequency of services, see the public transport services box on p48 (buses) and on p47 (trains). The latest information on public transport can also be obtained from the national public transport information line, **traveline** (☎ 0800-464 0000, 🖥 traveline.cymru).

The nature of the walk is such that bus services are infrequent and fragmented, with different operators establishing routes on their own patch to meet local demand, particularly school bus services and shopping needs. Both timetables and operators, especially in rural areas, tend to change at short notice, and summer and winter services can vary considerably. Check ahead to make sure that the service you want is running. Be aware that some community transport services operate only if pre-booked at least two hours in advance.

PLANNING YOUR WALK

HISTORY, ENVIRONMENT & NATURE

2

History of the Welsh rebellion

"Cruell [were the] *lawes against Welshmen made by Henrie the ffourth"*
Owen of Henllys, 16th-century Welsh historian

It seems it was a neighbours' dispute exacerbated by an ill-timed change of monarch which set off the most protracted and initially successful of Welsh rebellions that cost so much and went on to achieve so little. Visualising the sweep and dates of these events is a lot easier on the video map animation linked from the Owain Glyn Dŵr Society's website: 🖥 owain-glyndwr.wales (see box p45).

OWAIN GLYNDŴR'S EARLY LIFE

Owain Glyndŵr was born in the mid 1350s into the Welsh landed gentry in Sycharth (see box p52), north of Welshpool. He professed descent via Llywelyn the Great and the three great kingdoms of Cymru: Gwynedd, Powys and Deheubarth (southwest Wales) which had been briefly united under Rhodri Mawr in 872. The assassination of Owain Lawgoch in 1378 while planning an invasion from France saw the extinction of Gwynedd's powerful House of Aberffraw and so the bards and soothsayers sought a new rebel king with a lineage descended from Rhodri Mawr. For some, Owain Glyndŵr fitted that profile and around 1390 the celebrated Welsh bard, Iolo Goch, composed the praise poem *Owain Glyndŵr's Court*. In it he extolled the hospitality of '*the Light of Powys*', the splendour of his Sycharth estate (likened to Westminster Abbey and even a Neapolitan villa) while describing his many children as '*a fine nestful of chieftains*'.

Benefitting from a nobleman's education in London, Glyndŵr learned Latin, French and English and went on to become squire to the Earl of Arundel and maybe even to Henry Bolingbroke himself, future usurper and Glyndŵr's later nemesis. He honed his martial skills fighting with the English against the Scots and French and at some point married a teenage bride, Margaret of Hanmer, who bore some of his many children. Towards the end of the century he settled down into running his own estate at Glyndyfrdwy (see box below) in North Wales and from which his surname derives. As the 14th century turned, his life was to take a very different direction.

THE MARCHER LORDS

Backtracking a few centuries, Cymru's three dominant Celtic kingdoms had quickly reemerged following the departure of the Romans in the 5th century. Thereafter they engaged in the soon-to-be-familiar pattern of war, dynastic alliances and occasional union, while Saxon and later Norse incursions pressed from all sides. William the Conqueror's invasion of Britain in 1066 was predicated on ensuring his barons' loyalty with land and all its potential income. England fell relatively easily, but the task of subduing the Cymry or 'the people' ('Wallia' or Wales being a Saxon word for foreigners) was eventually outsourced to the Marcher or 'borderland' lords. The favoured were allocated estates across western Mercia (today's Welsh Marches) with frontiers that were fixed in the east but undefined westwards, allowing them to grab as much as they could retain. The Marcher lords' rapaciousness was matched with equal resistance across terrain ill-suited to the Norman cavalry-based war machine. It would take some two centuries to subdue the land.

The death of Llywelyn ap Gryffudd near Builth in 1282 ('Llywelyn the Last'; buried at Abbeycwmhir; see box p104) sealed the capitulation of Wales to the English under Edward I. Llywelyn's brother Dafydd fought on but was caught and taken to Shrewsbury a year later to be drawn [dragged], hung [partially strangled], then watch his disembowelled innards get cast onto a fire before being quartered (to give the correct order; this was the first recorded example of this macabre execution). His pieces were then displayed as deterrents across the four corners of the land. Following nearly a millennium of autonomy, Gwynedd and Powys became a principality within the English realm. To remind the Cymry who was in charge, between 1301 and 1969 the title of 'Prince of Wales' has been bestowed on the English monarch's heir at a ceremony in Caernarfon. The work which the Normans had started in 1066 had finally been achieved. By the end of the 14th century the Welsh principalities had reached a shaky accommodation with the new Anglo-Norman hegemony holed up in the 'ring of stone', a series of fortresses built during the reign of Edward I, the self-declared first 'king of England and Wales'.

> ❏ GLYNDŴR'S ANCESTRAL HOMES
> Both Sycharth and Glyndyfrdwy survive today as grassy mounds ringed by defensive ditches where a motte and bailey 'castle' or fortified lodge once stood. The former (💻 www.castlewales.com/sycharth) is a 15-mile drive north of Welshpool and the latter another 20 miles north around the Berwyn hills to a point marked 'Owen Glyndŵr's Mount' (💻 www.castlewales.com/gldwr_mt) alongside the A5 and River Dee, between Corwen and Glyndyfrdwy.

The south of the country which, as far back as the 9th century had sought Alfred of Wessex's protection against the belligerent northern kingdoms, was now controlled by Marcher lords or were enclaves of English support. But the upland north and west, like mountainous Gwynedd, Anglesey, and the hills of Powys, were known as *Pura Wallia* which only begrudgingly accepted the English yoke based out of *Marchia Wallia* in the east and south. In most cases a tribute was paid for the continued permission of the ruling elite to capitalise from their feudal fiefdoms.

THE RIGHTFUL PRINCE OF WALES

This was the brutal medieval world of dynastic rivalries into which Owain Glyndŵr was born. At this time the Black Death had nearly halved Britain's population, causing social upheavals which threat-

> *These signs have marked me extraordinary*
> *And all the courses of my life do show*
> *I am not in the roll of common men.*
> Owen Glyndower in *Henry IV, Part I*,
> **William Shakespeare**

ened to disrupt the ancient feudal order. Wat Tyler's Peasant Revolt of 1381 was eventually crushed by the teenage Richard II with the chilling threat '*For as long as we live we will strive to suppress you, and your misery will be an example in the eyes of posterity*'. The increasingly tyrannical king was deeply unpopular among his English barons and parliament, but did have the support of influential Welsh landowners like Anglesey's Tudur ap Goronway (a close relative of Glyndŵr). Returning from making war in Ireland, in 1399 Richard II was ambushed in North Wales, forcibly deposed, imprisoned and starved to death once plots for his restoration were uncovered. Though not the heir presumptive, Bolingbroke (Richard's cousin) convoluted a rightful claim and stepped on to the throne as Henry IV with his own network of allegiances. Less well disposed towards the upstart Celtic princes, it was to signal the end of Owain Glyndŵr's comfortable position.

The fuse of Glyndŵr's rebellion was lit following an earlier land-grab by neighbouring Marcher lord, Reginald Grey of Ruthin, who was now a member of the elite King's Council. Glyndŵr had dutifully followed legal protocols for such disputes, but with Grey's closer ties, Glyndŵr's claim on the land was rejected with the scathing jibe '*what care we for Welsh dogs?*'

Despite being now well into middle age and with years of service for the English, this slight to Glyndŵr was compounded when Grey deliberately delayed notifying him of a royal summons to provide men for the new king's Scottish wars. Glyndŵr's apparent failure to comply was a treasonous act and Glyndŵr's estates were deemed forfeit until he could prove his loyalty.

Forced into a corner, on September 16th 1400 the hitherto dependable Glyndŵr proclaimed himself the rightful 'Prince of Wales' – 'Tywysog Cymru'. That done, he first struck north against Grey at Ruthin, then swept in a clockwise arc through the Marches, sacking Denbigh, Flint and Oswestry among other places, but met defeat at the Battle of Vyrnwy near Meifod. A later offer of reconciliation by Grey turned out to be an ambush which Glyndŵr foresaw and dodged.

The rebellion seemed to stall until the sons of Tudur ap Goronway, Glyndŵr's cousins and scions of the prominent family, led a parallel rebellion in Anglesey. That too ended in defeat thanks to Henry IV's swift response and within a month it seemed the brief rebellion has been extinguished. Pardons were offered to all except Glyndŵr, with the repressive Penal Laws of 1401 imposing punitive sanctions on the Welsh. In fact, among many Welsh the uprising had revived thoughts of self-determination, with expatriates now returning home to fight for the cause.

On Good Friday 1401 Owain's Tudur cousins tricked their way into the impregnable fortress of Conwy while its Marcher lord was in church. Now finding themselves besieged, they eventually surrendered some of their own to the customary grisly fate in return for their freedom. In the meantime Glyndŵr had set up camp in the remote valley of Hyddgen just north of Pumlumon mountain (see p173), periodically raiding the countryside, including the abbey at Cwmhir (see box p104) where Llywelyn, his decapitated ancestor, lay buried. In June 1401 Glyndŵr's Hyddgen camp was surrounded by a much bigger army of English and Flemish mercenaries, but he prevailed against the odds. Following this victory a series of agile guerrilla raids flowed thick and fast, a technique which trailed no vulnerable supply line that could be easily cut by a garrison dispatched from the nearest Marcher castle. In early 1402 Owain's enemy Reginald Grey was caught and ransomed, leaving him ruined. At the same time a comet passing westwards over England and Wales was taken as a good omen for Glyndŵr's cause, but bode less well for Hywel, a distant cousin. He failed to assassinate Glyndŵr and paid with his life and the destruction of his estate.

A string of decisive victories

Under his able general Rhys Gethin 'the Fierce', a battle that summer at Bryn Glas, near Knighton, saw another decisive victory for Glyndŵr, ending with the capture of Edmund Mortimer when his native Welsh archers turned on him. What followed was a widely recorded savage mutilation of the dead and dying by camp followers; in Shakespeare's words (*Henry IV, Part I*):

… *Upon whose dead corpse there was such misuse, Such beastly shameless transformation, By those Welshwomen done as may not be without much shame retold or spoken of.*

Fearing the Mortimer family's legitimate claim to his throne, Henry IV's usual offer of ransom didn't materialise. As a result Mortimer switched sides and later married one of Owain's daughters, so aligning the Glyndŵr line a little closer to the English nobles.

When Abergavenny and Cardiff were sacked by Glyndŵr, the king, his son Bolingbroke and the earls of Arundel, Stafford and Warwick responded with a decisive, three pronged response along the length of the Welsh borderlands. The campaign failed:

…through art magicke…[bringing] *foul weather of winds, tempest, rain snow and hail … the like of which he had never seen.*

Bolingbroke was nearly killed in a storm by a collapsing tent, all helping to found the myth of Glyndŵr's supernatural ability to appear out of nowhere and to control the elements.

Around this time the hitherto ambivalent southern principalities (populated by Flemish weavers since the time of Henry I) came on side, as briefly did the king's ally, Harry Percy of Northumberland who, like Mortimer, had fallen out of Henry IV's favour. He died in 1403 with thousands more in a battle north of Shrewsbury (now the village of Battlefield) and appears as 'Hotspur' in Shakespeare's 1597 play, *Henry IV, Part I*, alongside 'Owen Glendower' and 'Prince Hal', the heir to the throne with his rotund fictional sidekick, Falstaff.

At this stage much of the land apart from the Marcher fortresses was under Welsh control. A fourth military intervention from Hereford by Henry IV again fell flat, while a few days later Glyndŵr rematerialised and took every major town between Usk and Cardiff. Expatriate Welshmen were now dropping their quills, hoes and trowels and, along with hundreds of Welsh archers and other soldiers seasoned in French and Scottish campaigns, joined the Welsh rebellion, as did French and ethnically Celtic Breton troops. It wasn't all good news for Glyndŵr however; his unoccupied estates at Sycharth and Glyndyfrdwy were razed by Prince Henry ('Hal'), never to recover.

By 1404 Glyndŵr had captured the key west coast castles of Aberystwyth and Harlech, where he brought his family and now based his court. With these successes and the English up to their necks with the restive Scots, there was now time to organise an official investiture in Machynlleth as 'Prince of Wales' before emissaries from Scotland, France and Castile (Christian Spain). The first parliament was held, promising a return to the progressive 10th-century 'Hywel's Law'. A better documented assembly was held in Harlech in 1406, the same year the Pennal Letter was written (see box p133). A manifesto and plea for support to the lunatic Charles VI of France, the letter foresaw the establishment of universities and an independent church in Wales pledging allegiance to the papacy in Avignon, not Rome, as England did. By early 1405 Glyndŵr felt confident enough to propose the Tripartite Indenture: dividing a soon-to-be conquered England between the Mortimer and Percy families while he settled for a substantially enlarged Wales.

The rebellion falters and collapses

This breathtaking pace couldn't last, despite a pact with the French who had been helpfully raiding southern English ports for over a year. In the far south battles at Grosmont and, later, Pwll Melyn near Usk saw the rebellion's first major defeats; the death of Glyndŵr's brother Tudur, and Rhys the Fierce, as well as the capture of Glyndŵr's son who would eventually waste away in the Tower. In the north, the English retook Anglesey; the rebellion was in trouble.

HISTORY, ENVIRONMENT & NATURE

Following a crossing delayed by bad weather, which cost them their valuable horses, a reluctant French force landed at Milford Haven and joined Glyndŵr to raze Haverfordwest, Tenby and other towns. Then Glyndŵr over-reached himself and invaded England, basing his forces at Woodbury Hill, northwest of Worcester. Out on a limb, after a few days and some skirmishes, the rebels withdrew, possibly under a brief truce. Henry regrouped and pursued, but was again cut off by storms attributed to Glyndŵr's dastardly supernatural powers.

The French sailed home and, according to one chronicle, '... *from that time forth in those parts the fortunes of Owen waned*'. Some accepted Prince Henry's pardons but Glyndŵr became a hunted outlaw, dodging outright confrontations for the guerrilla-style raids of his early successes. By 1407 the English were gaining ground and two years later cornered Glyndŵr and his court in Harlech where his family were captured and Edmund Mortimer was killed. Glyndŵr escaped and went on to harry the English for a few more years, rejecting pardons from the new Henry V which his son, Maredudd, eventually accepted. By 1412 most territorial gains had been lost and following one last ambush near Brecon, Owain Glyndŵr – the last Welshman to carry the title 'Prince of Wales' – vanished into the hills.

OWAIN GLYNDŴR'S LEGACY

Unlike the Scottish rebel William Wallace, popularised in the 1995 film, *Braveheart*, Owain Glyndŵr was neither betrayed nor captured. It's thought he died in 1415, the year of Henry V's famous victory at Agincourt, coincidentally secured with the help of lethal Welsh archers. The rebellion fizzled out, unable to resist the vastly greater resources of the English, and the Cymry ended up little better off than the massacred French. The years that followed saw the imposition of more restrictions in a land already crippled by years of warfare, made worse by 'scorched earth' tactics employed by both sides.

Nearly two centuries later, in a bid to consolidate his realm after his break with the Catholic church, Henry VIII's 1536 Act of Union amended Edward I's 1284 annexation of Wales to incorporation into the English realm. Parliamentary representation was offered, the Marcher lordships were scrapped and English law and language now took precedence.

In 2012, the discovery of Richard III's remains in a Leicester car park recalled the demise of the Plantagenets at Bosworth Field in 1485 by Henry Tudor, launching a new English dynasty with Welsh roots. But any remains of Owain Glyndŵr, or even the grave, have yet to be located. It's thought he spent his final years near the village of Vorchurch, a few miles west of Hereford, at a former seat of the Scudamore family into which Glyndŵr's daughter Alys had married. Others believe he's buried in nearby Kentchurch, near the Welsh border.

With his passing, the myth of Owain Glyndŵr and his deeds began to coalesce. Shakespeare portrayed him as an exotic, magical figure channeling ancient Druidic wisdom to '*call spirits from the vasty deep*'. (To which Hotspur tellingly replies: '*Why, so can I, or so can any man; But will they come, when you do call for them?*').

Since that time, among the Welsh Glyndŵr's reputation has grown massively, particularly as calls for greater autonomy from England mounted in the latter half of the 20th century. Meanwhile, on the death of Queen Elizabeth II in 2022, a flying royal visit to Wales by the new King Charles III fell, probably coincidentally, on September 16th, Owain Glyndŵr Day. A few days earlier the palace had announced the title of Prince of Wales had passed to William, Charles's son and heir, though this latest Prince of Wales very soon made it clear he had no plans for any kind of lavish investiture ceremony.

The environment & nature

Frequently we are made aware that interests from construction, development and the transport infrastructure make demands on our woods and fields, replacing them with concrete and brick. There are plenty of organisations determined to slow this pace of development, some of them listed on p59. Thanks to the efforts of these groups, many of them voluntary, the fight-back is holding its own.

GOVERNMENT AGENCIES, SCHEMES & GLOBAL INSTITUTIONS

In 2013 the Countryside Council for Wales (who funded the Way's upgrading to a National Trail in the late 1990s) was renamed Natural Resources Wales (NRW; 🖥 naturalresources.wales); the government body responsible for conservation and landscape protection in Wales. NRW has also taken over the functions of Forestry Commission Wales and the Environment Agency in Wales, and is also responsible for drawing up and reviewing the quality standards for National Trails in Wales. NRW and other agencies aim to give protection from modern development and to maintain the countryside in its present state. As in England, one of its roles is to designate national trails, national parks, national landscapes (the new name for AONBs – areas of outstanding natural beauty), sites of special scientific interest (SSSIs), and national nature reserves (NNRs), and to enforce regulations relating to all these sites.

National parks
National park status is the highest level of landscape protection available in Britain and recognises the importance of the area in terms of landscape, biodiversity and as a recreational resource. As in the US, some might say these places have become victims of their own success, sucking in sometimes unsustainable crowds with associated congestion, while nearby areas are overlooked. There are three national parks in Wales (Snowdonia, Pembrokeshire Coast and Brecon Beacons), covering around one-fifth of the country's total land area. For better or worse, Glyndŵr's Way does not pass through any of them which may explain its continued obscurity.

HISTORY, ENVIRONMENT & NATURE

> ❏ **MAINTENANCE OF GLYNDŴR'S WAY**
> The Glyndŵr's Way Management Service looks after the running of this national
> trail, replacing broken stiles, fallen posts or missing way marks to make sure the route
> is well signposted. Report issues encountered along the Way to the trail officer, Helen
> Tatchell (☎ 01597-827562, helen.tatchell@powys.gov.uk), who is based in
> Machynlleth and also looks after the Offa's Dyke Path. This task is assisted by vol-
> unteer wardens, some of whom may be your hosts along the Way.

Areas of outstanding natural beauty (AONBs/National Landscapes)
Land which falls outside the remit of a national park but which is nonetheless
deemed special enough for protection may be designated an AONB, the second
level of protection after national park status. There are five AONBs in Wales
including Anglesey, the Gower and the Llŷn Peninsula but again, Glyndŵr's
Way does not pass through any.

Sites of special scientific interest (SSSIs)
This is an important designation which affords extra protection to unique areas
against anything that threatens the habitat or environment. Although SSSIs are
not widely known, they range in size from small sites where orchids grow, or
birds nest, to vast swathes of upland, moorland and wetland. There are over a
thousand in Wales covering over ten per cent of the land surface. Glyndŵr's
Way has its share though you won't see any signs. Mostly they cover rivers,
some woods and for example, Dylife and its nearby gorge, the entire moorland
of the Pumlumon horseshoe (see pp173-80) and Glaslyn lake, the hills around
Lake Vyrnwy and parts of the Vyrnwy river valley below. 'Triple-S Is' are managed in partnership with the owners and occupiers of the land who must give
written notice of any operations likely to damage the site and who cannot proceed until consent is given.

National nature reserves (NNRs)
NNRs were set up to conserve the finest examples of wildlife habitats and geo-
logical features. There are 76 in Wales; all of them are also SSSIs. Some are
owned by NRW who select and designate them. NRW manages 58 but others
are managed by landowners or bodies such as Wildlife Trusts, the RSPB or a
local authority. Local nature reserves (LNRs) are designated by local authorities. There are none along the Glyndŵr's Way.

UNESCO sites
*The **UNESCO Dyfi Biosphere** inspires people and organisations to work together in creating sustainable futures we can all be proud of. It connects people with nature and cultural
heritage while strengthening the local economy.*　　🖳 **dyfibiosphere.wales**

The United National Education, Scientific and Cultural Organisation was
founded in post-war London in 1945 with the aim of fostering peace through
building mutual understanding between the peoples of the world. This global
organisation is grounded in local designations including World Heritage Sites,

Geoparks, Creative Cities and **Biospheres**. There are seven of the latter in the UK; Glyndŵr's Way passes through **Biosffer Dyfi** (see box p149), the only one in Wales.

CAMPAIGNING AND CONSERVATION ORGANISATIONS

Voluntary organisations started the conservation movement back in the mid-1800s and are still at the forefront of developments. Independent of government but reliant on public support, they can concentrate their resources either on acquiring land which can then be managed purely for conservation purposes, or on influencing political decision-makers by lobbying and campaigning.

The **National Trust** (NT; 🖳 nationaltrust.org.uk), with a membership of around 5.5 million, protects over 500 historic houses, gardens and ancient monuments as well as forests, woods, coastline, farmland, moorland and islands, the vast majority in England. NT properties on or close to the trail only include Powis Castle & Garden (see box p168). **Cadw: Welsh Historic Monuments** (🖳 cadw.gov.wales) is the Welsh organisation that protects, conserves and promotes an appreciation of the built heritage of Wales. The Bryntail mine (see box p122 & Map 25) is a Cadw site.

The **Royal Society for the Protection of Birds** (Welsh Office 🖳 rspb.org.uk/about-the-rspb/at-home-and-abroad/wales) has 1.2 million members and 220 nature reserves, including Lake Vyrnwy (see Map 25).

Active support for conservation work and sustainability comes from a number of organisations: the **Campaign for the Protection of Rural Wales** (CPRW; 🖳 cprw.org.uk) aims to conserve the landscape and quality of life in rural areas; the **Inland Waterways Association** (🖳 waterways.org.uk) looks after the interests of canal users; you'll end your walk alongside the Montgomery Canal in Welshpool. The **Wildlife Trusts** (🖳 wildlifetrusts.org) is an umbrella organisation that brings together the work of 46 individual Wildlife Trusts, of which there are five in Wales including Montgomeryshire (🖳 montwt.co.uk) and Radnorshire (🖳 rwt wales.org) wildlife trusts through which the walk passes. The trusts advise on land management which supports wildlife; and the **Woodland Trust** (🖳 woodlandtrust.org.uk) aims to conserve, restore and re-establish trees, particularly broadleaved species.

Increasing interest in environmental issues both from the public and the media in recent years underlines a greater awareness that such issues affect us

---

❏ **OTHER STATUTORY BODIES AND COUNTRYSIDE AUTHORITIES**
● **Clwyd-Powys Archaeological Trust** (CPAT; 🖳 cpat.org.uk) This organisation is one of the four Welsh archaeological trusts that works to help protect, record and interpret all aspects of the historic landscape.
● **Coflein** (🖳 coflein.gov.uk) is an online resource cataloguing many thousands of archaeological sites, monuments, buildings and maritime sites in Wales, including an index to the drawings, manuscripts and photographs held in the National Monuments Record of Wales (NMRW) archive collections.

all, and should not just be left to government agencies. What is emerging is the most powerful lobbying group of all: an informed electorate.

Flora and fauna

Like many of Britain's National Trails, Glyndŵr's Way passes through a diversity of landscapes and habitats that play host to a rich and varied wildlife. The path leads you through wooded ravines to sweeping hillsides and the expanse of the Cambrian Mountains. It offers the chance for seeing a wide range of wildlife and wild flowers, both familiar and unfamiliar. It would take a considerable library to do justice to the flora and fauna you might encounter on the way, so this can serve only as a brief introduction to the trail's most common species. Many of the B&Bs along the trail have field guides and environmental magazines that you can read at the end of the day's walk, while for additional input, the list of field guides on p144 should point you in the right direction.

In order to understand an environment it is important to appreciate the inter-actions between the plants and animals that inhabit it – and the impact of man on this relationship. If a greater awareness of these issues leads to an improve-ment in the way that we as walkers treat the countryside, and thus to our atti-tudes to conservation, that can only be a good thing.

TREES

The wide diversity of mature trees thriving alongside Glyndŵr's Way is one of the walk's highlights and efforts are being made to replant cleared plantations with local broadleaved species. On a less positive note, where felling takes place

❏ ASH DIEBACK

Described by The Tree Council as 'the most damaging tree disease since Dutch elm', Chalara ash dieback is caused by a fungus called *Hymenoscyphus fraxineus* which is native to eastern Asia. It was first identified in England in 2012 and initially causes blackening and wilting of leaves and shoots in mid- to late-summer, progressing from the leaves into the twigs, branches and eventu-ally the trunk of the tree. It is now present in most parts of the UK, potentially leading to the decline and possible death of the majority of ash trees in the country. See 🖥 treecoun-cil.org.uk for more information about the action plan, known as the Ash Dieback Toolkit, to help deal with the problem.

ASH (WITH SEEDS)

it can block or reroute the path, displace waymarks and leave an ugly, scarred landscape.

Deciduous

Trees are abundant along the Way with all the common indigenous species evident in large numbers. These include the **oak**, both English pedunculate oak (*Quercus robur*) and sessile oak (*Quercus petraea*), the difference being that with sessile oaks, the leaves are on stalks, not the acorns; **sycamore** (*Acer pseudoplatanus*), **ash** (*Fraxinus excelsior*), **beech** (*Fagus sylvatica*), **birch** (*Betula pubescens*), **lime** or linden (*Tiliax vulgaris*), **horse chestnut** (*Aesculus hippocastanum*) and **hornbeam** (*Carpinus betulus*).

Alder (with flowers)

Amongst mixed woodland you will also see trees such as **rowan** or mountain ash (*Sorbus aucuparia*) with its bright red berries from August. A favourite food for birds, drovers of old would pick a leaf for luck before setting off on their trek. Other trees include **silver birch** (*Betula pendula*), **aspen** (*Populus tremula*), **alder** (*Alnus glutinosa*), **wych elm** (*Ulmus glabra*), **poplar** (*Populus alba*) and **hazel** (*Corylus avellana*). The English elm (*Ulmus procera*) has been virtually wiped out by Dutch elm disease.

The **willow** most commonly seen along riverbanks and streams is the crack willow (*Salix fragilis*) which is often pollarded to encourage growth. The tree on which catkins appear is the goat or pussy willow (*Salix caprea*).

Conifers

Mid-Wales has experienced the same mass planting of conifers as Scotland, the Lake District and Northumberland, although the stretches of the trail passing through the sunless and silent environment of closely planted conifers are short and rather intriguing. The most common plantation trees are the **sitka spruce** (*Picea sitchensis*) introduced from North America and capable of growing 1.5m (approx 5ft) a year, **Norway spruce** (*Picea abies*; 'Christmas trees') which can reach a height of 40m (131ft), the European **larch** (*Larix decidua*) and the **Scots pine** (*Pinus sylvestris*).

❑ **OAK LEAVES WITH GALLS**
Oak trees support more kinds of insects than any other tree in Britain and some affect the oak in unusual ways. Some of these insects affect the oak in interesting ways: the eggs of gall-flies, for example, cause growths known as galls on the leaves. Each of these contains a single insect. Other kinds of gall-flies lay eggs in stalks or flowers, leading to flower galls, growths the size of currants.

HISTORY, ENVIRONMENT & NATURE

WILD FLOWERS

Hedgerows and field boundaries

In spring and early summer the variety of wild flowers in the hedgerows and along the verges of the minor roads and lanes which you will walk along will be rich indeed, primary among them being the **daffodil** (*Narcissus pseudonarcissus*), the national flower of Wales.

Even those with little knowledge will soon learn to recognise other species such as **red campion** (*Silene dioica*), **cowslip** (*Primula veris*), **primrose** (*Primula vulgaris*), **birdsfoot trefoil** (*Lotus corniculatus*) or 'bacon and eggs', **common speedwell** (*Veronica officinalis*) which is said to cure indigestion, gout and liver complaints, **bugle** (*Ajuga reptans*), **tufted vetch** (*Vicia cracca*)

❏ TIMBER GROWING

Forest and woodland areas make up almost 15% of the land area of Wales, of which almost a third is taken up by the sitka spruce, grown primarily for newsprint: 'paper from sustainable forestry'. The Glyndŵr's Way passes through several such plantations, the largest of which is at the Hafren Forest south of Machynlleth.

Originally **oak** and **ash** dominated the Welsh landscape until fast-growing **conifers** were introduced from America to produce pit props for the coal-mining industry. Even then, it was not until the latter part of the 20th century that large tracts of land were given over to conifer plantations, serving a massive softwood-processing industry that created thousands of jobs. Hand in hand with the new plantations went the desecration of moorland, blanketed with regimented rows of trees that became a familiar sight across upland Britain under the auspices of the Forestry Commission, supported by tax breaks that encouraged investment. These short-sighted policies produced the eyesores that defaced many wild places, the effect of which is still felt today.

The negative visual impression caused by the plantations is as nothing compared with the ecological impact. Thousands of acres of species-rich moorland were ploughed up and replaced by a monoculture of conifers. With it go birds such as the merlin and the golden plover. Once mature, the trees cannot support much wildlife as the close canopy allows little light to reach the forest floor. Nothing else can grow and as a consequence few animals venture into this sterile environment. As with all monocultures, pests easily thrive and have to be controlled with chemical agents. The deep ploughing and use of heavy machinery damages soil structure and also leads to a higher risk of flash floods as drainage patterns are altered. It has also been found that acid rain gets trapped in the trees and is released into the streams during heavy rain to the detriment of fish and invertebrates.

Fortunately the policy of blanket planting of conifers has fallen out of favour as environmental issues have been taken on board and a more responsible approach has been adopted. Even in already-forested areas, new policy initiatives have been put in place to reduce this negative impact on the environment, while more generally the Welsh authorities have devised a woodland strategy for improved management and control. Mixed varieties of trees are being planted to cover areas blighted by industry and mining, and to restore an appropriate habitat, with the aim of creating multi-purpose woodlands that will benefit tourism, agriculture and the environment.

HISTORY, ENVIRONMENT & NATURE

and **common dog violet** (*Viola riviniana*), all of which are easy to spot. Banks of the white **greater stitchwort** (*Stellaria holostea*) enliven the dullest stretch, often interspersed with **bluebells** (*Hyacinthoides non-scripta*).

Later, from May to September, these will be joined by **buttercup** (*Ranunculus acris*), the flowers of which were said to improve the milk when rubbed on a cow's udders, yellow **pimpernel** (*Lysimacia nemorum*), **goldenrod** (*Solidago virgaurea*) used in folk medicine to treat wounds, **viper's bugloss** (*Echium vulgare*), **harebell** (*Campanula rotundifolia*), **herb Robert** (*Geranium robertianum*), **foxglove** (*Digitalis purpurea*) which is poisonous and from which the drug Digitalin is extracted to treat heart disease, **field poppy** (*Papaver rhoeas*) and **ox-eye daisy** (*Leucanthemum vulgare*), also known as dog daisy or marguerite. The tall white flowering heads of members of the carrot family such as **cow parsley** (*Anthrisus sylvestris*), **yarrow** (*Achillea millefolium*), and upright **hedge parsley** (*Torilis japonica*) will be obvious along with, occasionally, **hogweed** (*Heracleum sphondylium*) which can grow to 1.75m (6ft) high.

Summer is when the climbers and ramblers come into their own. No introduction is needed for the common **bramble** (*Rubus fruticosus*) sought out in late summer by blackberry pickers. **Honeysuckle** (*Lonicera periclymenum*), also known as woodbine, makes its appearance growing through hedges from June to September, the fruits ripening to red in the autumn.

Hedge bindweed (*Calystegia sepium*), with its white trumpet-shaped flowers, and the related pink **field bindweed** (*Convolvulus arvensis*) are a common sight during summer months, as is the pale pink **dog rose** (*Rosa canina*), which later produces rosehips, an excellent source of vitamin C when taken as a syrup.

Woodland

In late spring, deciduous woodlands are often carpeted deep blue by **bluebells** (*Hyacinthoides non-scripta*), while in others the air is pungent with the smell of densely packed white **ramsons** (*Allium ursinum*), widely known as wild garlic. Equally common are two flowers whose petals close up at night and in bad weather: the **wood anemone** (*Anemone nemorosa*), and the smaller **wood-sorrel** (*Oxalis acetosella*), with its soft, light-green leaves.

From April to June **early purple orchids** (*Orchis mascula*) may be seen, often growing with bluebells, while far more in evidence from May onwards is the poisonous bittersweet or woody **nightshade** (*Solanum dulcamara*).

It is always a pleasure to see wild fruit growing. Wild **strawberry** (*Fragaria vesca*) and wild **raspberry** (*Rubus idaeus*) can be spotted in wooded areas, like near Bryntail mine. Other berries will be dark-blue sloes on the **blackthorn** (*Prunus spinosa*) bushes, the clustered heads of the **elderberry** (*Sambucus nigra*), and occasionally **bilberry** (*Vaccinium myrtillus*) – although this last is far more common on open moorland.

Moorland

Gorse (not spineless broom), and especially **bracken** (not fern) are commonly seen on the hillsides and open moorlands right up to the very last hours on Y

Golfa hill above Welshpool. Indeed the trail can be completely choked with thick bracken in places. Metre-high **thistles** will also erupt across some fields by late summer. You will also see **heather** or **ling** (*Calluna vulgaris*) and the gentle **broom** (*Cytisus scoparius*) with its characteristic seed-pods in the autumn. Here, too, you'll find great expanses of **bilberry** (*Vaccinium myrtillus*) among the heather, its tiny red bell-shaped flowers in evidence from April to July, followed in summer by tiny blue-black berries.

Riverbanks and wet areas

Lady's smock (*Cardamine pratensis*) and **ragged robin** (*Lychnis flos-cuculi*) are two pink flowers that are often seen in damp areas. **Watermint** (*Mentha aquatica*), **meadowsweet** (*Filipendula ulmaria*), which medicinally has the same properties as aspirin, and the poisonous **water-crowfoot** (*Ranunculus aquatilis*) make canals and ponds their habitat. Sometimes the prolific **policeman's helmet** (*Impatiens glandulifera*), distinctive by the shape of its flowers, will be found colonising riverbanks.

Rough ground and waste land

Uncultivated areas such as land that has been cleared of buildings or disturbed by construction seems to attract certain plants which move in and sometimes take over the whole area. These include the ubiquitous **rosebay willowherb** (*Epilobium angustifolium*), **ragwort** (*Senecio jacobaea*) which is poisonous to horses, **dandelion** (*Taraxacum officinale*) and **groundsel** (*Senecio vulgaris*). You will also see **Aaron's rod** (*Verbascum thapsus*) which used to be smoked like tobacco in a pipe, **rape** (*Brassica napus*), **knotgrass** (*Polygonum aviculare*), **field scabious** (*Knautia arvensis*) and **valerian** (*Valeriana officinalis*), the smell of which cats are said to love.

MAMMALS

You will often see **rabbits** (*Oryctolagus cuniculis*) on your walk, said to be responsible for an estimated £100m damage a year to crops in spite of being prey to buzzards, foxes, feral cats, stoats and man. Part of their secret is their famed ability to multiply rapidly, mating at just four months old. The sight of a rabbit's white tail bobbing for cover may appear delightful but to a countryman they're a pest.

The **brown hare** (*Lepus europaeus*) is bigger than the rabbit with large powerful hind legs and very long black-tipped ears. They're less commonly seen on farmland and rough grazing and survive on their ability to dash at up to 45mph (70km/h). In upland areas the **mountain hare** (*Lepus timidus*) replaces the brown, being distinguishable by its slightly blue colour that blends more easily with rocky terrain. In winter in mountain country their fur becomes white, supposedly for camouflage in the snow, although it has been suggested that the white fur offers a thermal advantage, creating a greenhouse effect on the outer layers of the skin.

Badgers (*Meles meles*) are nocturnal animals and so are rarely seen, lying up in their underground burrows known as setts with litters of cubs being born

Common Vetch
Vicia sativa

Harebell
Campanula rotundifolia

Red Campion
Silene dioica

Lousewort
Pedicularis sylvatica

Germander Speedwell
Veronica chamaedrys

Common Dog Violet
Viola riviniana

Common Fumitory
Fumaria officinalis

Heather (Ling)
Calluna vulgaris

Bell Heather
Erica cinerea

Foxglove
Digitalis purpurea

Rosebay Willowherb
Epilobium angustifolium

Early Purple Orchid
Orchis mascula

Gorse
Ulex europaeus

Meadow Buttercup
Ranunculus acris

Marsh Marigold (Kingcup)
Caltha palustris

Bird's-foot trefoil
Lotus corniculatus

Water Avens
Geum rivale

Tormentil
Potentilla erecta

Primrose
Primula vulgaris

St John's Wort
Hypericum perforatum

Honeysuckle
Lonicera periclymemum

Common Ragwort
Senecio jacobaea

Hemp-nettle
Galeopsis speciosa

Cowslip
Primula veris

Rowan (tree)
Sorbus aucuparia

Dog Rose
Rosa canina

Forget-me-not
Myosotis arvensis

Scarlet Pimpernel
Anagallis arvensis

Self-heal
Prunella vulgaris

Herb-Robert
Geranium robertianum

Ramsons (Wild Garlic)
Allium ursinum

Common Hawthorn
Crataegus monogyna

Bluebell
Hyacinthoides non-scripta

Common Knapweed
Centaurea nigra

Yarrow
Achillea millefolium

Hogweed
Heracleum sphondylium

Top: Most of the walk is through farmland and hills; you'll see far more sheep than other walkers. **Centre**: Flowering from late February to April Wales's national flower, the daffodil, is also abundant. **Bottom**: On some hills you'll find groups of horses roaming free.

in February. Unlike rabbits they are protected by law. There is, however, some suggestion that cattle can catch the TB virus through contact with badgers which has led to them being culled in some areas.

Red **foxes** (*Vulpes vulpes*) are becoming common in spite of occasional persecution by man. Readily identifiable by their colour and bushy tail, foxes are shy animals that come out mainly at night to hunt for food; in fact you've more chance seeing one sniffing out the rubbish in cities than on the Glyndŵr's Way. Their habit of killing all the hens in a coop and taking only one is apparently not the result of animal cruelty but done to take advantage of abundance while it is available to compensate for times when food is scarce.

The **red squirrel** (*Sciurus vulgaris*) is the only squirrel indigenous to the British Isles and is protected by law. There are only a few thousand left in Wales, primarily in coniferous woodland. The species is threatened with extinction for a number of reasons, including disease, loss of habitat and the dominance of the grey squirrel. Active during the day, the red squirrel is recognised by its colour which varies from deep brown to chestnut to grey brown but its

---

❑ **SHEEP**

Since sheep are the one animal you'll see every single day of your walk (and probably in your nightly dreams, too) it's worth trying to recognise the diverse breeds that graze across northern Powys. Most animals you'll see will be cross-breeds, usually referred to as mules, and reared for their meat. Fleeces no longer command a worthwhile price in today's markets and sheep reared solely for their wool are a rarity.

Among the different varieties which may be noticed look out for the following:

● **Black Welsh Mountain** Small, black sheep with no wool on their face or legs below their knee and hock. Rams are typically horned and ewes hornless. The meat obtained is much prized.

● **Balwen Welsh Mountain** Black with a white blaze on its face, white feet and a white tail, the Balwen is said to have been placed as a landmark on the hills in order to help the farmer to recognise his flock. It's a small, hardy breed which can get by on very little when food is scarce.

● **Welsh Mountain Badger Faced** Ancient breed, once common, it has a distinctive broad stripe on its face with a black band from its jaw extending under the belly to the tail. The fleece is used mainly for the carpet industry.

● **Kerry Hill** A well-balanced, sturdy sheep with ears set high and free from wool, a black nose and sharply defined black and white markings on its head and legs. The ewe is a perfect mother, adaptable and a good forager producing strong, lean lambs. One of Wales's oldest drovers' roads passes through the village of Kerry, north of Felindre.

● **Shropshire** A sheep with a gentle disposition, the Shropshire has a white fleece and black face with wool on its head. The lambs are hardy, vigorous and meaty and the ewes make wonderful mothers.

● **Hill Radnor** A hill or mountain breed found in Powys and Gwent; a hardy sheep with a grey aquiline nose and a tan face and legs. Rams have long curved horns and ewes are hornless.

HISTORY, ENVIRONMENT & NATURE

> ❏ **CATTLE**
>
> Apart from the breeds common to the British Isles generally, you will almost certainly come across the **Welsh Black** along the Glyndŵr's Way. A native British breed descended from cattle of pre-Roman origin, they are entirely black in colour, and are well suited to the rough upland country that is characteristic of the area. Bred for beef production, they are hardy and adapted to a rough environment and can be out-wintered. Prolific milkers, they thrive on poor pasture. They make excellent mothers and grow heavier and more quickly than most other British breeds, once seeing them driven in their thousands to the markets of England.
>
> Elsewhere on the trail you may come across unusual breeds such as **Red Poll**, a breed of rich brown cattle without horns; an excellent cheese is made from their milk.

size and tufted ears easily distinguish it from the much larger grey. The **grey squirrel** (*Sciurus carolinensis*) was introduced to this country from North America in the 19th century and is an altogether more robust species than the red, adaptable to the changing habitat of our woodland and perfectly at home in parks and domestic gardens.

The **weasel** (*Mustela nivalis*) is one of our smaller carnivores, found in a wide range of habitats and not a protected species. It is considered an enemy of gamebirds and is sometimes trapped and killed by gamekeepers. Mainly nocturnal and preferring dry areas, the weasel is smaller than the **stoat** (*Mustela erminea*), the tip of whose tail is always black.

It is possible that you may catch sight of an **otter** (*Lutra lutra*) along one of the riverbanks, where they live their secretive semi-aquatic life, as the species is now increasing in numbers after an alarming decline in the mid 20th century. They eat mainly fish but will take moorhens and their chicks, and in spring frogs are an important food source. Litters of cubs can be born at any time of the year. Their dens, or holts, are usually in holes in riverbanks or under a pile of rocks. Not dissimilar at first glance is the smaller, darker American **mink** (*Mustela vison*), an escapee from fur farms in the 1950s which gained a hold on British rivers.

Recent sightings have been reported in the Welsh Borders area of two rare animals: the **pine marten** (*Martes martes*) and the **polecat** (*Mustela putorius*), both similar in size to the mink, and the latter with a distinctive white 'face mask'.

The species of deer you are most likely to see is the **roe deer** (*Capreolus capreolus*); these are quite small with an average height of 60-70cm (about 2ft) at the shoulder. They are reddish brown in summer, grey in winter and have a distinctive white rear end which is conspicuous when the deer is alarmed. Males have short antlers with no more than three points. Abundant in mixed coniferous and deciduous woodland, they are active at dawn and dusk and can sometimes be heard barking. If you come across a young kid apparently abandoned, leave it alone; it's normal behaviour for the mother to leave her kid concealed while she goes off to feed.

HISTORY, ENVIRONMENT & NATURE

REPTILES AND AMPHIBIANS

The **adder** (*Vipera berus*) is the only venomous snake in Britain but poses very little risk to walkers and will not bite unless provoked; if you're lucky enough to see one, don't disturb it. You are most likely to encounter them in spring when they come out of hibernation and during the summer, when pregnant females warm themselves in the sun. They are easily identified by the striking zigzag pattern on their back and a 'V' on the top of their head behind their eyes. The venom is designed to kill small mammals such as mice and shrews; human deaths are very rare.

Grass snakes (*Natrix natrix*) are Britain's largest reptile, growing up to a metre in length. They prefer rough ground with plentiful long grass in which to conceal themselves, laying their eggs in warm, rotting vegetation such as garden compost heaps, the young hatching in August. They are sometimes killed by people mistaking them for adders but are neither venomous nor aggressive and should be left alone. The grass snake's body has vertical black bars and spots running along the sides and usually has a prominent yellow collar round its neck.

The **slow worm** (*Anguis fragilis*) looks like a snake but is actually a legless lizard. It has no identifying marks on its body, which varies in colour from coppery brown to lead grey, and is usually quite shiny in appearance. Like lizards, they are able to blink; snakes have no eyelids. Slow worms are completely harmless, love to sun themselves and are found in old buildings under stones or discarded roofing sheets.

The closest encounter you're likely to have with a **frog** (*Rana temporaria*) with be squashed flat on the road or as clumps of frogspawn and perhaps tadpoles in shallow puddles in early spring.

BIRDS

Streams, canals, rivers

The familiar sight of a **mallard** (*Anas platyrhynchos*), **coot** (*Fulica atra*) or **moorhen** (*Gallinula chloropus*) may be all that is immediately apparent to the walker following the path along water courses but there will be occasional surprises to add to your enjoyment of the natural environment. The **grey heron** (*Ardea cinerea*) is a striking sight as it takes off on its ungainly and unhurried flight or is spotted standing sentinel at the water's edge.

A **kingfisher** (*Alcedo atthis*) is a rare sighting since they fly at great speed; often all that's spotted is a flash of blue, there one minute and gone the next. The **grey wagtail** (*Motacilla cinerea*) and the **dipper** (*Cinclus cinclus*) are two delightful birds which can be seen year-round bobbing up and down on boulders in fast-flowing streams. With a blue-grey head and bright-yellow underside the grey wagtail is the most striking of the wagtails. The dipper's flight is unmistakable, with its rapid wingbeat, white bib and tail held upright all helping in identification. These two are joined in summer by the **common sandpiper** (*Tringa hypoleucos*), a long-legged long-billed wader whose characteristic stance is with the body tilted forward, head lowered and the tail bobbing up and down almost continuously.

Swallows (*Hirundo rustica*), **house martins** (*Delichon urbica*) and **swifts** (*Apus apus*) love to swoop low over water to drink or take flies. The swift cannot perch like the swallow and martin: its legs are mere hooks and it is unable to walk. The less-common **sand martin** (*Riparia riparia*) nests in colonies in holes in steep riverbanks and has a curious low buzz for its call. The **reed bunting** (*Emberiza schoeniclus*) frequents reed beds and is recognisable by its white collar, black hood and bib.

Woodland

The familiar woodland residents such as **chaffinches** (*Fringilla coelebs*), **robin** (*Erithacus rubecula*), **blue tit** (*Parus caeruleus*) and **great tit** (*Parus major*), **song thrush** (*Turdus philomelos*) and **blackbird** (*Turdus merula*) are joined by birds that are less common in our gardens, including the **coal tit** (*Parus ater*) which has a black head with white on the cheeks and nape of the neck; it's often seen in coniferous woodland. Its relative, the **long-tailed tit** (*Aegithalos caudatus*), is smaller in size and has a very long tail which distinguishes it from other tits; it tends to frequent woodland fringes and clearings.

In spring the very different songs of the almost identical **willow warbler** (*Phylloscopus trochilus*) and **chiffchaff** (*Phylloscopus collybita*) ring across the Welsh valleys, the descending trill of the willow warbler contrasting with the sharp, mechanical 'chiffchaff' of the bird of the same name. The chiffchaff is

❑ THE RAVEN

There are said to be about 10,000 breeding pairs of ravens in the British Isles, and Wales is home to the largest population, supposedly thanks to upland farmers leaving their sheep out all winter. Ravens feed mainly on carrion and seem to be particularly partial to dead sheep, which get them through the winter. Ravens are territorial and having once adopted a territory they stick to it. They can be seen year-round in many of the areas through which the Way passes, particularly in the few places where crags are in evidence, their favourite nesting places.

When fully grown the mature raven measures 60cm (2ft) from beak to tail, much larger than its cousin the crow with which it is sometimes confused. Its call is a lower, guttural 'kraa': once heard, never mistaken for a crow's higher pitched 'caw'. Ravens breed early in the year, making a flimsy nest of twigs lined with moss and sheep wool, usually high on a cliff-face ledge or quarry wall. The birds are often seen in pairs although they can sometimes gather in quite large numbers, with first-year birds usually flocking together. In the early months of the year ravens perform aerial acrobatics, swooping and diving and looping the loop in an extraordinary display which is part of their courting ritual.

RAVEN
L: 650MM/25"

generally rather browner than the willow warbler and its legs are blackish. The **whitethroat** (*Sylvia communis*) is easier to identify since its characteristic behaviour is its constant activity, never keeping still. You may also see the **pied flycatcher** (*Ficedula hypoleuca*) which prefers deciduous woods, especially oak, and darts after insects in the air, seldom returning to the same perch after an aerial sally.

GREEN WOODPECKER
L: 330MM/13"

The **green woodpecker** (*Picus viridis*) is a striking bird with its bright green body and red head and its curious call, a kind of laughing cry that carries a long way. Its near kindred, the **great spotted woodpecker** (*Dendrocopos major*), with its striking black-and-white plumage, and the smaller **lesser spotted woodpecker** (*Dendrocopos minor*), both habitually drum on trees, usually to mark their territory and extract insects rather than to bore holes for a nest site.

Of the finches, the **goldfinch** (*Carduelis carduelis*) is relatively common while the **greenfinch** (*Chloris chloris*) and **linnet** (*Linaria cannabina*) less so. Thanks to the conifer plantations which are their habitat you might also spot the **siskin** (*Carduelis spinus*); it has similar greenish plumage to the greenfinch but is much smaller and more streaked. The **brambling** (*Fringilla montifringilla*) often mixes with chaffinches in winter but is easily distinguished from them by its distinct white upper rump. The **bullfinch** (*Pyrrhula pyrrhula*) has a slow and deliberate movement and a rosy red underside as it feeds on berries, buds and seeds in the trees and bushes. A much smaller bird is the **goldcrest** (*Regulus regulus*) which is the smallest European bird, recognised by its yellow crown with black edges.

A darting movement on the trunks of trees may reveal the **treecreeper** (*Certhia familiaris*), a small brown bird with a curved bill which creeps spirally up trees searching for insects, dropping down to the bottom of another when one has been explored, or the **nuthatch** (*Sitta europaea*) which has a bluish-grey upper side and is very acrobatic, often climbing down tree trunks head first which woodpeckers cannot do.

It is highly likely that the **magpie** (*Pica pica*) will be seen and the **jay** (*Garrulus glandarius*) is becoming more common everywhere; both are highly efficient at cleaning eggs out of birds' nests and even taking young birds.

Less often seen and not heard as much now is the **cuckoo** (*Cuculus canorus*), which is grey or very occasionally brown in colour which makes it easy to confuse with birds of prey such as kestrels and sparrowhawks.

Among the dove family, **wood pigeons** (*Columba palumbus*) and **collared doves** (*Streptopelia decaocto*) are seen everywhere but you may try to distinguish the **stock dove** (*Columba oenas*) which is a darker, smaller bird than the wood pigeon, and nests in holes.

Open farmland and upland areas

The two birds you're most likely to see are the **wheatear** (*Oenanthe oenan-the*), the male of which has a steel grey back and crown and often bows and flicks its tail and perches on walls or rocks, and the **stonechat** (*Saxicola torquata*), much smaller and darker in plumage and identifiable by its call, a single sharp 'teck'.

Among the smaller birds seen on open moorland are the **meadow pipit** (*Anthus pratensis*) and the **skylark** (*Alauda arvensis*), which is often heard long before it is seen, its clear song delivered as it soars overhead. You may also see the **ring ouzel** (*Turdus torquatus*) which looks like a blackbird but with a white bib. In autumn huge flocks of **redwings** (*Turdus iliatus*) and **fieldfares** (*Turdus pilaris*) fly over from Scandinavia to feed on the berries.

Pheasants (*Phasianus colchicus*), **partridges** (*Perdix perdix*) and **lap-wings** (*Vanellus vanellus*) are likely to be seen practically everywhere. In sum-mer in upland areas the bird whose bubbling call will first alert you before you spot its characteristic flight is Britain's largest wader, the **curlew** (*Numenius arquata*), a large brown bird with a long down-curved bill that is as at home in moorland as on the coast.

The **oystercatcher** (*Haematopus ostralegus*) is another perhaps surprising wader that is quite common in the breeding season, with its distinctive black-

RED KITE
L: 650MM/25"

❏ THE RED KITE

Centuries ago red kites were common throughout Britain and were known to scavenge the streets of London, but since were shot, trapped or poisoned to such an extent that by the end of the 19th century they'd retreated to a tiny colony in Wales. They were saved from extinction by a ded-icated group of conservationists and, with the help of the Nature Conservancy Council, the Joint Nature Conservation Committee and the RSPB, they were re-introduced to avian society from 1989 onwards. This project has been one of Britain's greatest conservation successes and the latest figures we have are that there are now a very healthy 4400 breeding pairs in the UK.

Although it is commonly believed that kites feed on lambs, they don't have the strength to tear the carcass of a lamb, let alone kill a live animal. They'll feed on scraps left by ravens and buzzards but wait their turn, knowing better than to get involved with these fiercer birds. Kites' main prey are small mammals, insects and earthworms: it's been estimated that a growing kite consumes the equivalent of a small rabbit each day.

Glyndŵrists will have no trouble spotting a kite – they're quite numerous in the skies above Clywedog. The main problem is actually distinguishing them from the common buzzards, a similar bird that looks heavier and is less graceful in flight. Get a close enough view of the kite and you'll also be able to spot its deeply forked tail and the reddish-brown-to-dull-orange plumage.

For further information see 🖳 welshkitetrust.wales.

and-white plumage and orange pointed bill and legs. You may also put up a snipe (*Gallinago gallinago*), which has a zig-zag flight when flushed, or in wooded areas the **woodcock** (*Scolopax rusticola*), easily distinguished from the snipe by its larger size and more rounded wings. Its camouflage makes it difficult to observe during the day.

Much larger than the **carrion crow** (*Corvus corone corone*), the **raven** (*Corvus corax*; see box p68) is now quite common in upland areas.

Most conspicuous of the birds of prey are the **kestrel** (*Falco tinnunculus*), the **sparrowhawk** (*Accipiter nisus*) and the much larger **buzzard** (*Buteo buteo*), with its brown colouring and cruel yellow talons. **Red kites** (*Milvus milvus*) can now be seen once again in mid-Wales; their forked tails distinguish them quite clearly from other birds of prey in flight; see also box opposite.

If you're very lucky you may even spot the **merlin** (*Falco columbarius*) which has a darkish bluish back and tail and flies fast and low over the ground chasing pipits and larks.

There's also a large population of **redstarts** (*Phoenicurus phoenicurus*) in Wales and you may see the tell-tale flash of the male's orange tail as it flits amongst hedgerows and bushes.

BUTTERFLIES AND DRAGONFLIES

Given the numerous factors that militate against the survival of **butterflies** including high winds and heavy rain throughout the year, the use of pesticides and loss of habitat and the removal of hedgerows and intensive farming, it is surprising how often butterflies are seen on the trail during the summer months.

Breeding in nettle patches left alone by most grazing animals, the nettle feeders include **peacock** (*Inachis io*), **tortoiseshell** (*Aglais urticae*), **red admiral** (*Vanessa atalanta*) and **painted lady** (*Cynthia cadui*). They are in colourful contrast to the **meadow brown** (*Maniola jurtina*), **wall** (*Lasiommata megera*) and **small heath** (*Coenonympha pamphilus*), all of which are likely to be seen on warm, sunny days.

Large whites (*Pieris brassicae*) and **small whites** (*Artogeia rapae*) are common everywhere but should not be disregarded, having their place in the ecological chain. Although rarer nowadays you could still see the **common blue** (*Polyommatus icarus*), the **orange tip** (*Anthocaris cardamines*) and the **green-veined white** (*Artogeia napi*), especially in areas such as the disused quarries along Montgomery Canal.

Dragonflies fall into two groups: hawkers and darters. Hawkers restlessly patrol their territory by a river, lake or canal which the male, much more brightly coloured than the female, defends against intruders; most common is the **brown aeshna**, the wingspan of which is 10cm (4in). Darters are less restless than hawkers and have a sturdier body, spending time clinging to vegetation and making occasional darts after prey. Males have a blue bloom on their bodies.

MINIMUM IMPACT & OUTDOOR SAFETY

Minimum impact walking

As more and more people enjoy the freedom of the countryside so the land comes under increasing pressure and the potential for conflict with other land-users is heightened. Everyone has a right to this natural heritage, but with it comes a responsibility to care for it too. By following some simple guidelines while walking you can have a positive impact, not just on your own well-being but also on local communities and the environment, thereby becoming part of the solution.

ENVIRONMENTAL IMPACT

By choosing a walking holiday you have already made a positive step towards minimising your impact on the wider environment. Following these suggestions you can also tread lightly along the path.

Use public transport whenever possible
Using public transport rather than private cars benefits both visitors and locals, as well as the environment. Unfortunately, away from the four towns, infrequent local buses (see pp48-9) serve some of the villages through which you pass. To fill in the gaps, local taxi firms and some B&B proprietors are happy to ferry walkers and/or their luggage around, though the latter is an avoidable and less environmentally acceptable option even if it helps the local economy.

Never leave litter
Leaving litter shows a disrespect for the natural world and others coming after you. As well as being unsightly, litter can harm wildlife, pollute the environment and be dangerous to farm animals. Please dispose of your rubbish in a bin in the next village and pick up litter left by others too.
● **Is it OK if it's biodegradable?** Not really. Apple cores, banana skins, orange peel are all unsightly, encourage flies and wasps and ruin the spot for others.
● **The lasting impact of litter** A piece of orange peel left on the ground takes six months to decompose; silver foil 18 months; a plastic bag 10 years; clothes 15 years and a fizzy drink can 85 years.

Buy local

Look and ask for local produce to buy and eat. Not only does this cut down on 'food miles' (the amount of pollution and congestion that the transportation of food creates), it also ensures you're supporting local farmers and producers.

Erosion

Stay on the waymarked trail. The effect of your footsteps may seem minuscule on the usually deserted Glyndŵr's Way, but avoid taking shortcuts, widening the trail or creating more than one path.

Respect all wildlife

Tempting as it may be to pick wild flowers, leave them for the next person who passes. Don't break branches off or damage trees in any way, unless they're blocking the path.

If you come across wildlife keep your distance. Your presence can cause stress to adults with their young or in winter when food scarce. Young animals are rarely abandoned; if you come across deer calves or young birds that are apparently alone, keep away so that their mother can return.

The code of the outdoor loo

As more and more people discover the joys of the outdoors this is becoming an important issue. Human excrement is not only offensive to our senses but, more importantly, can infect water sources.

● **Where to go** Wherever possible try to use a toilet. Though few, public toilets are marked on the trail maps and you'll also find facilities in pubs, cafés and on campsites.

If you do have to go outdoors choose a site well away from running water. Carry a **small trowel** and dig a small hole about 15cm (6") deep in which to bury your excrement. It decomposes quicker when in contact with the top layer of soil or leaf mould. Use a stick to stir loose soil into your deposit as well as this speeds up decomposition. Do not squash it under rocks as this slows down the composting process. If you have to use rocks to hide it make sure they're not in contact with your faeces.

● **Toilet paper and tampons** Toilet paper takes a long time to decompose whether buried or not. It is easily dug up by animals and could then blow into water sources or onto the trail. The best method for dealing with it is to pack it out. Put the used paper inside a paper bag which you place inside a plastic bag (or two). Then simply empty the contents of the paper bag at the next toilet you come across and throw the bag away. You should also pack out disposable tampons and sanitary towels in a similar way; they will almost certainly be dug up and scattered about by animals and they take years to decompose.

Wild camping

Without consent from the landowner, wild camping is not permitted along the Glyndŵr's Way or anywhere else in Wales or England, but some go ahead and do it anyway. If that includes you, it goes without saying that you should leave your pitch without any obvious signs of having overnighted there. More on p22.

ACCESS

Almost all of the Glyndŵr's Way crosses **farmland**, frequently passing farm buildings as well as grazing livestock to the point that it's impossible to be unaware of the business of farming. You'll become a master at evaluating the orderliness of farm yards on a scale of ten. Farmers are faced with a harsh environment, a short grazing season and challenging weather conditions; so let's not add the nuisance of long-distance walkers to their situation.

The landscape of the countryside and its wildlife has been created to a large extent by farming. Deforestation of native woodlands started in the Neolithic era and centuries of sheep grazing has produced the close-cropped grassy hillsides characteristic of mid-Wales. Hill farming has shaped the land into that which is so appealing to walkers and other visitors. The hill farm helps sustain a service and supply industry, from feed suppliers to transport, fuel, machinery, farm labour, fencing, vets and auction markets. It should be seen as a part of the vital rural infrastructure rather than an isolated farmstead at the end of a long and winding trail.

Rights of way

As a proudly designated National Trail, Glyndŵr's Way is a public right of way, a path that anyone has the right to use on foot, or in certain sections with bikes and horses, provided that they stay on the path and don't damage or obstruct it in any way. Broadly speaking, public rights of way in Britain fall into one of three colour-coded categories:

● A footpath (yellow) is open to walkers only
● A bridleway (blue) is also open to horse-riders and cyclists
● A byway (red) is open to motorised traffic as well as to walkers, riders and cyclists

That said, not all footpaths are necessarily rights of way. Sometimes an arrangement is made with a landowner to allow walkers to cross their land. This is known as a **permissive path** and there are a few on the Glyndŵr's Way, most often to divert the trail around a farmyard.

It may come as a surprise to learn that the responsibility for maintaining rights of way is not the job of National Trail but largely down to the landowner, with some support from the county council or local authority through whose area it passes. You'd think farmers have enough on their plate, but they or land managers must ensure that paths aren't impeded by overgrown vegetation, or

---

❑ **LAMBING**

This takes place from mid-March to mid-May and is a critical time for hard-pressed hill farmers. Please don't interfere with livestock farming in any way. If a ewe or lamb seems to be in distress contact the nearest farmer. Dogs should not be brought on land where sheep are grazing throughout this season so that pregnant ewes are not disturbed.

❏ **THE COUNTRYSIDE CODE**
The Countryside Code, originally described in the 1950s as the Country Code, was revised and relaunched in 2004. It was updated again in 2012, 2014 and was last updated in 2022. The Code seems like common sense but sadly some people still appear to misunderstand how to behave the countryside they walk in. With the key words 'Respect. Protect. Enjoy.' the most pertinent bullet points from the 2022 Code for England and Wales have been gathered below:

Respect other people
- be considerate to those living in, working in and enjoying the countryside
- leave gates and property as you find them

Protect the natural environment
- keep to marked paths unless wider access is available
- take your litter home – leave no trace of your visit
- do not light fires
- always keep dogs under effective control; dog poo – bag it and bin it

Enjoy the outdoors
- plan ahead and know what to expect
- follow advice and local signs

otherwise obstructed by fallen trees as well as locked or broken gates – all things you'll regularly encounter along the Glyndŵr's Way. If there are crops growing over the path (almost unheard of on Glyndŵr's) you have every right to walk through them, following the right of way as closely as possible. In the real world some farmers don't prioritise these responsibilities along the Glyndŵr's Way, probably due to the scant footfall, but should you find a path blocked or impassable, you can try reporting it to the appropriate highway authority (see box p59) or the National Trail Officer (see box p58).

Open Access land ('Right to roam')

Southerners may envy Scotland's enlightened attitude to 'right to roam' but thanks to the concerted efforts of groups such as Ramblers (see box p43) and the British Mountaineering Council, the wild corners of England and Wales are not so badly off. Not unlike Scotland, generally **Open Access land** is hill country over 400m which the Glyndŵr's Way traverses most days. There are sensible restrictions of course, and farmland may be excluded, but you can pretty much walk anywhere across open moorland, which may include crossing fences or walls, ideally without doing them or yourself an injury. Whether you'd *wish* to do so, given the vegetation or drainage involved, is another matter, as our excursion around Pumlumon Fawr shows (see pp173-80).

Though they supposedly exist (a circular brown symbol with a person walking over hills) you'll rarely see handy signs welcoming you to Open Access land. The easiest way to identify it is on an OS Explorer (1:25k) map which shades Open Access areas with faint green tint (usually moorland or common) and a brighter green tint for forest, all enclosed with an orangey-brown band. Full details are on 🖳 naturalresources.wales/days-out (search Open Access land), along with zoomable OS mapping.

Health and outdoor safety

HEALTH

Preventative measures

● **Water and dehydration** You need to drink at least two litres a day depending on the weather. If you're feeling drained, lethargic or just out of sorts it may be that you haven't drunk enough. **Thirst is not a reliable indicator** of how much you should drink. The frequency and colour of your urine is better; follow the maxim, 'a happy mountaineer always pees clear', that is to say, a pale colour to the urine. Dark yellow urine is more concentrated with the toxins it's trying to flush out and implies insufficient water intake.

● **Sunburn** Even on overcast days, the Welsh sun still has the power to burn. Not everyone likes slathering themselves in greasy sunscreen, so covering up and wearing a **hat** will do the same job.

BLISTERS AND SORE FEET

Blisters are primarily caused by friction, pressure, moisture, heat and bone movement.

We've pinched that fun fact from 🖳 blisterhelp.co.uk which, while hoping to sell you socks and foot care kits, also gives loads of good advice on avoiding the long distance walker's scourge. Blisters are your body's response to reduce persistent pressure or friction by producing a lubricant. Given time, the fluid will be reabsorbed into the body and the lifted skin either reform or dry up and peel off.

You can prevent blisters by wearing **worn-in, comfortable boots**. Many people set out on a big walk in new boots and soon regret it. But many others will suffer the same agonies simply by virtue of walking 15 miles a day for over a week. Now that we're no longer lithe hunter gatherers, long-distance walking can be tough on our underused, 21st-century bodies.

Above all, **look after your feet**. They're all you have to get you to the end of the trail. Today's ubiquitous use of miracle membranes in hiking footwear means feet get **hot and sweaty** despite claims of breathability. **Air your feet** at lunchtime while giving them **a darn good rub**. Pull your socks off inside out and give them an airing too. Take your time to **readjust laces** as the terrain or your feet require – usually soon after setting off. With proper hiking boots this is an easy, low-friction affair. Keep your feet clean and endeavour to change your socks daily.

If you feel any 'hot spots' forming while walking, stop immediately and apply some zinc oxide tape or smooth backed Elastoplast, then re-apply pre-emptively for as long as necessary. If you've left it too late and a blister has developed, apply Compeed or similar 'blister plasters' to reduce the abrasion and spread the pressure.

Types of blister

It's worth considering exactly where and why blisters form on our feet in the hope of avoiding their formation, while appreciating that scoffing painkillers is something of a last resort if you're not to damage your feet.

● **Soles** Blisters on your soles suggest your footwear's tread is too soft for the task and the weight they're bearing and your feet are getting pulverised by the rough ground underfoot. Many of today's trail walking shoes have soles as flexible as trainers. They feel great right out of the box but a Sunday afternoon towpath amble is not the same as repeated 15-mile days on backroads, stony tracks and gnarly climbs. Aside from trading them in for something stiffer, you might try fitting a thicker or **harder insole** to make up for the mushy sole (stock insoles often resemble pieces of cheap foam). Sole blisters won't go away until you stop walking so protect your feet, or substantially lighten your load.

● **Between toes** These are usually caused by wide feet getting jammed into a boot with a too-narrow toe box, or a too-soft shoe which flexes like a slipper. The compressed or constantly mashed toes rub against each other (or the little toe on the boot's inner surface) and eventually a blister forms somewhere. Aside for getting **wider, round-toed boots** (better hiking boot manufacturers offer 'wide fit' models), an easy remedy is to wrap the damaged toes in tape or fit inter-toe foam spacers found in the foot-care section of pharmacies – ideally doing either before things get too bad. Blisters on the inside ball of your feet (the big toe's 'knuckle') are also caused by too narrow boots, though this is usually an area of hardened skin.

● **Back of the heel** These are probably the most common blisters, caused by the heel moving up and down inside the loose boot on each step. A too-stiff sole

---

❏ **THE HILL-WALKING ENIGMA**

Is walking up and down inclines further than on the flat? It's a question commonly pondered as you pant up a 1-in-1 slope. Representing your hillside as a right-angle triangle with two equal sides (called an 'isosceles right triangle'; a square divided diagonally) with the right angled sides or equal length representing distance over ground and elevation gain, the hypotenuse (angled slope) is indeed 42% longer than either side. So walking up the diagonal hypotenuse of an isosceles right triangle with right angled sides of 1km adds up to 1.4km, nearly half as far again!

A 1-in-1 slope is an extreme example with the longest hypotenuse, but still, it makes you think because one thing's for sure: a length of hypothetical string trailed from Knighton to Welshpool will end up a whole lot longer than 134 miles.

can also be a culprit, not flexing with your foot as you walk and causing the same movement at the heel, or your heel and the boot's heel cup are simply ill-matched. This could possibly be remedied by adjusting your socks or the insoles to set your heel lower or more snugly in the boot. On lacing your boot, always **kick your foot back** snugly into the heel cup and then lace the front up firmly to minimise any movement.

Heel blisters can become particularly agonising if untended for a few days. Aside from optimising and modulating your lacing, **act early** to limit the effects of the rubbing by applying smooth-backed tape or Compeed-like plasters that will then **slide, not rub** inside your socks. As a result of ignoring this advice and letting things go too far, we've resorted to wrapping a blistered heel in a crisp packet with sellotape for the last day's Ibuprofen-assisted hobble into Welshpool!

Walking lore suggests that **bursting a blister** can lead to infection, but outside of the tropics you'd have to be pretty neglectful to let things get that bad. If the skin is broken, keep the area clean and cover with a non-adhesive dressing held in place with tape. If not too sore, remove the dressing at night to let it all breathe and dry out.

Eight hours of tramping across the pastures and moorland of mid-Wales can result in **sore feet**. Again, today's soft trail shoes combined with your overall mass can be the problem. As suggested, a midday or more frequent airing and rub can work wonders. After that you might apply some of the exotic Nordic foot balms overnight to help recovery. Sometimes the simple facts can't be ignored: a full day's walk in the countryside will result in sore feet, along with soreness elsewhere too.

JOINTS AND MUSCLES

If you're susceptible to joint problems – in particular knees and hips – invest in a pair of **walking poles** and use one or both, especially during steep ascents or descents. Properly used, they reduce the impact on your joints, with the arms and chest muscles getting a bit of a work out along the way. Poles (or just a longer, thicker staff) also reduce the effort needed in keeping your balance on rough terrain (especially with a heavy camping backpack) plus being something to brandish at aggressive dogs or to probe boggy mires before hopping over.

Even the fittest athlete **warms up** before exercise and **stretches** afterwards – and so should you. It's surprising how much easier it is to set off in the morning without aching muscles, and this, too, reduces the risk of injury.

AVOIDANCE OF HAZARDS

The Glyndŵr's Way is not an undertaking that would put the average walker in any greater risk than a regular day's ramble in the countryside. But unlike other National Trails, **few people** use this path so you'll be on your own. Always make sure you've sufficient spare clothes to keep you warm and dry, whatever the conditions. You'll be thrilled to hear a **charged smartphone** turned on only when needed might be your biggest emergency asset, backed up by the good sense to **react to changing circumstances**, be they you, members of your group or the deteriorating conditions around you. 'First-aid kits' are often blithely added to this list, but a few Band Aids and an aspirin won't solve an incapacitating injury the way signalling or communications devices will.

Carry enough **food** to sustain you during the day and always set out with at least a litre of **water**. A stagnant drain in a region of intensive agriculture area is one thing, but despite the oft parroted 'hill-walkers' lore', drinking from fast-flowing **upland streams** or **peaty tarns** is much less harmful than becoming dehydrated. If you're worried, carry a water filter. You're burning many more calories so expect to **eat more** than normal. Branded high-energy snack bars are overpriced gimmicks; there's no secret to nutrition and energy. Bring chocolate or a home-made trail mix of your favourite nuts and dried fruit for mouth-watering morale boosters, rather than worthy, overpriced health foods.

Endeavour to **keep track** of where you are throughout the day. Besides the Pumlumon excursion which is a grade or two above the average day on Glyndŵr's, Beacon Hill Common on Day 1 is more than the usual hour out on

---

❑ WALKING THROUGH FIELDS OF CATTLE

It is very rare that cows will attack walkers but people have been crushed to death and the Welsh Black is known to be flighty. Cows get particularly agitated in the presence of **dogs** and cows with calves can get even more twitchy. Don't be alarmed; Glyndŵr's Way passes through relatively few cattle fields and most of the time they will just watch you pass or edge away. If you feel nervous or unsure about a herd, you're entitled to walk round the edge of the field to avoid them and rejoin the path later. Very rarely they'll wander over out of curiosity. Ramblers (see box p43) offer the following guidelines:

● Try not to get between cows and their calves.
● Be prepared for cattle to react to your presence, especially with a dog.
● Move quickly and quietly, and if possible walk around them; if that's not possible it's best to wait for the cattle to move.
● Keep your dog close and under proper control.
● Don't hang onto your dog. If you are threatened by animals let your dog go as the cow will chase after that.
● Don't put yourself at risk. Find another way round the cows and rejoin the footpath as soon as possible.
● Don't panic! Most cows will stop before they reach you. If they follow just walk on quietly. Consider reporting problems to the highway authority.

Beware of the bull!

Sometimes a field full of cows will be accompanied by a bull. This is, in fact, in contravention of the law, especially if they endanger the public. In theory, bulls aged more than 10 months must not be allowed in a field through which a public footpath passes. In practice, if the farmer who sees a Glyndŵr's walker once a fortnight decides to let his bull out in a field there's not much you can do about it. The best thing is to give it a wide berth. If it seems to be taking notice of you, speed up.

the moors above 400m. These places can feel quite intimidating when the clouds darken. The easiest way is to refer regularly to our superbly detailed maps and anticipate what landmarks lie ahead. Otherwise, refer to a tracklog laid over a familiarly readable digital map (see p19) on your phone. If bad weather comes in, you'll then be able to make a sensible decision, which can mean **turning back**. Take note of locations of possible **shelters** as you pass them, like partly roofed ruins or barns; there aren't very many but we mark them on our maps for just this reason. Where present, we also unsportingly identify **short-cuts** by backroad or alternative footpaths to speed you to your night's destination. On some days it doesn't have to be an outright emergency for you to have had enough and want to get off the trail sooner than later.

Many who enjoy **walking alone** understand the increased risk and act accordingly, telling someone where they're going. Your booked accommodation will probably have asked you for an expected arrival time. Try to contact them if you're running late, and if you leave word with someone else, don't forget to let them know you've arrived safely.

Dealing with an accident

● Ensure that both you and the casualty are out of further risk of danger, but otherwise do not move someone who may be seriously injured.
● Use basic first aid to treat the injury to the best of your ability.
● Work out exactly where you are in case you have to call emergency services.
● See if you have a phone signal; climbing to higher ground may help. If you have, call ☎ 999 and ask for the police or other rescue service. Report the exact position of the casualty (the proven 🖳 what3words app, see p20, can make this easier) and their condition.
● Otherwise, try to attract the attention of anybody else who may be in the area. The emergency signal is six blasts on a whistle, or six flashes with a torch.
● If you have to go for help, ideally leave someone with the casualty. If that's not an option, make sure the casualty is as comfortable as possible. Leave spare clothing, water and food within easy reach, as well as a phone, whistle and/or torch for attracting attention and communication.

WEATHER

Anyone familiar with the British weather will know that it can change quickly, especially in upland areas which have their own rules. What starts out warm and sunny in the valley can turn chilly and wet by lunchtime. Television and local

---

❏ TICKS AND LYME DISEASE
Those who walk in Scotland will be familiar with the risk of collecting a tick that carries the bacterial infection Lyme disease. Luckily the disease is rare in Wales, but visit 🖳 111.wales.nhs.uk then search 'Lyme disease' for more information, and be tick-aware.

radio give regular daily forecasts and there are any number of **weather apps** if you have internet. Try ⌨ metoffice.gov.uk, ⌨ bbc.co.uk/weather, ⌨ xc.com, ⌨ yr.no or ⌨ mwis.org.uk/forecasts/english-and-welsh/brecon-beacons (as close as this service gets to mid-Wales). If things look rough consider changing your plans, while appreciating that a forecast for Machynlleth close to sea level might not match what's going on 500 metres up in the nearby Cambrian mountains, just a few miles away.

HYPOTHERMIA AND HYPERTHERMIA

Also known as exposure, **hypothermia** occurs when the body can't generate enough heat to maintain its core temperature. Since it is usually as a result of being wet, cold, unprotected from the wind, tired and hungry, it's easily avoided by wearing suitable clothing (see pp40-1), carrying and eating enough food and drink, responding to the weather conditions, and checking on the morale of your companions.

Early signs to watch for include feeling cold and tired with involuntary shivering. **Find shelter** as soon as possible and warm the person up with a hot drink and chocolate or other high-energy food. Remove wet clothing, give them some more warm and dry clothing then allow them to rest until they feel better.

If the condition is allowed to worsen, strange behaviour, slurring of speech and poor co-ordination will become apparent and the victim can quickly progress into unconsciousness, followed by coma and death. Quickly get the victim out of the wind and rain, **improvising a shelter** if necessary.

Rapid **restoration of body warmth** is essential and best achieved by bare-skin contact: someone should get into the same sleeping- or bivi-bag as the patient, both having stripped to their underwear, with any spare clothing laid under and over them to build up heat. This is an emergency: call or go for help.

At the other end of the scale, near-identical sounding **hyperthermia** occurs when the body overheats. Compared to exposure it's not a common occurrence in the Welsh countryside, but recall the three SAS reservists who died in the Brecon Beacons on one of the hottest days of 2013, covering a typical Glyndŵr's 16 miles/25.8km in an equally reasonable 9 hours (albeit with 27-kilo packs).

Heat exhaustion is often caused by water depletion and is a serious condition that can lead to death; remember, it's usually a lot easier to warm up than to cool down. Symptoms include thirst, fatigue, giddiness, a rapid pulse, raised body temperature, low urine output and, later on, delirium and coma. The only remedy is to re-establish the balance of water. If the victim is suffering severe muscle cramps it may be due to salt depletion.

It does not have to get that serious. **Cramps** in the legs are also a common sign of salt and other vital minerals getting lost in sweat. In warm weather routinely pop an isotonic or **rehydration tablet** like 'High 5' or 'Nuun' into your water container. And when things get serious (it may not be you) have a couple of sachets of Dioralyte or less expensive supermarket branded versions. These sachets aren't the same as the pre-emptive tablets; they're a medicine with a specific balance of minerals to take with 200ml of water when you've left it too long and are getting dizzy.

Heat stroke is caused by failure of the body's temperature-regulating system, and is extremely serious. It is associated with a very high body temperature and an absence of sweating. Early symptoms can be similar to those of hypothermia, such as aggressive behaviour, lack of co-ordination and so on. Later the victim goes into a coma or convulsion, and death follows if effective treatment is not given. Sponge the victim down or cover them with wet towels, then vigorously fan them. Get help immediately.

Using this guide

In this guide the trail has been divided into nine stages, each roughly corresponding to a day's walk, although this is not the only way to plan your trek.

On pp34-37 are tables to help you plan an itinerary. To provide further help, practical information is presented on the trail maps, including walking times, places to stay, camp and eat, as well as shops where you can buy supplies, taps (for drinking water) and public toilets. Further service details are given in the text under the entry for each settlement. See also the colour maps (with profile charts) at the back of the book.

TRAIL MAPS [see key map inside cover; symbols key p191]

Direction
See p32 for a discussion of the pros and cons of walking south to north (clockwise) or north to south (anti-clockwise). In the text and maps that follow, look for the **Welshpool direction arrow symbol**

◀WELSHPOOL which indicates information for those walking **north/clockwise from Knighton to Welshpool** and the

KNIGHTON▷ **Knighton direction arrow symbol** with shaded text (also on the maps) for those walking **south/anti-clockwise from Welshpool to Knighton**.

Scale and walking times
The trail maps are to a scale of just under 1:20,000 (1cm = 200m; 3⅛ inches = one mile). Walking times are given along the edge of each map and the arrow shows the direction to which the time refers. The black triangles indicate the points between which the times have been taken. **See box on walking times below**.

❏ **IMPORTANT NOTE – WALKING TIMES**
Unless otherwise specified, **all times in this book refer only to the time spent walking**. You will need to add 20-30% to allow for rests, photography, checking the map, drinking water etc, not to mention time to simply stand and stare. Also remember to factor in any additional distance to reach your accommodation for the night.

The time-bars are a tool and are not there to judge your walking ability. There are so many variables that affect walking speed, from the weather conditions to the weight of the pack you're carrying, the state of your feet and how many beers you drank the previous evening. After the first hour or two of walking you will be able to see how your speed relates to the timings on the maps.

Up or down?

The trail is shown as a red dashed line. An arrow across the trail indicates the slope; two arrows show that it is steep. Note that the arrow points towards the higher part of the trail. If, for example, you are walking from A (at 80m) to B (at 200m) and the trail between the two is short and steep, it would be shown thus: A – – – >> – – – – B. Reversed arrow heads indicate a downward gradient.

Accommodation

Accommodation marked on the map is either on or within easy reach of the path. If arranged in advance, some B&B proprietors based a mile or two off the trail will collect walkers from the nearest point on the trail and take them back the next morning (charges may apply).

For **B&B-style accommodation** the number and type of rooms is given after each entry: **S** = single room (one single bed), **T** = twin room (two single beds), **D** = double room (one double bed), **Tr** = triple room and **Qd** = quad. Note that many of the triple/quad rooms have a double bed and either one/two single beds, or bunk beds, thus in a group of three or four, two people would have to share the double bed, but it also means the room can be used as a double or twin.

Unless stated otherwise, **rates** quoted for B&B-style accommodation are **per person (pp) based on two people sharing a room for a one-night stay**; rates are sometimes discounted for longer stays. Where a single room **(sgl)** is available the rate for that is quoted if different from the rate per person. The rate for single occupancy **(sgl occ)** of a double/twin may be higher and the per person rate for three/four sharing a triple/quad may be lower. At some places, generally chain hotels, the only option is a **room rate**; this will be the same whether one or two people (or more if permissible) use the room. Unless specified, rates are for **bed and breakfast**. See p23 for more information on rates. Some, but not all, B&Bs and campsites accept **credit/debit cards** but most guesthouses and nearly all hotels and hostels do.

Rooms either have **en suite** (bath or shower) facilities, or **private** or **shared** facilities just outside the bedroom. Most of these have only a shower. In the text ▼ signifies that at least one room has a bathroom with a **bath**, or access to a bath, for those who prefer a relaxed soak at the end of the day.

Nowadays almost all places to stay or eat, including many campsites, have **wi-fi** which is free unless otherwise stated. If a business has a Facebook page **(fb)** it can be useful to check this for updates to opening times, especially for small and seasonal businesses. The text indicates if **dogs** (🐾 – see also p30 and pp183-4) are welcome in at least one room (subject to prior arrangement, additional charge may apply). And finally it shows if **packed lunches** (Ⓛ) can be prepared, again subject to prior arrangement.

Other features
Features are marked on the map when pertinent to navigation. In order to avoid cluttering the maps and making them unusable not all features have been marked each time they occur.

KNIGHTON (TREF Y CLAWDD)
[see map p87]

Situated just over the English border since the 1535 Act of Union, 'Tref y Clawydd', the Welsh name for Knighton (🖥 visit knighton.co.uk, **fb**) means 'the town on the Dyke', which is literally true: the town bestrides Offa's Dyke as well as the River Teme, an ancient Brittonic name sharing roots with the better known Thames and Tamar rivers. Knighton has been a strategic border town since Saxon and even Roman times, when local 1st-century AD hero King Caratacus (Caradog), a proto Glyndŵr figure, harried the invaders then, once defeated and captured, managed to talk his way into a pardon in front of Claudius in Rome.

Apart from the handy train link, one reason the walk might start here is that one of Glyndŵr's most decisive victories against the English took place at the Battle of Bryn Glas in 1402, near the village of Pilleth, three miles south-west of town. At the same time Knighton's Norman castle, occupied by the well-connected Mortimer family (see p54), was reduced to rubble. You'll pass close to the site as you walk down Castle Road on the way out of town. The Mortimers were amongst the 'Marcher lords' invested by the English king to guard the border or **Welsh Marches**, as this part of the country has since become known.

Besides the **Offa's Dyke Centre** (see Services p86), the attractions of Knighton

---

❏ THE HINDWELL ENCLOSURE – A SUPERSIZED STONEHENGE
Though there's precious little to actually marvel at, just seven miles south of Knighton is the site of what is currently western Europe's largest known timber Neolithic structure. Flying over farmland in certain conditions revealed vestiges of ancient works, in this case part of a broad arc resembling a ditch showed a series of huge, closely dug post holes. The arc was a small section of a huge oval ring composed of some 1400 oak trunks weighing up to four tons each. They produced a palisade (wall) some 6m (20') high with a diameter of 880m by 580m, with a second smaller double-walled palisade at the southern end. Later the site was used as a fort on a Roman road. The remnants of such **henges** are commonly found around Britain and western Europe, but none on this scale. The site is thought to date back to 2700BC, some three centuries after work on the similar but much smaller Stonehenge was believed to have started and which spanned several centuries. Like Stonehenge, it's thought the site would have been used for ceremonial or religious purposes. Read more at 🖥 coflein.gov.uk/en/site/309366/.

Wales is densely packed with many other remains of ancient sites, from the late Neolithic to medieval times. Megalithic structures like cromlechs (tombs) are particularly prolific in the peninsular west: Anglesey, Llyn and the west coast down to Pembrokeshire, as these would have been the first re-inhabitable areas when the ice sheet started retreating 10,000 years ago, while the mountainous interior remained largely icebound. Larger Iron Age hill forts became more numerous on the eastern side of the country and later were commonly adopted or repurposed as defensive structures by or against those that followed (Romans, Saxons, Normans), just as sites of pagan worship would become churches and cathedrals. Wales has more castles per square mile than any other country, with 400 still standing or in ruins.

ROUTE GUIDE AND MAPS

amount to a couple of antique shops on the High St and the volunteer-run **museum** (Apr-Oct; free) with exhibits reflecting the social history of the area, including a 1950s kitchen, scullery and school room. The **Knighton Show** (see p17) is held on the last Saturday in August.

Transport

[See pp46-50] Knighton **train** station is a stop on the Heart of Wales line from Shrewsbury (55 mins) and is by far the most practical way of getting here by public transport.

Minsterly Motors No 738/740 **bus** services connect Knighton with Ludlow across the border, while Knighton **Taxis** (☎ 01547-528165; 🖳 knightontaxis.co.uk) take up the slack.

Services

The **tourist information centre** up on West St also houses the **Offa's Dyke Centre** (☎ 01547-528753, **fb**; Wed-Sun 10am-4pm) with a fine display on all aspects of the Dyke as well as a little on Glyndŵr's Way too, plus books and maps and a café run by volunteers. There's an outdoor **ATM** on the way back to the town centre and another in the Premier **supermarket** (6am-8pm) on Broad St (the high street) with a Costcutter (7am-9pm) nearby. The **post office** (Mon-Fri 8am-6pm, Sat 8am-2pm) is in the Co-op (Mon-Sat 7am-8pm, Sun 10am-4pm) at Texaco at the south end of town.

You'll find a **doctors' surgery** (☎ 01547-528523, 🖳 wylcwmstreetsurgery.co.uk) on Wylcwm St, which runs parallel to Broad St.

Market day is Thursday, though since the mid 1850s it's no longer permitted to sell your wife for a shilling.

Where to stay

Knighton has several old coaching inns with **rooms**. At the **George & Dragon** (☎ 01547-528067, 🖳 thegeorgeknighton.co.uk, **fb**; 3T/2D all en suite; Ⓛ; 🐾) on Broad St, B&B will set you back £42.50pp (sgl occ £45). The **Horse & Jockey** (☎ 01547-520062, 🖳 thehorseandjockeyinn.co.uk, **fb**; 3D/4T/1Qd, all en suite; Ⓛ; 🐾) offers

eight comfortable rooms overlooking a courtyard from £50.45pp (sgl occ £92.95) and the **Red Lion Inn** (☎ 01547-428080, 🖳 booking.com; 1T/2D/1Tr all en suite; Ⓛ; 🐾) by the clock is another option from £47.50pp (sgl occ £65).

That leaves the **Knighton Hotel** (🖳 booking.com & similar sites; call centre ☎ 01547-520530; 1S/3D/2Tr/1Qd all en suite) down the hill. Rooms go from just £21pp (sgl occ £36) and are perfectly fine, just don't expect full-time staff or a restaurant, and you might like to skip the £6 'dry snack' breakfast.

B&Bs include **Pannas** (off map opposite; ☎ 01547-740046, 🖳 staypannas knighton.co.uk; 1D en suite in an apartment; Ⓛ; 🐾) at 15 The Dingle, nearly a mile south-east of the clock, costing from £27.50pp (£40 sgl occ). They offer a 'breakfast basket' for £6 and evening meals are available by prior arrangement.

The Laurels (Map 1; ☎ 07748-328554, 🖳 laurelsknighton.wales; 2D/1T/1Tr shared bathroom) is at the start of Penybont Road in town. There are some en suite rooms in a separate cottage and all costing from £37.50pp (£55 sgl occ).

The most central option is the **Garden House** (☎ 07453-006011; 🖳 booking.com; 1D/1T en suite; ➴) on Church Road, with rates from £32.50pp (£56 sgl occ).

Campers should march northwards about 15 minutes to riverside **Panpwnton Farm** (Map 1; ☎ 07503-186166, 🖳 pan pwntonfarm@gmail.com, **fb**; Easter-Oct; £10pp).

Where to eat and drink

You're well served for pub grub. The **George & Dragon** (see Where to stay; **fb**) has mains starting from £9.50 with food daily at lunchtimes and evenings. They have regular evening theme nights featuring Thai and Italian menus, steak nights and two sittings for their popular Sunday carvery (noon & 2pm, booking essential). Booking is advised at the popular **Horse & Jockey** (see Where to stay; **fb**; food daily noon-2pm & 6-9pm) where 'Jockey Classics' include the likes of chicken and bacon enchilada (£12.95).

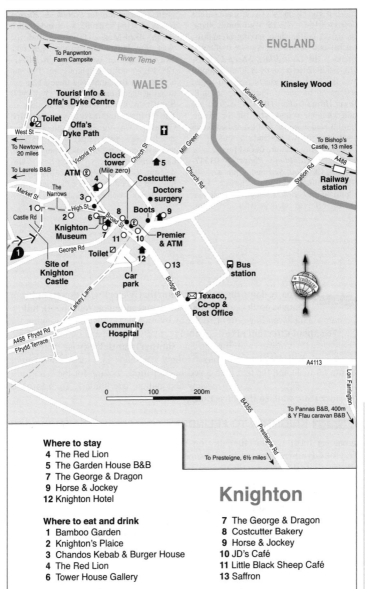

ENGLAND

River Teme

WALES

Kinsley Wood

Kinsley Rd

**Tourist Info &
Offa's Dyke Centre**

To Panpwnton
Farm Campsite

Toilet

West St

**Offa's
Dyke Path**

To Newtown,
20 miles

To Laurels B&B

Victoria Rd

Church St

Mill Green

To Bishop's
Castle, 13 miles

Station Rd

A488

**Clock
tower**
(Mile zero)

Church Rd

**Railway
station**

ATM £

4

Market St

The Narrows

3

High St

1

Castle Rd

2

6

8

Broad St

£

Costcutter

5

**Doctors'
surgery**

Boots

9

**Knighton
Museum**

7

11

10

**Premier
& ATM**

George Rd

Toilet

12

13

**Bus
station**

**Site of
Knighton
Castle**

Larkey Lane

**Car
park**

Bridge St

**Texaco,
Co-op &
Post Office**

A488 Ffrydd Rd

Ffrydd Terrace

**Community
Hospital**

A4113

Lon Farrington

0   100   200m

To Pannas B&B, 400m
& Y Ffau caravan B&B

B4355

Presteigne Rd

To Presteigne, 6½ miles

Knighton

Where to stay
4 The Red Lion
5 The Garden House B&B
7 The George & Dragon
9 Horse & Jockey
12 Knighton Hotel

Where to eat and drink
1 Bamboo Garden
2 Knighton's Plaice
3 Chandos Kebab & Burger House
4 The Red Lion
6 Tower House Gallery

7 The George & Dragon
8 Costcutter Bakery
9 Horse & Jockey
10 JD's Café
11 Little Black Sheep Café
13 Saffron

ROUTE GUIDE AND MAPS

If it's a caffeine shot you're after, *JD's Café* (☎ 01547-528218; Wed-Sun 8.30am-2pm) is a coffee shop serving breakfasts, lunches and takeaways. A more traditional option is the *Little Black Sheep Café* (☎ 01547-520224; **fb**; daily 8.30am-3.30pm) over the road, with gluten-free and vegan options on the menu. Further up the hill, *Tower House Gallery* (☎ 01547-529530, 🖳 galleryknighton.co.uk, **fb**; Tue-Sat 10am-4pm) is said to do the best tea and coffee in town, with sandwiches and cakes too.

The guilty pleasure of **fast food** can be satiated at *Knighton's Plaice* (☎ 01547-520943; **fb**; Mon-Wed noon-2pm & 4.30-10pm, Thur-Sat 11.30am-2pm & 4.30-10pm) up the Narrows, which has fresh pizzas on offer as well as fish and chips.

There's also *Chandos Kebab & Burger House* (☎ 01547-528085; 🖳 chandoskebab .co.uk; Wed-Mon 3-11pm) behind the clock. For Indian food to eat in or take away it's got to be *Saffron* (☎ 01547-528510; 🖳 saffronknighton.com; Tue-Sun 6-11pm) on Bridge St, and there's Chinese to go at the *Bamboo Garden* (☎ 01547-520010; Wed-Sun 5-10pm) at the top of The Narrows, right next to your very first Glyndŵr's Way sign leading out of town.

It is now time to get stuck into your walk so early risers make your way to *Costcutters* **bakery** (Mon-Sat 7am-4.45pm, Sun 9am-3pm) for hot *oggies* (pasties) and other baked delicacies to fuel the full day's walk to Felindre.

The route guide

WELSHPOOL If you're doing this walk in an **northerly/clockwise direction** (from south to north starting in Knighton and ending at Welshpool), follow the maps in an ascending order (from 1 to 54) and the text as below, looking for the **Welshpool direction arrow symbol** on overview text and on map borders.

KNIGHTON If you're walking in a **southerly/anticlockwise direction** (Welshpool to Knighton) follow the maps in a descending order (from 54 to 1) and the text with a **red background**, looking for the **Knighton direction arrow symbol** on overview text and on map borders. **Turn to p172 to start your walk in this direction**.

WELSHPOOL KNIGHTON TO FELINDRE   [MAPS 1-7]

What for most is their first day on the Way of Glyndŵr turns out to be a superb hike that sets the pace for the typical daily distance, but with relatively few gates. Allow at least 8 hours with **no prospect of resupply or any other services** direct-

Distance	15¼ miles (24.5km)
Ascent	2536ft (773m)
Time	8 hours
	WALKING TIME ONLY
	SEE P83 – ADD 20-30%

ly on the Way, other than whatever you can trap. So, with your time-keeping device synchronised with Knighton's pre-atomic town clock and a hearty cry of 'God for Owain, Cymru and St David!' strike forth out of town.

Bailey Hill (Map 2) Once up the Narrows, from Castle Road cast one last view south-east over the town spread across the Teme valley and the now uncontested English border before back lanes squirrelling between the houses bring you

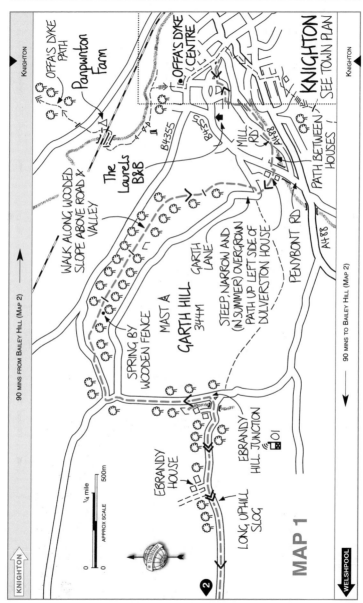

OFFA'S DYKE PATH

Panpwnton Farm

KNIGHTON

OFFA'S DYKE CENTRE

KNIGHTON
SEE TOWN PLAN

B4355

The Laurels B&B

MILL RD

B4355

A488

PATH BETWEEN HOUSES!

WALK ALONG WOODED SLOPE ABOVE ROAD & VALLEY

GARTH LANE

STEEP, NARROW AND (IN SUMMER) OVERGROWN PATH UP LEFT SIDE OF DULVERTON HOUSE

PENYBONT RD

A488

90 MINS FROM BAILEY HILL (MAP 2)

KNIGHTON

90 MINS TO BAILEY HILL (MAP 2)

SPRING BY WOODEN FENCE

MAST

GARTH HILL
344M

EBRANDY HOUSE

EBRANDY HILL JUNCTION

LONG UPHILL SLOG

¼ mile

500m

APPROX SCALE

MAP 1

2

WELSHPOOL

KNIGHTON

ROUTE GUIDE AND MAPS

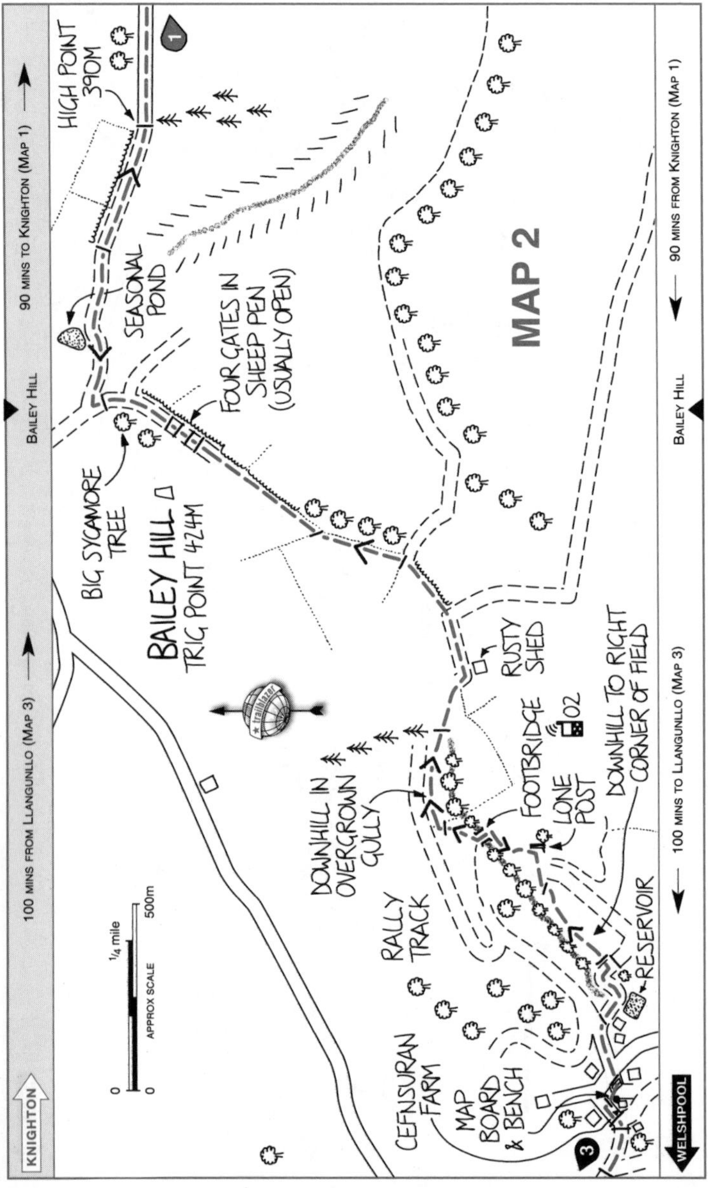

KNIGHTON

100 MINS FROM LLANGUNLLO (MAP 3) →

BAILEY HILL ►

HIGH POINT 390M

90 MINS TO KNIGHTON (MAP 1) →

SEASONAL POND

FOUR GATES IN SHEEP PEN (USUALLY OPEN)

BIG SYCAMORE TREE

BAILEY HILL △ TRIG POINT 424M

MAP 2

90 MINS FROM KNIGHTON (MAP 1) →

BAILEY HILL ►

RUSTY SHED

FOOTBRIDGE

LONE POST

DOWNHILL TO RIGHT CORNER OF FIELD

100 MINS TO LLANGUNLLO (MAP 3) →

DOWNHILL IN OVERGROWN GULLY

RALLY TRACK

RESERVOIR

CEFNSURAN FARM

MAP BOARD & BENCH

WELSHPOOL ►

¼ mile
APPROX SCALE
500m

0

to the wooded northern flanks of Garth Hill. A road stage follows with an irksome climb up a quiet country lane delivering you to the airy ovine expanse leading to **Bailey Hill**, already at over 1300ft (400m).

Dropping down past a motorsports track to Cefnsuran Farm, by late morning you amble into seemingly deserted **Llangunllo**.

Llangunllo (Map 3)   Here at the drinks-only *Greyhound Inn* (☎ 01547-550400, **fb**; Wed-Fri 5-11pm; Sat & Sun 2-11pm), the nearest you'll get to Soup of the Day is 'whisky with ice croutons'. Chances are the pub is closed anyway, so unless your visit coincides with a 'Big Breakfast' social at the village hall (🖥 llangunllo.co.uk/events) you might settle for a sit-down by the old bus-shelter-cum-village-book-exchange before crossing over the infant River Lugg which rises on Beacon Hill and, after recrossing a tributary (nice lunch spot), you rejoin a road to pass under the **Heart of Wales** rail line.

If you've had enough already, Llangunllo (also known as Llangynllo) **train**
[cont'd on p94]

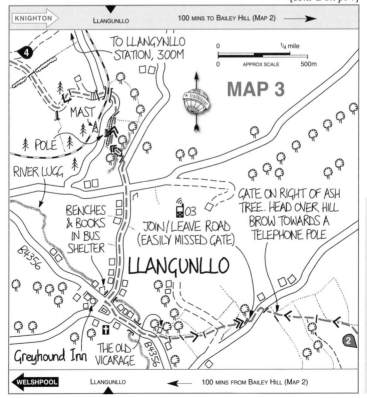

KNIGHTON ▶   LLANGUNLLO   100 MINS TO BAILEY HILL (MAP 2) ⟶

TO LLANGYNLLO STATION, 300M

0 — ¼ mile
0 — APPROX SCALE — 500m

MAP 3

MAST

POLE

RIVER LUGG

BENCHES & BOOKS IN BUS SHELTER

B4356

📱03
JOIN/LEAVE ROAD (EASILY MISSED GATE)

LLANGUNLLO

GATE ON RIGHT OF ASH TREE. HEAD OVER HILL BROW TOWARDS A TELEPHONE POLE

Greyhound Inn   THE OLD VICARAGE   B4356

◀ WELSHPOOL   LLANGUNLLO   ⟵ 100 MINS FROM BAILEY HILL (MAP 2)

ROUTE GUIDE AND MAPS

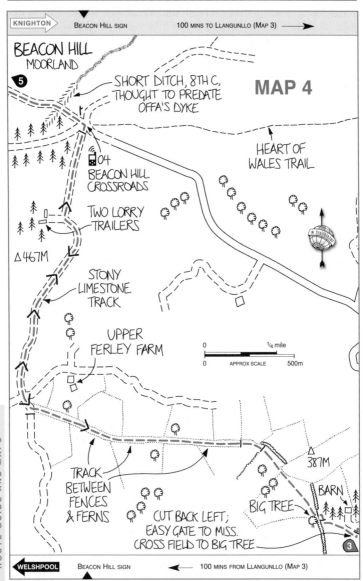

BEACON HILL
MOORLAND

5

SHORT DITCH, 8TH C,
THOUGHT TO PREDATE
OFFA'S DYKE

MAP 4

HEART OF
WALES TRAIL

04
BEACON HILL
CROSSROADS

TWO LORRY
TRAILERS

△ 467M

STONY
LIMESTONE
TRACK

UPPER
FERLEY FARM

0 ___ ¼ mile
0 ___ APPROX SCALE ___ 500m

△ 387M

TRACK
BETWEEN
FENCES
& FERNS

BARN

BIG TREE

CUT BACK LEFT;
EASY GATE TO MISS.
CROSS FIELD TO BIG TREE

3

ROUTE GUIDE AND MAPS

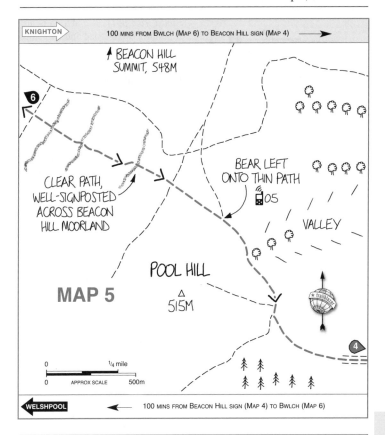

↑ BEACON HILL
SUMMIT, 548M

6

CLEAR PATH,
WELL-SIGNPOSTED
ACROSS BEACON
HILL MOORLAND

BEAR LEFT
ONTO THIN PATH
📱05

🌳🌳🌳🌳

VALLEY

POOL HILL

MAP 5

△
515M

⊻

★ trailblazer

4

0   1/4 mile

0   APPROX SCALE   500m

🌲🌲🌲🌲🌲🌲

❑ JOHN DEE: THE 'WELSH WIZARD'

Just near the Offa's Dyke Centre in Knighton is a cul-de-sac curiously called Conjuror's Drive, recalling a time when ancient Radnorshire was linked with the *dynion hysbys*: 'clever men', sorcerers or perhaps just healers. Some 19th century sources claimed that Beguildy was the birthplace of Ieuan Ddu, better known as the late Tudor mathematician and alchemist, Dr John Dee. He was tutor to Elizabeth I, the last of the Tudor dynasty which, of course, originated in Wales. Dee's immediate ancestors did come from nearby Pilleth, site of Glyndŵr's 1402 Battle of Bryn Glas.

Thought to be the inspiration for Shakespeare's sorcerer, Prospero, in *The Tempest*, like many renaissance 'physicians' (not least Isaac Newton), Dee immersed himself in Hermetic studies and sought to commune with angels in a bid to unravel the secrets of the universe. Less esoterically, Dee is also credited with coining the term 'British Empire' in support of colonisation of the New World.

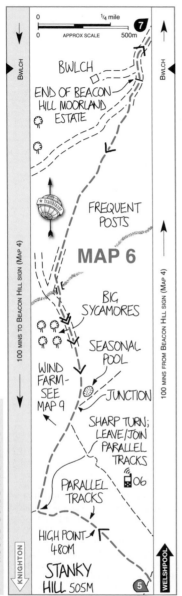

MAP 6

0 ... 1/4 mile

0 ... 500m

APPROX SCALE

BWLCH

BWLCH

BWLCH

END OF BEACON HILL MOORLAND ESTATE

FREQUENT POSTS

100 MINS TO BEACON HILL SIGN (MAP 4)

100 MINS FROM BEACON HILL SIGN (MAP 4)

BIG SYCAMORES

SEASONAL POOL

WIND FARM – SEE MAP 9

JUNCTION

SHARP TURN; LEAVE/JOIN PARALLEL TRACKS

06

PARALLEL TRACKS

HIGH POINT 480M

KNIGHTON

WELSHPOOL

STANKY HILL 505M

ROUTE GUIDE AND MAPS

[*cont'd from p91*]   station is just 10 minutes up the road and two stops back to Knighton (see p46-7 for more details).

Beacon Hill common Otherwise from here you will spend the rest of the day inching towards – and then over – the bracing windswept mass of the Beacon Hill common. At the start of the moorland section by a plantation you'll cross the indistinct remains of **Short Ditch** (Map 4), an 8th century structure thought to predate Offa's Dyke. Continuing west and north, you reach the high point of 1570ft (480m) near the Hill's brow and the waymarking and path remain clear until the descent rolls back into sheep pasture and patchy woodlands before dropping steeply into **Felindre**, right back on the River Teme and the border.

> **Walking to and from Beguildy**
> Just over a mile before Felindre consider diverting 1½ miles (2.4km) east along a lane down to **Beguildy** (see below) for the village **shop** (with rooms), followed by a visit to the adjacent pub for a proper **meal**. From there, either return to the trail to tick off the last mile, or it's 2 miles (3.2km) by road to **Felindre**.

BEGUILDY   **[off Map 7]**
Food is on offer at the *Radnorshire Arms* (☎ 01547-510634, 🖳 radnorshirearms-beg.wix site.com/radnorshirearms, **fb**; Tue-Sat noon-2pm & 6-11pm, Sunday noon-3.30pm & 6-11pm) with mains such as smoked haddock & pea risotto (£12.95). Booking is recommended.

Here the village **shop/PO** (☎ 01547-510631; Mon-Fri 8am-6pm, Sat & Sun 8am-1pm) will offer walkers a single night in the Airbnb **apartment** (1D; 1S en suite; 🐾) from £37.50pp (sgl occ rates on request).

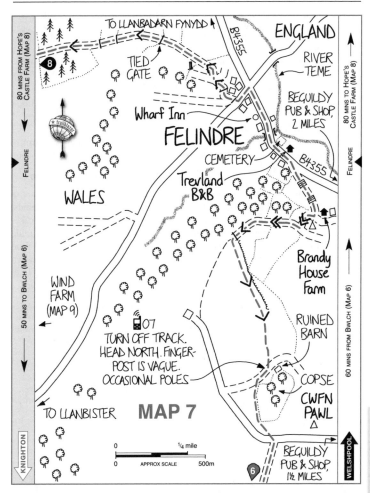

8

TO LLANBADARN FYNYDD

TIED GATE

Wharf Inn

ENGLAND

B4355

RIVER TEME

BEGUILDY PUB & SHOP, 2 MILES

FELINDRE

CEMETERY

B4355

Trevland B&B

WALES

WIND FARM (MAP 9)

Brandy House Farm

07 TURN OFF TRACK. HEAD NORTH. FINGER-POST IS VAGUE. OCCASIONAL POLES

RUINED BARN

COPSE

TO LLANBISTER

MAP 7

CWFN PAWL △

0   ¼ mile

0   500m
APPROX SCALE

BEGUILDY PUB & SHOP, 1½ MILES

6

FELINDRE   **[Map 7]**

After a stage of not much at all, it's a short-list of two lodging options at day's end in Felindre on the B4355 (just over 10 miles/16km to Knighton if you need to return there).

You'll find *Brandy House Farm* (☎ 01547-510282, 🖥 brandyhousefarm.co.uk; shared facilities; no wi-fi; (L); 🐾) right on

the Way just south of the village. Besides cottages (min 3-nights), the farm offers a vintage **caravan** (1D) and three basic camping **pods** (each sleeps 4, bedding not provided) from £25pp (sgl occ £50). Call to check single-night availability for Glyndŵr's Way walkers. **Campers** can pitch their tent for £15pp. With advance notice the owners can also lay on an

evening meal from £11.50 as well as a hearty breakfast from £7.50. Where the trail joins the road is ***Trevland*** (☎ 01547-510211; 1S/1D/1T en suite; 🐾; (Ⓛ)) with B&B from £40pp as well as evening meals and a packed lunch for another £19 inclusive.

The welcoming village pub is the ***Wharf Inn*** (☎ 01547-510659), open evenings from 6pm daily and 4pm on Saturday. It's drinks only so if you want a meal as well your best bet is probably the 2-mile walk along the Knighton road to the pub at **Beguildy** (see p94).

KNIGHTON **FELINDRE TO KNIGHTON**   [MAPS 7-1]

You'll start with the by-now familiar stiff climb into the hills and will keep climbing over the bleak moors of **Beacon Hill** common until well past lunchtime, before dropping down under the Heart of Wales railway line (Map 3) into the vil-

Distance **15¼ miles (24.5km)**
Ascent   **2192ft (668m)**
Time   **8 hours**
WALKING TIME ONLY – ADD 20-30%

lage of **Llangunllo** by which time the pub (no food) may be open on weekends. Otherwise, there's nothing much for you here other than a bench and another series of ascents topping out near **Bailey Hill** (Map 2) before an agreeable glide down into **Knighton** and a range of well-earned choices in lodgings and food with which to sign off your double crossing of the Celtic badlands of Glyndŵr. And so you wind your way along the back alleys and lanes before coming in to land at the foot of Knighton's town clock. Your time is up – congratulations!

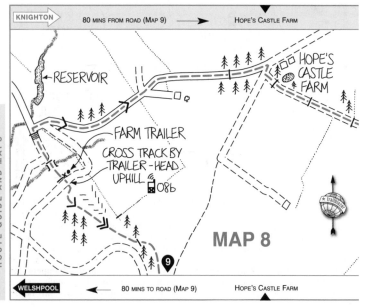

⬛WELSHPOOL FELINDRE TO ABBEYCWMHIR [MAPS 7-13]

This second stage is another fine walk that climbs out of the Teme valley to around 1500ft/457m on occasions, while mostly traversing grassy, sheep-speckled pastures. It's also blessed with a handy **shop** and **café** close to the halfway mark at Llanbadarn Fyndd.

Distance	15½ miles (24.9km)
Ascent	2441ft (744m)
Time	8 hours
	WALKING TIME ONLY
	SEE P83 – ADD 20-30%

Garreg Lwyd Hill You pass below the Garreg Lwyd Hill **Wind Farm** (Maps 8 & 9) you'll have spotted yesterday afternoon and which on a good day supplies electricity to over a third of Powys' homes.

Castell y Blaidd Right after, you'll need greater powers of visualisation to see more than docile sheep grazing the weathered ramparts of 'Wolf's Castle' or Castell y Blaidd (Map 9; 💻 coflein.gov.uk/en/site/306154; excellent aerial images), an Iron Age hill fort whose evocative name sounds a lot better than it looks from ground level, like so many of these mysterious ancient mounds along the trail. A long road walk drops you from the woolly hilltops into the village of **Llanbadarn Fynydd.**

Llanbadarn Fynydd (Map 10) Village of the year in 1998, one of the walk's few **community shops** (☎ 01597-840448, 💻 llanbadarnfynydd.org/llanbadarn-

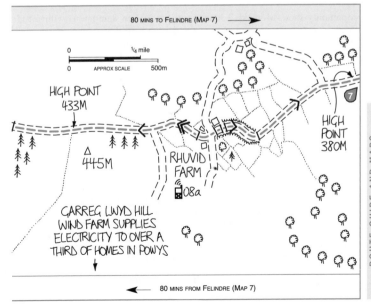

80 MINS TO FELINDRE (MAP 7) ➔

0 ¼ mile

0 APPROX SCALE 500m

HIGH POINT 433M

△ 445M

RHUVID FARM 📱08a

HIGH POINT 380M

7

GARREG LWYD HILL WIND FARM SUPPLIES ELECTRICITY TO OVER A THIRD OF HOMES IN POWYS

◄── 80 MINS FROM FELINDRE (MAP 7)

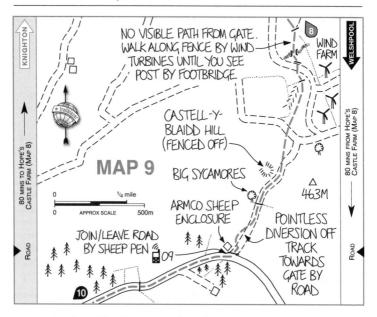

community-shop, Mon-Fri 7.30am-5pm, Sat & Sun 8am-noon) with a rudimentary **café** offers a rare chance for a proper sit-down snack-lunch while appraising the vast selection of mugs. It's said a mug emblazoned with the Welsh flag (see box p110) can bring good luck for the way ahead; it certainly makes a nice souvenir.

❑ OF KINGS AND FOOLS

Along the B4355 south of Beguildy, local traditions claim that an earlier iteration of the Norman-era Knucklas castle (another Glyndŵr casualty from 1402) was the site of the marriage of King Arthur and Gwynhwyfar (Guinevere), and that Crug-y-Byddar, just north of Felindre, was where Uther Pendragon – Arthur's father – had his castle. Doubtless many other localities across western Britain claim similar connections, but although popularised and embellished centuries later in 12th-century medieval romances, the Arthurian legend of the Celtic leader who fought off Germanic Saxon invaders around 500AD has a strong claim in Wales, based on chronicles including the *Mabinogion* and earlier *Welsh Triads*.

Triads relate to groups of three, usually with a heading indicating the point of likeness, thought probably to be a mnemonic aid for the Welsh bards or poets and dating from the 8th century. These myths depict heroic victories over supernatural beings or pagan (Saxon) entities. Tellingly the Triads include the famous verse: "*Three things* [are] *not easily restrained*[:] *the flow of a torrent, the flight of an arrow, and the tongue of a fool.*" Consider yourself suitably chastised.

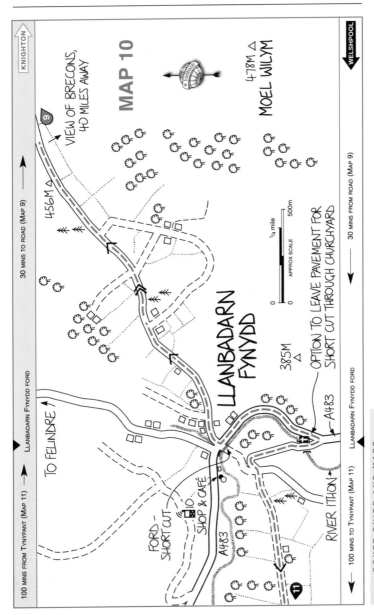

MAP 10

KNIGHTON

WELSHPOOL

VIEW OF BRECONS, 40 MILES AWAY

478M △ MOEL WILYM

9

456M △

30 MINS TO ROAD (MAP 9)

LLANBADARN FYNYDD FORD

30 MINS FROM ROAD (MAP 9)

385M △

OPTION TO LEAVE PAVEMENT FOR SHORT CUT THROUGH CHURCHYARD

LLANBADARN FYNYDD FORD

A483

LLANBADARN FYNYDD

TO FELINDRE

FORD - SHORT CUT

SHOP & CAFÉ

A483

RIVER ITHON

100 MINS FROM TYNYPANT (MAP 11)

100 MINS TO TYNYPANT (MAP 11)

11

¼ mile
APPROX SCALE
0   500m

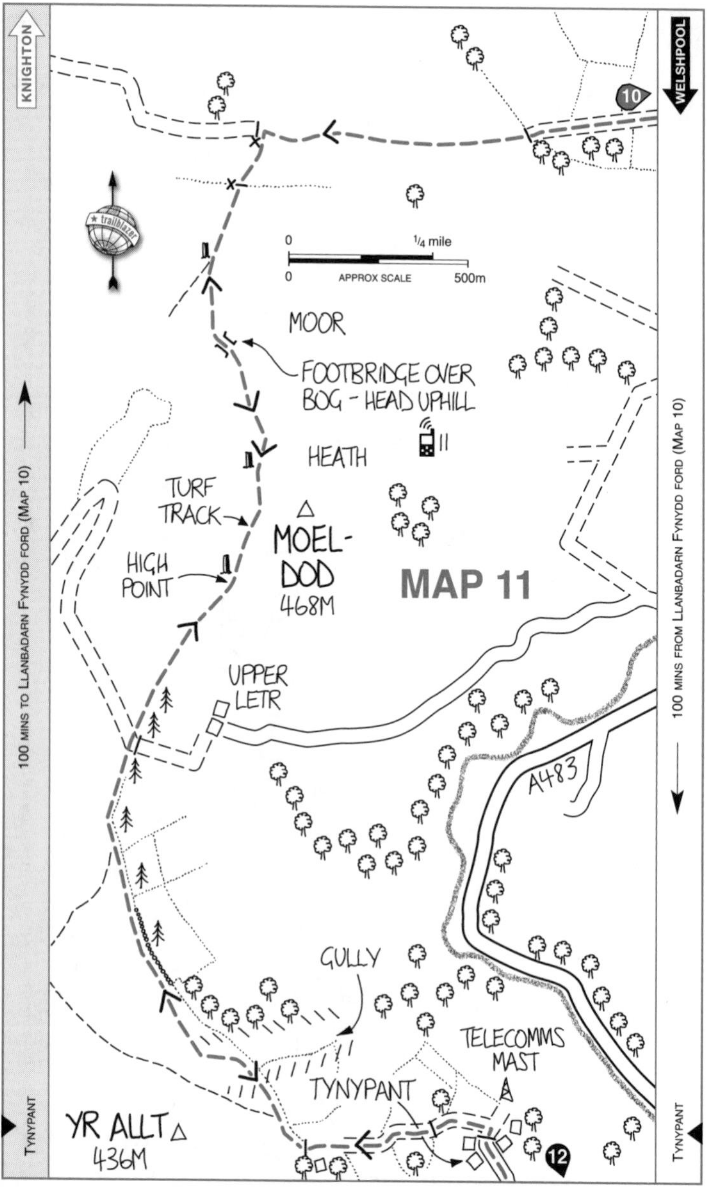

KNIGHTON

WELSHPOOL

★ trailblazer

0 ¼ mile
0 APPROX SCALE 500m

MOOR

FOOTBRIDGE OVER
BOG – HEAD UPHILL

HEATH

TURF
TRACK

MOEL-
DOD
468M

HIGH
POINT

MAP 11

UPPER
LETR

A483

GULLY

TELECOMMS
MAST

TYNYPANT

YR ALLT
436M

10

12

100 MINS TO LLANBADARN FYNYDD FORD (MAP 10)

100 MINS FROM LLANBADARN FYNYDD FORD (MAP 10)

ROUTE GUIDE AND MAPS

TYNYPANT

TYNYPANT

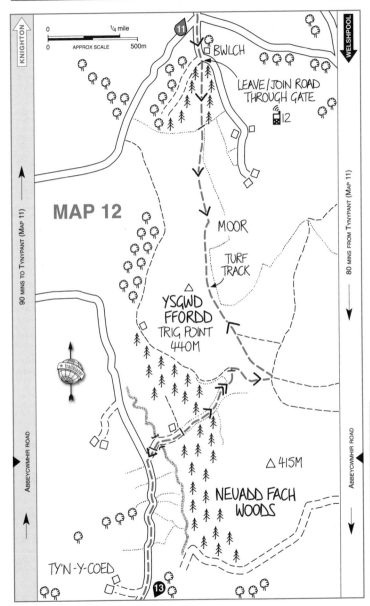

KNIGHTON

WELSHPOOL

0   ¼ mile
APPROX SCALE
0   500m

11

BWLCH

LEAVE/JOIN ROAD
THROUGH GATE

12

MAP 12

90 MINS TO TYNYPANT (MAP 11)

80 MINS FROM TYNYPANT (MAP 11)

MOOR

TURF
TRACK

△
YSGWD
FFORDD
TRIG POINT
440M

△ 415M

NEUADD FACH
WOODS

ABBEYCWMHIR ROAD

ABBEYCWMHIR ROAD

TY'N-Y-COED

13

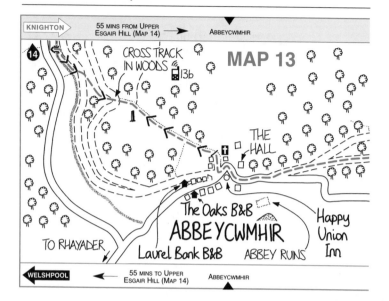

Moel Dod With your immediate future assured, either wade across the nearby River Ithon's ford, or stick diligently to the route (an extra 900m), with a tempting short-cut through the lych gate leading into St Padarn's ancient churchyard. Weather permitting, ahead lies a very agreeable afternoon traversing the grassy crests of Moel Dod, Yr Allt (Map 11) and Ysgŵd Ffordd (Map 12) hills, before a steep drop through the Neuadd-fach Wood leads to another deserted country lane amble and the final, sometimes tangled approach into **Abbeycwmhir**.

KNIGHTON ▷ **ABBEYCWMHIR TO FELINDRE** [MAPS 13-7]

After the previous section's sometimes tortuous routing, today's penultimate stage is a more straightforward up and over a line of hills to **Llanbadarn Fynydd** (Map 10; shop/café, see p97), followed by a similar, if more gradual

Distance	15½ miles (24.9km)
Ascent	2454ft (748m)
Time	8½ hours
WALKING TIME ONLY – ADD 20-30%	

ascent below the Garreg Lwyd Hill Wind Farm onto sheep pastures ending with a gentle drop down to the Teme valley and **Felindre** (Map 7).

Right from the steep start through Neuadd-fach Wood, be prepared for a fair amount of upping and downing.

[*Next route overview p96*]

ROUTE GUIDE AND MAPS

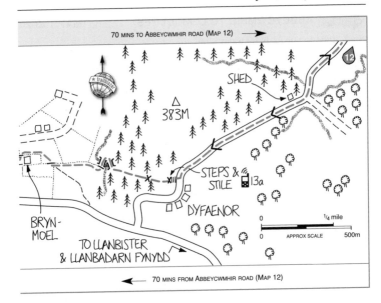

ABBEYCWMHIR   [Map 13]

The ruins of the 12th-century **Cistercian abbey** (see box p104) lie through a gate on the eastern approach to the village.

In the village centre by the aged petrol pump, the brooding churchyard, unusual 19th-century neo-Byzantine tower and the traditional stained-glass interior of **St Mary Virgin** gives eyes and lenses something more concrete to fix on.

Although the grand, neo-Elizabethan **Abbeycwmhir Hall** was lavishly restored in the late 1990s and was open for public tours prior to 2020, at the time of writing it appears to be a victim of prolonged Covid closures. Like the previous church, the nearby 17th-century manor of Dyfaenor, and doubtless a few other local dwellings, the Hall reused stone from the abbey.

After the thrill of Llanbadarn Fynydd's village shop, Abbeycwmhir (🖥 abbeycwmhir.org.uk) returns to the Way's modest offerings: two B&Bs and a drinks-only pub.

Opposite the church the squat, brick *Happy Union Inn* (☎ 01597-851203, **fb**; Tue-Sat 7.30-11pm) boasts a curious pub sign of a portly squire, tankard and Ploughman's in hand and a leek in his hat band, riding a sanguine white goat. A happy union of man and beast or a biting satire on English subjugation? A couple of pints should settle it.

The two **B&Bs** are on the road west out of the village. *The Oaks* (☎ 07967-298725, 🖥 Airbnb.co.uk/rooms/49720019, 1S/1T shared facilities; 🛏; Ⓛ) costs £35pp (sgl occ £55) with great food, morning and evening. *Laurel Bank* (☎ 01597 851240, 🖥 laurelbankabbeycwmhir.co.uk, 1D/2T en suite or private bathroom; Ⓛ) over the road is £42.50pp (sgl occ £85). Both can provide **packed lunches**. The only alternative will be crisps from the pub.

It's said that **wild camping** discreetly on the edge of the village will not result in a baying mob of irate locals, pitchforks and flaming torches in hand.

🔲WELSHPOOL ABBEYCWMHIR TO LLANIDLOES [MAPS 13-20]

Start limbering up early for today's trek to
the bright lights of Llanidloes. With two
lengthy days already done, you may find
today's longer road stages and erratic
routing outpace your enthusiasm. It's not
helped by the fact that there's nothing but

Distance	**15¼ miles (24.7km)**
Ascent	**2743ft (836m)**
Time	**8-9 hours**
WALKING TIME ONLY – ADD 20-30%	

farm taps and hay feeders to sustain you. So unless you've buried food caches
in advance or anticipated your needs at Llanbadarn Fynydd's shop, order a
packed lunch from your B&B to power you through; today may feel further
than it looks.

Esgair Hill (Map 14) The path rising above the church cuts across Sugar Loaf
hill for a short road stage, passing Fishpool Farm where the abbey's monks once
nurtured their eels and trout, before climbing onto the grassy sweep of Esgair
Hill. On a clear day there are fine views south to the Brecons and west into the
Cambrian mountains which await you patiently, like a sleeping Welsh prince.

🔲 CISTERCIANS – THE WHITE MONKS

A reformist offshoot of the Benedictine order seeking to get back to the old ways, the
Cistercians were founded in Cîteaux, near Dijon in 1098 and, all things considered,
proliferated across Europe like a shock wave, at their peak totalling hundreds of
abbeys or similar houses from Sicily to Ireland, and Sweden to Hungary. By this time
Christian persecution had long since ceased, and a monastic life replaced martyrdom
as the pinnacle of religious devotion.

The Cistercians got to work and supported vibrant communities of farmers,
brewers, millers, animal breeders and of course, master builders and engineers, creating the earliest manufactories – an 'industrial revolution' of its day, all with a
healthy dose of self-denial. Seen as a prestigious institution by ostensibly pious
rulers, both wealthy Norman Marcher lords and Welsh princes lent patronage to the
French order in the bid to legitimise their authority, partake of wider European rather
than Celtic influences, and to help expedite their passage to salvation.

Abbeycwmhir's own 12th-century **Cistercian abbey** (🖥 abbeycwmhir.org) was
one of over a dozen in Wales including Neath, Strata Florida and magnificent Tintern
(1131) near Chepstow. Although a grand abbey was never completed, in its day it was
one of Britain's largest churches, the order's industrious austerity supposedly chim-
ing with local lore channelling abstemious Celtic Saints who were among Britain's
earliest Christians. Llywelyn ap Gruffudd, the last of the native Princes of Wales (see
p52) is said to be buried here. Killed near Builth in 1282, his death ended a rebellion
against Edward I who had his head paraded around London.

Considering Gruffudd's Glyndŵr-like significance to the Welsh, there's a rather
discreet memorial slab at the ruin's east end. Even Glyndŵr's claims of descent from
ap Gruffudd didn't stop him ransacking the place in 1402, suspecting the monks of
spying for the English. Henry VIII's Dissolution of 1535 added further depredations,
and a few years later some of the fine nave bays were moved to Llanidloes' church,
p112). Civil War skirmishes in the 17th-century picked over the remains. As it is
today, with little more than a crumbling outline and some unpilfered carved pedi-
ments, prepare to be disappointed; it's no Cambrian Angkor Wat.

FALLEN GATE

TO BWLCH

0   ¼ mile

0   APPROX SCALE   500m

450M

UPPER ESGAIR HILL

WATER TROUGHS

JUNCTION OF ROAD & LANE FOR ESGAIR FARMS 14

LONE OAK

UPPER ESGAIR

VIEW OF BRECONS

LOWER ESGAIR

MAP 14

FISHPOOL FARM – ONCE SUPPLIED FISH FOR ABBEY MONKS

13

UPPER ESGAIR HILL   ← 55 MINS FROM ABBEYCWMHIR (MAP 13)   WELSHPOOL

Talking of the sleeping princes, as you join the stony track leading down to Bwlch y Sarnau (Map 15), half a mile in the opposite direction is **Castell y Garn** (below).

Castell y Garn   [off Map 15, p106]
Marked on OS maps, three fence lines converge on a hill top around faint traces of a 14-metre wide ring cairn. It's said in 1858, a *cist* (pre-Christian coffin) containing human bones was unearthed here, indicating a burial site dating from the Bronze Age (🖳 coflein.gov.uk/en/site/305885). But just as with yesterday's Wolf's Castle (Map 9) don't undertake the diversion unless you are able to let the imagination soar like a red kite. Even older *cromlechs* (tombs) and standing stones like Maen-serth just a few miles to the south-west can impress more easily.

Bwlch-y-Sarnau (Map 15) Without the detour, after just 90 minutes from Abbeycwmhir you're in Bwlch-y-Sarnau. It's the only village you'll see today

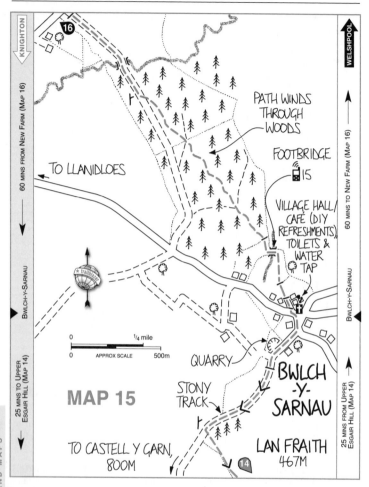

but the promisingly named *Glyndŵr's Way Café* in the **community hall** (🖳 bwlchysarnau.org.uk; **fb**) is volunteer run and generally only opens by prior arrangement for large groups, it seems. However, there are **tea and coffee making facilities** (Apr-Oct; honesty box) and toilets in the community hall's porch, plus a water tap outside. Refreshed or not, there's nothing left but to get stuck in for the next few hours.

Pistyll (Map 16) You'll pass through some woods, then follow more asphalt before a long stage contouring Pistyll and Domen-ddu along a forestry track.

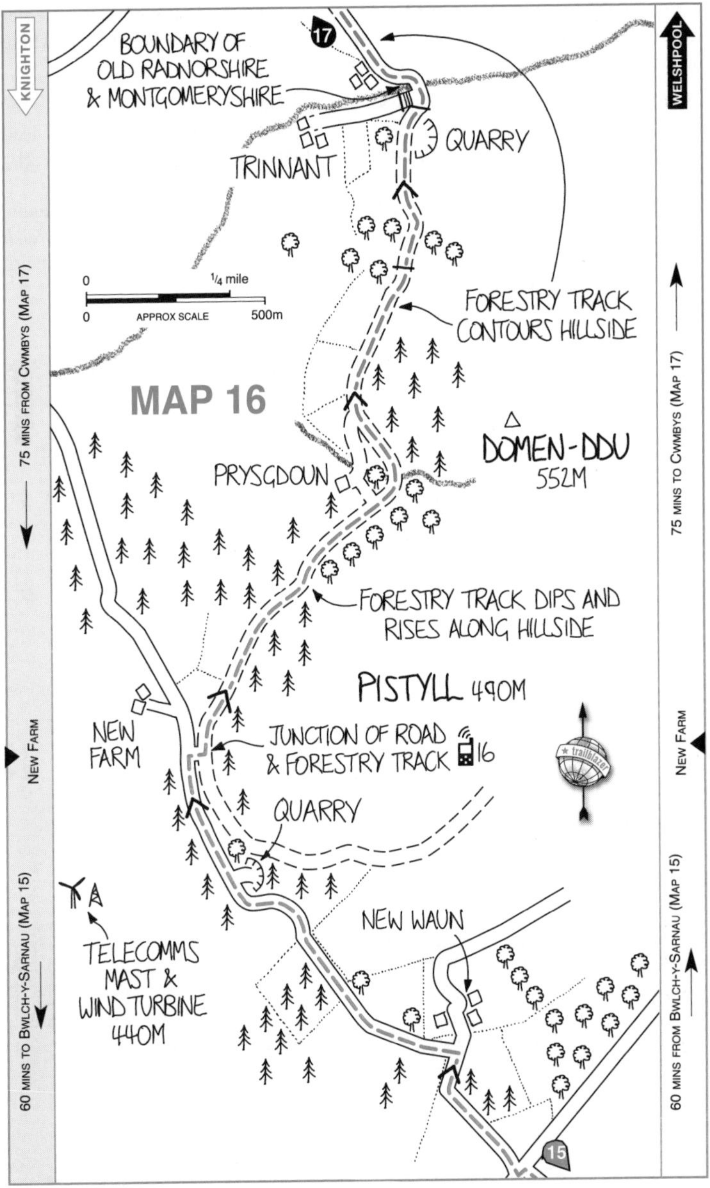

KNIGHTON

WELSHPOOL

BOUNDARY OF
OLD RADNORSHIRE
& MONTGOMERYSHIRE

17

QUARRY

TRINNANT

FORESTRY TRACK
CONTOURS HILLSIDE

0   1/4 mile
0   APPROX SCALE   500m

MAP 16

△ DOMEN-DDU
552M

PRYSGDOUN

FORESTRY TRACK DIPS AND
RISES ALONG HILLSIDE

PISTYLL 490M

NEW
FARM

JUNCTION OF ROAD
& FORESTRY TRACK 16

QUARRY

NEW WAUN

TELECOMMS
MAST &
WIND TURBINE
440M

15

75 MINS FROM CWMBYS (MAP 17)

75 MINS TO CWMBYS (MAP 17)

NEW FARM

NEW FARM

60 MINS TO BWLCH-Y-SARNAU (MAP 15)

60 MINS FROM BWLCH-Y-SARNAU (MAP 15)

ROUTE GUIDE AND MAPS

Crossing the brook at **Trinnant Farm**, you're leaving old Radnorshire to enter what was Montgomeryshire, while above sits the Llandinam Wind Farm where a hundred turbines turn wind into watts.

Nant Feinion Contouring **Pegwyn Bach** (Map 17), the forestry track ends and a path, other tracks and short road sections past backwoods farms lead steeply down to the **Nant Feinion stream** (Map 18) a tributary of the nearby Severn.

These elevation drops must be dutifully repaid in a series of seismographic switchbacks which take you directly past Prospect Farm and the home of *Welsh Mountain Cider* (see box p110) which also offers no frills **camping** in one of their fields, with views of the mountains.

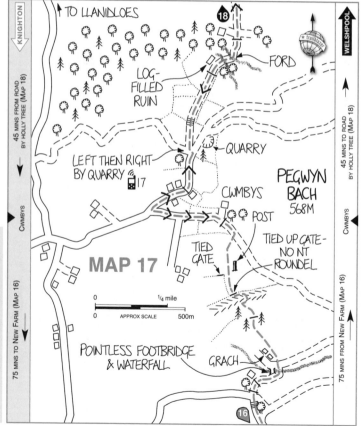

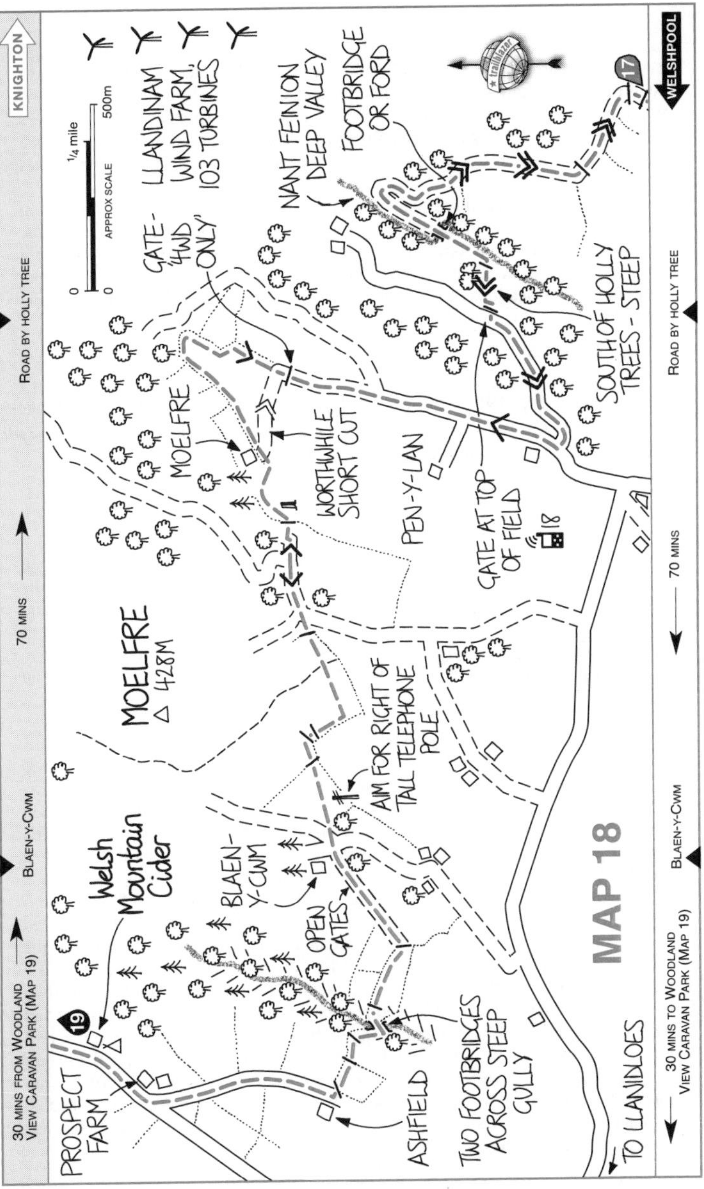
KNIGHTON
30 MINS FROM WOODLAND VIEW CARAVAN PARK (MAP 19)
BLAEN-Y-CWM
70 MINS
ROAD BY HOLLY TREE
PROSPECT FARM
19
Welsh Mountain Cider
ASHFIELD
TWO FOOTBRIDGES ACROSS STEEP GULLY
BLAEN-Y-CWM
OPEN GATES
AIM FOR RIGHT OF TALL TELEPHONE POLE
MOELFRE
△ 428M
MOELFRE
WORTHWHILE SHORT CUT
PEN-Y-LAN
18
GATE AT TOP OF FIELD
GATE- '4WD ONLY'
APPROX SCALE
0
1/4 mile
0
500m
LLANDINAM WIND FARM, 103 TURBINES
NANT FEINION DEEP VALLEY
FOOTBRIDGE OR FORD
SOUTH OF HOLLY TREES - STEEP
trailblazer
17
WELSHPOOL
MAP 18
TO LLANIDLOES
30 MINS TO WOODLAND VIEW CARAVAN PARK (MAP 19)
BLAEN-Y-CWM
70 MINS
ROAD BY HOLLY TREE

❏ **WELSH MOUNTAIN CIDER**   **[MAP 18, p109]**
At Prospect Farm (☎ 07790-071729, 🖥 welshmountaincider.com, **fb**) they have
established something you may not have expected to encounter while traversing the
Welsh mountains – a cider orchard. They specialise in growing apple and pear trees
at high altitude and if you fancy sampling their wares, they are open for **tours** on the
first and third Saturday afternoons of the summer months (Apr-Oct) or at other times
by appointment.

They also offer **camping** (call or email to book; £10 per tent) with mountain
views on their basic, no-frills field site (water, composting toilets). Catering can be
provided for groups by prior arrangement. Better still, if you time it right you could
give yourself the weekend off and book onto one of their occasional summer
Saturday Cider Sessions (see website for dates) to enjoy cider, food and live music
with camping.

Gorn Road (Map 19)   Continuing through Newchapel, those switchbacks
eventually spit you out onto quiet upper end of Gorn Road, past *Plasnewydd
Bunkhouse* (see p114) leading down into 'Llani'.

❏ **GLYNDŴR AND THE WELSH FLAG**

You'll see the Welsh red dragon motif all along
your walk, from flags fluttering outside public
buildings and private houses, to magic mugs and
car bumper stickers. The use of the red dragon to
represent the *Cymry* (Welsh people) dates back to
at least the 7th century and King Cadwaladr ap
Cadwallon of Gwynedd. Some also like to link it
to the legendary Arthurian 'Pendragon' dynasty.

It was this standard which Glyndŵr raised against the English at the start of his
campaign for Welsh autonomy in 1400 and which you'll see on waymarkers (see
p17). A few decades later the first Tudor monarch, Henry VII, introduced the now-
familiar green and white backgrounds from his own coat of arms. Welsh archers had
dressed in green and white as far back as the Battle of Crecy in 1346, possibly the first
national military uniform in Europe at this time. The distinctive flag then regained
popularity early in the 20th century and was adopted as the flag of Wales in 1959.

The reason it was never incorporated into the 'Union Jack' as with other coun-
tries of the United Kingdom is because that flag as we know it today first appeared
in 1801 on the creation of the 'United Kingdom of Great Britain and Ireland'. At the
time a red-on-white saltire – St Patrick's Cross (supposedly representing Ireland) –
was incorporated into the 'Flag of Great Britain'. That flag came into being in 1606
by merging England's Cross of St George), a red cross dating from the Crusades and
Knights Templar, with the Scottish white-on-blue saltire (established from the 14th
century) following the Union of the Crowns in 1603. By the time these flags were
adopted, Wales had been formally '… *incorporated, united and annexed to and with
this his* [Henry VIII's] *Realm of England…*' to quote the 'Laws of Wales Act' of 1535.
In other words, Wales was not considered a separate country at the time, and so had
no representation in the union flag.

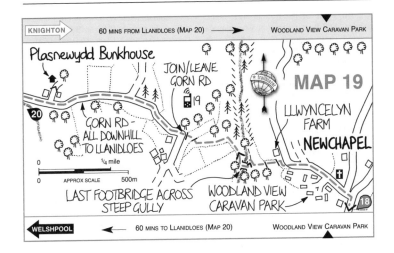

KNIGHTON

60 MINS FROM LLANIDLOES (MAP 20)

WOODLAND VIEW CARAVAN PARK

Plasnewydd Bunkhouse

JOIN/LEAVE
GORN RD

19

20

GORN RD -
ALL DOWNHILL
TO LLANIDLOES

MAP 19

LLWYNCELYN
FARM

NEWCHAPEL

0   ¼ mile
0   APPROX SCALE   500m

LAST FOOTBRIDGE ACROSS
STEEP GULLY

WOODLAND VIEW
CARAVAN PARK

18

WELSHPOOL

60 MINS TO LLANIDLOES (MAP 20)

WOODLAND VIEW CARAVAN PARK

LLANIDLOES [map p115]

After three full days on the trail with the prospect of at least another 29 miles (47km) across the Cambrian mountains to Machynlleth, you might ask yourself: is it too soon for a day off? **Llanidloes** (🖳 llanidloes.com) or 'Llani' has a nice vibe and certainly offers more than is on offer at other stage end points, as well as easy transport links to the outside world if you're doing the walk in short stages. With food and lodgings the most plentiful along the Way, bar either terminus, Llani's draw can be hard to resist.

Located on the south bank of the nascent 'Hafren' or Severn river (Britain's longest) where it joins the Clywedog and where it was most easily forded and later, bridged, Llanidloes traces its roots back to the 7th century Celtic Saint, Idloes (pronounced 'Id-loiz' – so, 'Hlanid-loiz').

Mined since the Bronze Age in the nearby Hafren Forest, a **lead mining** revival in the 1870s saw fortunes made and lost over a couple of decades; you'll pass one site below the Clywedog dam wall west of town. There's more on that subject as well as other local histories at the town **museum** (🖳 en.powys.gov.uk/llanidloes

museum; Mon 10am-1pm, Wed 10am-1pm & 2-6pm, Fri 10am-1pm & 2-4pm, Sat 10am-noon; free) in the **library** up a side lane off Great Oak St.

Much like abbeys, 500 years earlier, many of the temperate chapels were funded by wealthy benefactors at which time the main street adopted its facade, much of which survives today. In the surrounding hills sheep farming survives too, occasionally subsidised by a smart cabin with a hot tub. Like many such small rural towns in England and Wales, a post WW2 decline has now been somewhat reversed by the boom in campervanning and glamping.

Said to be the oldest of its kind in Britain, the half-timbered **Market Hall** in the town's centre dates from around 1600 though harks back to 1280 when Llanidloes (like many in Wales at this time) received its market charter from the king. Today's street plan can be traced back to that era and in the old days a bell was rung each evening to call time for vendors to shut up shop. Over the years the Market Hall has seen use as a courthouse, jail and Quaker Meeting House (see p160); John Wesley himself preached here in 1748.

By the main Severn bridge and a

wooden statue of the Roman river deity, Sabrina, **St Idloes church** boasts columns pilfered from Abbeycwmhir abbey (Map 13). A small modern Catholic church on the other side of the Severn from the Co-op is dedicated to Richard Glyn, a locally born and Oxbridge-educated bard and school teacher who suffered numerous persecutions before finally being hung, drawn and quartered as an obstinate *recusant* (refusing to attend Anglican church services) in Wrexham in 1584. One of many avowed Welsh Catholics who defied post-Reformation strictures, in 1970 he was canonised by the Pope.

Transport

[See pp46-50] Without your own transport, the easiest way to get out of town is to hop on a Celtic Travel No X75 **bus** (office on New St) north to connect with the Aberystwyth–Shrewsbury **rail** line, either at Caersws or busier Newtown (35 mins), with Welshpool and Shrewsbury the next stops. There are much less frequent Celtic Travel No X47 buses leaving west for Aberystwyth, or south as far as Llandrindod Wells to connect with the other mid-Welsh rail line between Swansea and Shrewsbury (via Knighton).

Note there are no buses out of Llani on a Sunday; your best bet will be a **taxi** to Caersws station (Llani Cars ☎ 07495-306840, **fb**).

Services

Banks being a thing of the past, you'll find **ATMs** in the **supermarkets**. The biggest of these is the Co-op at the south end of town (Mon-Sat 7am-10pm, Sun 10am-4pm); there's also a Spar (daily 7am-11pm) with **post office** on Long Bridge St and further up, a Costcutter (daily 8am-9pm) at the Texaco petrol station. There's a **launderette** (daily 8am-8pm) opposite the free car park on Church Lane.

Independent veggie-friendly **food shops** include *Great Oak Foods* (☎ 01686-413222; 14 Great Oak St; Mon-Tue, Thur-Fri 9am-5pm, Wed & Sat 9am-3pm) and *Natural Foods* (☎ 01686 412306; Mon-Tue & Thur-Fri 9am-5pm, Wed & Sat 9am-3pm) right over the road at number 17.

Back on Long Bridge St you'll find a **pharmacy** (Mon-Sat 9am-1pm & 2-5.30pm). If you need to see a **doctor**, Arwystli Medical Practice (☎ 01686-412228; Mon-Fri 8am-6.30pm) is on Mount Lane. Now in its 8th century, there is a Saturday **market** on Great Oak St. If

---

☐ CHARTISM IN SOUTH WALES

Chartism was a nationwide workers' movement that had gained traction in the industrial centres of northern England and South Wales, seeking voting reform and relief from destitution following the introduction of workhouses a few years earlier. It was especially militant in the mills and foundries of South Wales where twenty were killed during the Newport Uprising of 1839. Tellingly, Dickens' *Oliver Twist* had been serialised between 1837-9 and you'll find one of Wales' best preserved workhouses in Llanfillyn (🖳 the-workhouse.org.uk/history) a few miles east of Lake Vyrnwy (see p152).

Owain Glyndŵr's rampaging had set Llanidloes' prosperity back several decades before cottage industry weaving put the town back on the map. In the early 19th century the work moved into factories which did not pass without discord. Months of peaceful Chartist activity came to a head in April 1839 when a riot was provoked by a twitchy local mayor. Three locals were detained in the Trewythen Arms (now known as the Trewythen Hotel); a mob stormed the hotel and they were released. Reinforcements soon arrived from Powis Castle (see p168) to find order restored, but with a £100 reward on their head, the Llanidloes fugitives were found, tried and transported to Australia.

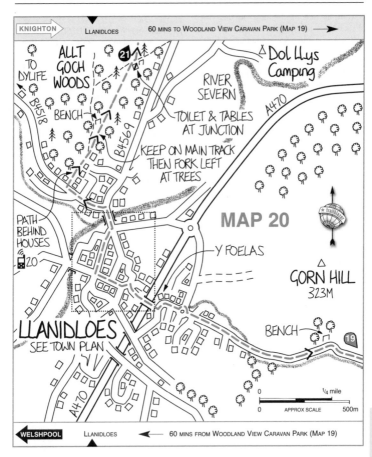

ALLT GOCH WOODS

TO DYLIFE

B4518

BENCH

B4569

RIVER SEVERN

A470

△ Dol Llys Camping

TOILET & TABLES AT JUNCTION

KEEP ON MAIN TRACK THEN FORK LEFT AT TREES

PATH BEHIND HOUSES

📱 20

MAP 20

Y FOELAS

△ GORN HILL 323M

LLANIDLOES
SEE TOWN PLAN

BENCH

trailblazer

0   ¼ mile
0   APPROX SCALE   500m

you need camping gear, see what the Co-op might have, but for camping gas canisters it'll have to wait till Machynlleth (see p134), so plan ahead.

If your **bicycle** needs fixing or you've had enough of walking and want to rent one Llani Bikes (☎ 07425-176826; 🖥 llani bikes.co.uk; 2 Great Oak Street; Tue-Fri 10am-4pm, Sat 10am-2pm) can help.

Is a **bookshop** a service? We like to think so, and in Llani it's provided by the *Great Oak Bookshop* (35 Great Oak St;

Mon-Sat 9.30am-5pm, Sat 9.30am-4.30pm) opposite Llani Bikes.

Where to stay

Like a medieval pilgrim, allow yourself to gaze awestruck at the lavish spread of lodging options in Llani; it won't get any better.

There's not much competition but for **campers** *Dol Llys Farm Camping* (Map 20; ☎ 01686-412694, 🖥 dolllyscaravan campsite.co.uk; Easter-Oct; 🐕), a mile north of town on the north bank of the

Severn, is one of the best on the Way. Walkers can use their kitchen/lounge with fridge, kettle, microwave and free wi-fi. It's £10pp and you'll need 20p coins for the shower block.

You'll have passed the spacious ***Plasnewydd Bunkhouse*** (Map 19; ☎ 01686-412431; 💻 plasnewyddbunkhouse.co.uk; sleeps 27 in 2 dorms & 1 family room) on Gorn Rd. It has a self-catering kitchen, large dining room and a drying room. Bring your own sleeping bag or hire bedding (£3). From £20, it's your cheapest bed in Llani.

Back in the town centre are several high street **pubs** with restaurants and rooms right on the route, like the ***Trewythen Hotel*** (☎ 01686-411333; 💻 trewythenhotel.wales; 3D/1Tr/2Qd, en suite) on Great Oak St where the Chartists were held in 1839, though probably not in lavish rooms for £72.50pp (sgl occ £115).

On Long Bridge St, the ***Red Lion Hotel*** (☎ 01686-412270, 💻 redlionllanidloes.com; 1S/2D/4T/1Tr/1Qd, en suite; Ⓛ; 🐕) has smart and simple rooms from £40pp (sgl occ £40-45), while accommodation at the adjacent ***Unicorn Hotel*** (☎ 01686-411188; 💻 unicornllanidloes.co.uk; 5D/2T, ensuite ; ▾; Ⓛ; 🐕; adults only) costs from £50pp (sgl occ £75) with direct booking discounts Mon-Thur.

Still on Long Bridge St, the ***Queens Head Hotel*** (☎ 01686-413409, 💻 queensheadhotel.co.uk; 1D/1D or T/2Tr, en suite; Ⓛ) is £50pp (sgl occ £75) for room only. Breakfast is available at the ***Traveller's Rest*** café (see Where to eat) next door for an additional charge.

Just south of the Market Hall is the 12th century ***Mount Inn*** (☎ 01686-412247, 💻 mountinn.com, **fb**; 3D/2T/2Tr/2Qd; 🐕) with en suite rooms from £40pp (sgl occ £55). Keep going south for the ***Coach & Horses B&B*** (☎ 01686-413758, 💻 coachandhorsesbandb.co.uk; 1D/2Tr, en suite; ▾) on the road to the Co-op, with spacious rooms from £45pp (sgl occ £55).

Down Short Bridge Street the ***Whistling Badger*** (☎ 01686-412583, 💻 thewhistlingbadger.co.uk, bookings via 💻 airbnb.co.uk preferred, **fb**; 1D en suite, 1D/1T private bathroom) has football in the Sports bar, live music and quirky rooms from £32.50pp (sgl occ £65) for room only.

And if all else fails, try 💻 airbnb.co.uk for rooms from £40, right in town.

Where to eat and drink

For evening meal, a walk along Great Oak St and Long Bridge St armed with our town map and a good appetite will take you past just about all of Llani's offerings.

For a special treat, pay a visit to ***Chartists 1770*** restaurant (Mon-Wed & Fri 10.30am-8.30pm, Thur to 9pm) in the ***Trewythen Hotel*** (see Where to stay), with mains such as fillet of turbot with scallop, samphire and lobster sauce (£24) or truffle potato gnocchi (£18).

If **pub grub** is more to your taste head down Short Bridge St and see what's vegan and veggie on the menu at the ***Whistling Badger*** (see Where to stay; **fb**; food Mon & Tue 5pm-midnight, Wed-Sun noon-midnight). Of the restaurants in the other hotel-pubs, round the corner on Long Bridge St, the ***Unicorn Hotel*** (see Where to stay; **fb**; food Tue-Thur 8am-4.30pm, Fri & Sat 8am-10pm, Sun 9am-3pm) has some rather special main dishes such as confit duck leg (£22.95) alongside the more usual burgers, while next door the ***Red Lion Hotel*** (see Where to stay; **fb**; food Mon-Sat noon-9pm, Sun noon-3pm) has evening menu options such as braised steak (from £8) and a lunchtime carvery on Sundays. On Mount Lane, the eponymous ***Mount Inn*** (see

❑ **WHERE TO STAY: THE DETAILS**

In the descriptions of accommodation in this book: ▾ means at least one room has a bath; Ⓛ means a packed lunch can be prepared if arranged in advance; 🐕 signifies that dogs are welcome in at least one room; **fb** indicates a Facebook page. See also p84.

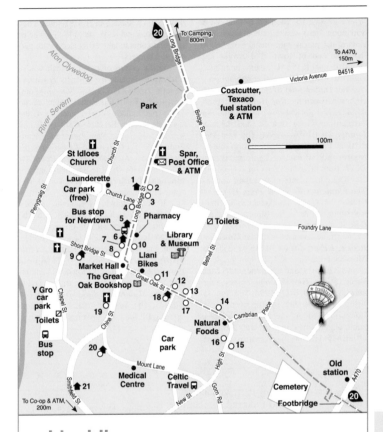

Llanidloes

Where to stay; **fb**; Mon-Fri 6-9pm, Sat & Sun noon-3pm) serves pub classics plus curries and pizzas with mains from £9. At the east end of town, the *Angel Inn* (☎ 01686 414635; **fb**; daily noon-midnight) at 3 High St is another pub option.

For **Indian** food to eat in or takeaway, choose between the *Raj Mahal* (☎ 01686-412432; 🖥 rajmahal-powys.com; Tue-Sun 5-10pm) on Great Oak St, and the *Goa Lounge* (☎ 01686-449344; **fb**; Wed-Mon 5-10pm, Fri & Sat to 10.30pm) opposite the Market Hall, which has classic mains from £8.95. Both offer discounts for collections.

There are plenty of **fast food** options. The *Llanidloes Kebab & Pizza House* (☎ 01686-412183; 🖥 llanikebab.co.uk; daily 4-9.30pm, Fri & Sat to 10pm,) at 6 Great Oak St, also offers burgers and fried chicken, not to be confused with the *Llanidloes Fish & Kebab Bar* (☎ 01686-413251; **fb**; Mon-Sat noon–2pm & 4.30–9pm, Fri & Sat from 11.30am) round the corner at 53 Long Bridge St. The *New Welcome* Chinese takeaway (☎ 01686-413898; Tue-Sun 5-9.30pm, Fri & Sat to 10pm) is at 44 Longbridge St. At the Market Hall head south along China St for *Evan's Fish Bar* (☎ 01686-412734; 🖥 evansfishbar.co.uk;

Thur-Sat 11.30am-2pm & 4.30-9pm). They are licenced and serve seafood to eat in or fish and chips to take away along with pizzas and burgers.

If it's coffee or a light lunch you're after, **cafés** include the no-frills *Travellers Rest* (☎ 01686-412329; Tue-Sun 8am-3pm) next to the Red Lion Hotel, which can do you a fried brekkie or roast lunch. On Great Oak St, there's the *Rose Café* (☎ 01686 412463; Mon-Sat 9am-4pm, Sun 9am-3pm) at No 5, or nip round the corner to the quaint and cosy *Cobblers Tea Room* (☎ 07871-897036; **fb**; Tue-Sat 9am-4pm) for traditional Welsh rarebit and finish off with some homemade gelato.

If you're looking for picnic ingredients, the *Fish Deli* (☎ 01686-413676; **fb**) Wed-Fri 9am-2pm, Sat 9am-noon) on Great Oak St has ready-to-eat seafood, coffee, meats and Welsh cheeses. You've the *Little Welsh Bakery* (☎ 07983-073952; 🖥 thelittlewelshbakery.co.uk; Mon-Sat 8.30am-4pm) for snacks on the long trail to Dylife and the *Talerddig Bakery* (☎ 01686 412973; **fb**; Tue-Sun 10am-4pm; Fri to 5pm) to fill the gaps, both right on the trail on Long Bridge St.

KNIGHTON ▷ **LLANIDLOES TO ABBEYCWMHIR**   [MAPS 20-13]

Today gets off to a slow start, with a long walk up **Gorn Road** followed by clambering in and out of gullies, across farmyards and country lanes ringing with the clang of a gate's sprung bolt. But this interrupted flow is all part of Glyndŵr's Way diversity.

Distance	15¼ miles (24.7km)
Ascent	3058ft (932m)
Time	8-9 hours
WALKING TIME ONLY – ADD 20-30%	

Taking in the switchbacks of the **Nant Feinion** valley, by the time you climb up to **Cwmbys** (Map 17) below **Pegwyn Bach** (1866ft/569m), you're ready to get on a roll that contours the base of the hillside to your left along a stretch of forestry track and road.

A turf path through some woods brings you up to **Bwlch-y-Sarnau** (Map 15), today's sole hamlet with a slim chance of a brew in the village hall's self-service 'porch café'. Revived or not, you can now enjoy the remains of the day across the breezy heights of **Esgair Hill** (1476ft/450m), hopefully with great views in all directions, before the last couple of miles down and up and down into **Abbeycwmhir**.   *[Next route overview p102]*

◄WELSHPOOL **LLANIDLOES TO DYLIFE** [MAPS 20-25]

The next two stages might be the crux of your trek, as places to stay and eat are scattered and sparse. But if you've got those pinned down and the weather is good, they could also be amongst your highlights, as you pass the Bryntail mine

Distance	**13¼ miles (21.4km)**
Ascent	**869m (2851ft)**
Time	**6-7 hours**
WALKING TIME ONLY – ADD 20-30%	

below the Clywedog dam wall, and then wend your way around the reservoir into the eastern remnants of the Hafren forest and the Cambrian mountains beyond.

By now you'll have got used to passing nothing more than rolling pastures and farmyards while far above the peel of **red kites** (see box p70) pierces the moaning soundtrack of the Cambrian wind which seems to sigh '*Owain… Owain…*'. This stage may be shorter than average but it's a staggered ascent. Less than an hour in you're lower than you started, but of course this is mid-Wales so the climbs are over in minutes.

Allt Goch woods Out of Llani the track up through the Allt Goch woods (Map 20) breaks out onto the edge of a **golf course** (Map 21), whereafter a multitude of field gates and a couple of backroad crossings bring you back to the B4518 Dylife and Machynlleth road.

Clywedog reservoir (Map 22) Just up the way you hop off the B4518 to the safety of a field below Penwar hill, before approaching and then dodging Bryntail Farm's yard and bearing down on the convex edifice of the **Clywedog dam wall**.

Haul yourself out of the Clywedog valley which you'll be paralleling for the remains of the day and stop for a cuppa at the **Caffi Clywedog** (see below) overlooking the dam wall. Suitably refreshed, you're now ready to carry on navigating around the reservoir's spurs and inlets. [*cont'd on p121*]

CLYWEDOG DAM [Map 22, p119]
With lessons learnt from Capel Celyn and the Tryweryn dam scandal a few years earlier (see p151), no villages were drowned in the making of this dam, completed in the late 1960s and among the tallest in the UK. A small embankment was even built at Bwlch y Gle to plug a side valley west of Van and which now carries the B4518 to Dylife; a lay-by makes a popular viewpoint. With this, the reservoir's capacity was maximised to 11 million gallons after a wet spell – something a good winter in mid-Wales can reliably supply.

Overlooking the dam wall is *Caffi Clywedog* (01686-41107; 🖥 cafficlywedog.co.uk, **fb**; 🐾; Wed-Sun 10am-4pm,

winter hrs vary) where you can choose drinks, snacks and desserts from their entirely plant-based menu to eat in or take away.

If you're following a non-conformist schedule, there is a possible option to spend the night here too. All alone at 6½ miles (10.3km) from Llani, *Ty Capel B&B* (☎ 07484-143877; 🖥 tycapelbandb.co.uk; 3D/1T en suite; 🛥; 🐾; Ⓛ) is a lovely spot right on the trail. Prices are from £37.50 to £65pp (sgl occ from £60) and evening meals are available (request at least 48 hrs in advance).

It's said that informal **camping** is occasionally allowed alongside the reservoir: ask locally.

ROUTE GUIDE AND MAPS

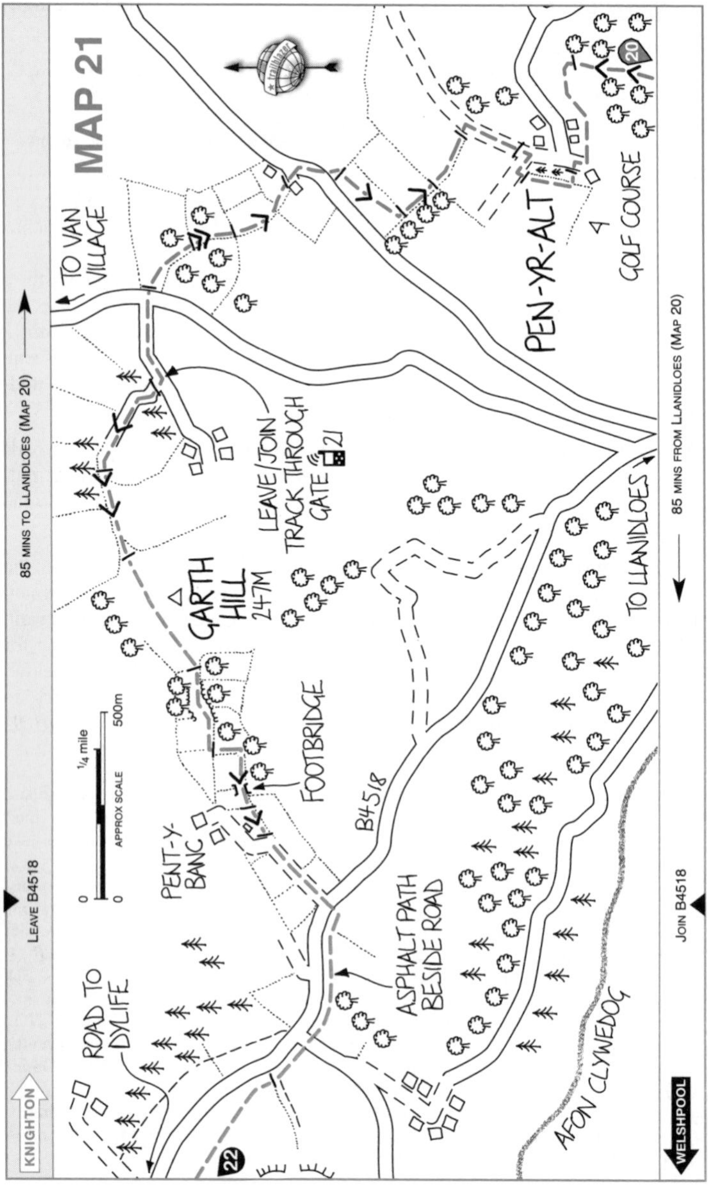

MAP 21

KNIGHTON

Leave B4518

85 MINS TO LLANIDLOES (MAP 20)

TO VAN VILLAGE

GARTH HILL 247M

LEAVE/JOIN TRACK THROUGH GATE 21

PEN-YR-ALT

GOLF COURSE

¼ mile
APPROX SCALE
0   500m

PENT-Y-BANC

ROAD TO DYLIFE

FOOTBRIDGE

B4518

ASPHALT PATH BESIDE ROAD

AFON CLYWEDOG

22

TO LLANIDLOES

85 MINS FROM LLANIDLOES (MAP 20)

JOIN B4518

WELSHPOOL

20

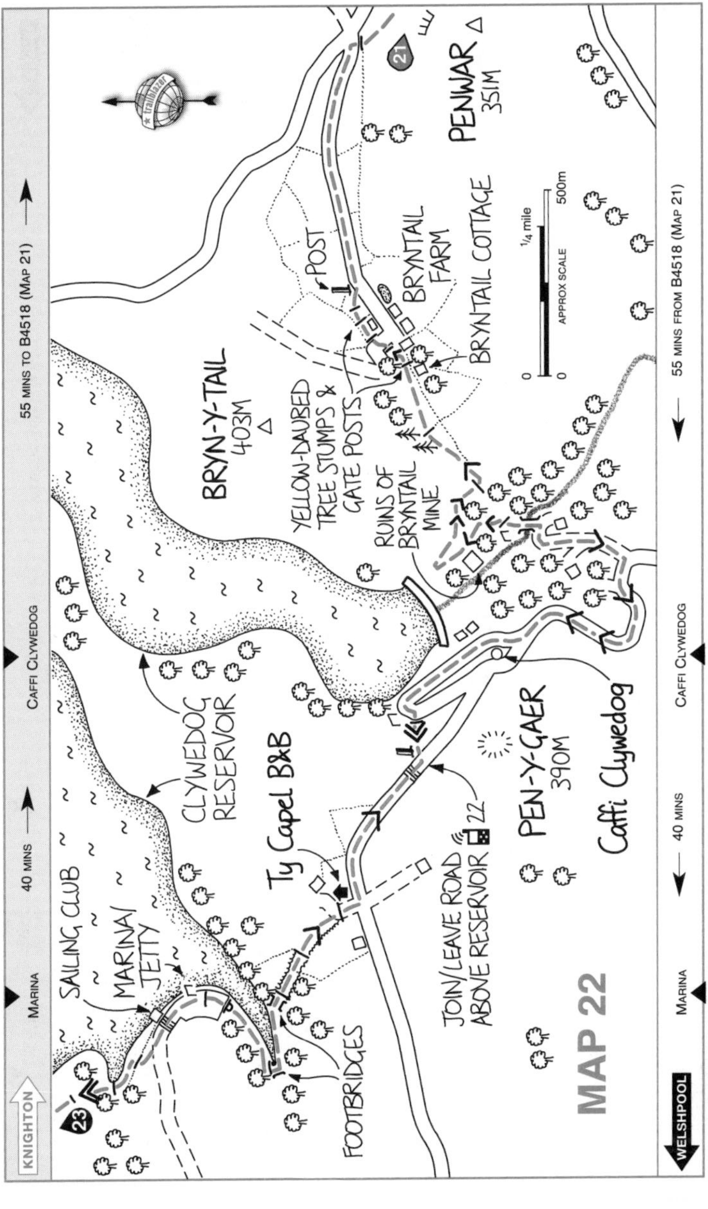

MAP 22

KNIGHTON

MARINA — 40 MINS — CAFFI CLYWEDOG — 55 MINS TO B4518 (MAP 21) →

← MARINA — 40 MINS CAFFI CLYWEDOG 55 MINS FROM B4518 (MAP 21) →

WELSHPOOL

PENWAR △ 351M

21

BRYNTAIL FARM

BRYNTAIL COTTAGE

POST

BRYN-Y-TAIL △ 403M

YELLOW-DAUBED TREE STUMPS & GATE POSTS

RUINS OF BRYNTAIL MINE

0 — 500m
0 — ¼ mile
APPROX SCALE

CLYWEDOG RESERVOIR

SAILING CLUB

MARINA/ JETTY

Ty Capel B&B

PEN-Y-GAER 390M

JOIN/LEAVE ROAD ABOVE RESERVOIR 📷 22

Caffi Clywedog

FOOTBRIDGES

23

ROUTE GUIDE AND MAPS

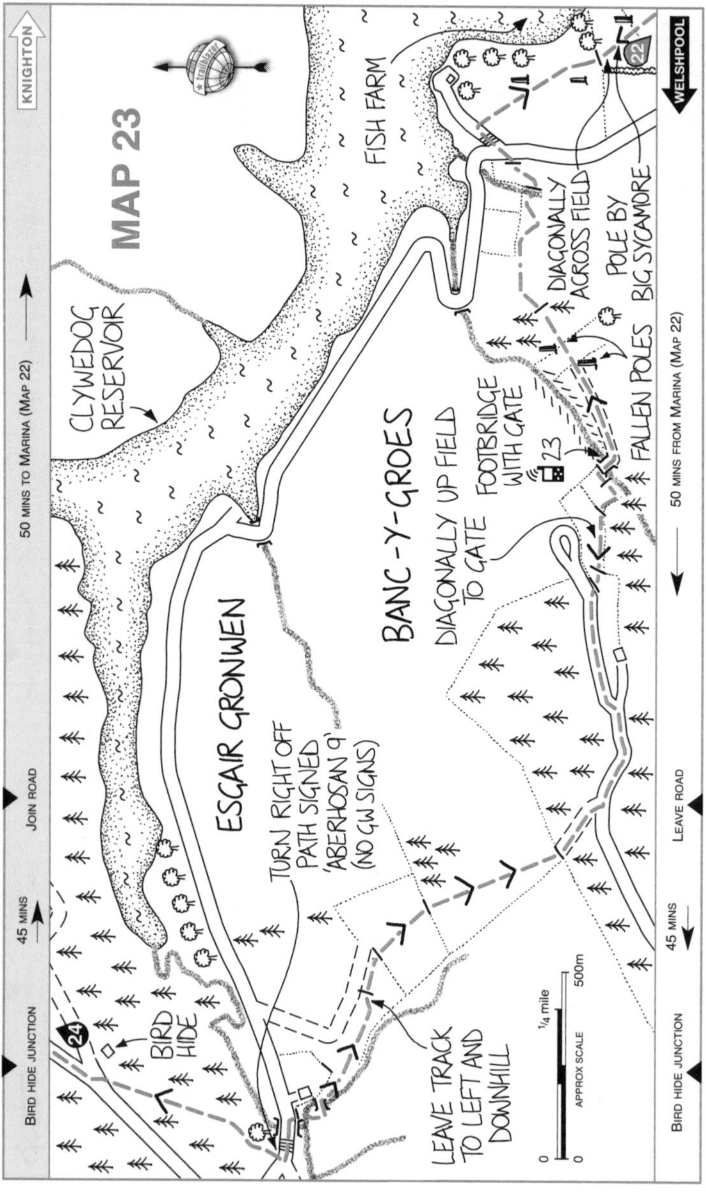

KNIGHTON

MAP 23

FISH FARM

CLYWEDOG RESERVOIR

50 MINS TO MARINA (MAP 22)

ESCAIR GRONWEN

BANC-Y-GROES

WELSHPOOL

DIAGONALLY ACROSS FIELD

POLE BY BIG SYCAMORE

FALLEN POLES

50 MINS FROM MARINA (MAP 22)

FOOTBRIDGE WITH GATE

🏕 23

DIAGONALLY UP FIELD TO GATE

45 MINS   JOIN ROAD

TURN RIGHT OFF PATH SIGNED 'ABERHOSAN' (NO GW SIGNS)

BIRD HIDE JUNCTION

24

BIRD HIDE

LEAVE TRACK TO LEFT AND DOWNHILL

LEAVE ROAD

45 MINS

BIRD HIDE JUNCTION

¼ mile

APPROX SCALE

0   500m

[*cont'd from p117*]   Rejoining the road above the lake, there's an Iron Age **hill fort**, Pen-y-Gaer (Map 22), with metres-thick foundations just to the south and with an even better view over the reservoir.

Hafren Forest (Maps 23 & 24) Follow the road down past Ty Capel B&B and the sailing club before leaving the valley to glance across the edge of the Hafren

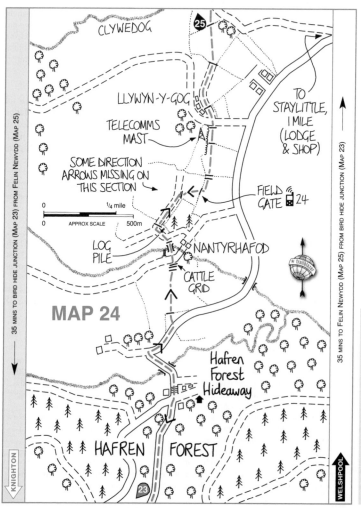

Forest (see below for details of lodge accommodation), Hafren being the Welsh name for Severn, or Sabrina to the Romans. The first trees were planted in the 1930s and it has gradually become a haven for birds including buzzards, goshawks, red kites, merlins, sparrowhawks, crossbills and nightjars.

HAFREN FOREST   [Map 24, p121]

Nearly 11 miles (17.2km) after leaving Llani, you'll pass *Hafren Forest Hideaway* (☎ 07871-740514; 🖥 hafrenforesthideaway .com; 1T/2Qd/1 sleeps 6; ✕; (Ⓛ), a cosy woodland lodge with a well-equipped kitchen. The lodge sleeps a total of 16, all in bunkbeds or single beds, and you can hang your dripping waterproofs in the drying room before relaxing in front of the wood-burner in the large lounge. Bedrooms have allocated shower-rooms and towels are provided. They usually require a two-night minimum stay but may accept single night bookings at quieter times (Mon-Thur) from £45pp (sgl occ £50) plus £30 for optional half board (meals by prior arrangement) if you're not cooking.

Walking to and from Staylittle Following World War 2 the village of Llwyn-y-gog was created next to **Staylittle** (Penffordd-las; shop & lodge accommodation) by the Forestry Commission to house workers needed to develop the pine, larch and spruce plantation. Known as 'Stay-a-little' on old maps, the distinctive name is supposedly attributed to a particularly efficient local blacksmith who could shoe a cattle drover's horse in record time. To reach Staylittle, only a mile before this stage ends above Dylife, leave the trail just before bridging the Clywedog stream (boundary of Map 24 & Map 25) below Felin Newydd farm (on Map 25). The diversion's elevation loss is minimal.

STAYLITTLE (PENFFORDD-LAS)
[off Map 24, p121 & Map 25]

The mile's diversion east of the Way to neo-alpinesque *The Lodge Staylittle* (☎ 01686-449354, 🖥 thelodgestaylittle.co.uk; 2T/2D/6 rms sleep 4-6; (Ⓛ; ✕) is another option worth keeping up your parka. Sleeping up to 40 in 10 rooms from £40pp (bedding and towels provided), there's a large comfortable lounge, a well-equipped kitchen, laundry facilities and a drying room. Breakfast, packed lunches and evening meals are all available on request.

There's a **shop/PO** in the village too (Staylittle Stores; ☎ 01686-430208, **fb**; Mon-Sat 8am-7pm; Sun 9am-noon).

❏ LEAD MINING IN MID-WALES

Right below the Clywedog dam wall lie the part-restored ruins of the **Bryntail Lead Mine** (Map 22; 🖥 cadw.gov.wales, daily 10am-4pm, free) dating from the early 18th century when, as today, the river was used as a power source. In the final boom of the 1870s, this part of Wales produced more lead than the rest of the world put together, much as Parys mountain on Anglesey had done with copper a century earlier.

The inevitable bust followed a few years later and the Bryntail mine closed in 1884. What's left today are the remains of crushing houses, ore bins, roasting ovens, smithy and the mine manager's office.

Other local lead mines include **Van** (off Map 21), which was among the biggest and most successful of the late 19th century, while at **Dylife** a thousand workers toiled under the *Rhod Goch* (Red Wheel), one of the largest waterwheels in Britain, to produce up to 2000 tons of ore annually, before it too fell silent in 1884.

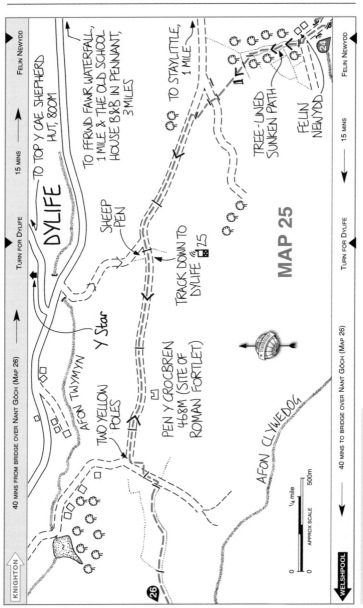

KNIGHTON

40 MINS FROM BRIDGE OVER NANT GÔCH (MAP 26)

TURN FOR DYLIFE

15 MINS

FELIN NEWYDD

TO TOP Y CAE SHEPHERD HUT, 800M

DYLIFE

TO FFRWD FAWR WATERFALL, 1 MILE & THE OLD SCHOOL HOUSE B&B IN PENNANT, 3 MILES

TO STAYLITTLE, 1 MILE

SHEEP PEN

TRACK DOWN TO DYLIFE 15

TREE-LINED SUNKEN PATH

FELIN NEWYDD

24

MAP 25

AFON TWYMYN

Y Star

TWO YELLOW POLES

PEN Y CROCBREN 468M (SITE OF ROMAN FORTLET)

AFON CLYWEDOG

26

APPROX SCALE

¼ mile

500m

0

0

FELIN NEWYDD

15 MINS

TURN FOR DYLIFE

40 MINS TO BRIDGE OVER NANT GÔCH (MAP 26)

WELSHPOOL

ROUTE GUIDE AND MAPS

Unless they've been fixed, it's around here that you'll notice the annoyance of missing direction arrows (see box p18) as well as fallen marker posts which, without a tracklog, can briefly lead you astray. A couple more farm yards and soon you're astride the lofty ridge and rut-worn Roman road, rising to overlook the humble hamlet of **Dylife** ('Deeleefah') just to the north.

DYLIFE [MAP 25, p123]

Another ancient lead mine site (see box p122), now all that remains of Dylife is a dispersed collection of dwellings. Crossing the road on the way to *Y Star* (see below), directly ahead lie the foundations of St David's church. A school house once stood nearby; now just a few tombstones remain. If you've a bit more left in the tank, just a mile east of Dylife is the 130-foot **waterfall** of Ffryd Fawr close to the road and near the **impressive lookout** down the Twymyn valley or 'Dylife Gorge', carved out of the sandstone at the end of the last Ice Age.

The end of this stage in Dylife is typically a place where tent folk have to resort to **wild camping**. Provided you have the water and all the rest, it's a great place to spend a night out (notwithstanding Pen y Crocbren – see box opposite).

Otherwise, half a mile below the trail there's the 17th-century *Y Star* (☎ 07563-034493; 2T/1D en suite; 🐾; book via 💻 airbnb.co.uk), a former inn predating the mining era, now disguised by modern cladding. These days it's a self-catering guesthouse from £45pp (sgl occ £50) with a shared kitchen-diner/lounge so you'll need to feed yourself. There are plans to erect some pods too.

Just five minutes walk further north is *Top Y Cae* or Cwt Mwynwr shepherd's hut (☎ 07779-718692; 1D, from £45pp, book via 💻 airbnb.co.uk) which can supply self-catering breakfast packs and evening meals such as veggie curry, bolognese or chilli for you to heat up yourself for a very reasonable £5 per meal, per person.

And though four miles away, with advance notice the *Old School House B&B* (☎ 01650-521486; 💻 theoldschoolhouse

---

Knighton-bound, yesterday may have been the walk's toughest day, not least the final climb onto Foel Fadian. So today you can enjoy the staged descent to the Babylonian delights of Llanidloes, plus probably a bit of extra distance from

Distance	**13¼ miles (21.4km)**
Ascent	**1985ft (605m)**
Time	**5½-6½ hours**
WALKING TIME ONLY – ADD 20-30%	

your 'off-piste' lodgings. After cutting through a corner of the **Hafren Forest**, up ahead lies the glittering expanse of the **Clywedog reservoir** and eventually, the **café** (see p117) overlooking the dam wall.

It's a steep walk down and back out of the Clywedog river valley for the final two-hour ramble across the fields and farm tracks before ending with a descent through the **Allt Goch woods** (expect confusion; generally take the left forks in the track) delivering you to the outskirts of **Llanidloes** where the range of lodgings is only outdone by the variety of eateries. A chance to stock up for the final days and some great walking to Knighton.

[*Next route overview p116*]

wales.co.uk; 1T/1D with private bath, 🛥;
(L) in **Pennant** village will pick up and
drop off walkers and cyclists from Dylife,
Machynlleth and Llanbrynmair meaning
you can settle in for three nights. They'll

also lay on an evening meal and packed
lunches (if pre-booked). Rooms go from
£47.50pp (sgl occ £95). Make sure you call
for your pickup from the ridge above Dylife
where there ought to be a signal.

❑ **GRUESOME JUSTICE ON GIBBET HILL**

Meaning 'gibbet hill', **Pen y Crocbren** (Map 25) was so named for an 18th century
tale of Sion Jones, known as Sion y Gof. He was an unfaithful blacksmith from near
Aberystwyth who murdered his wife and family after they paid him an unexpected
visit. Once their bodies were discovered in disused mine shafts, he was caught, tried
and sentenced to death.

His last task was to fabricate his own iron gibbet (cage) which was erected where
he was hung on Pen y Crocbren hill. The gallows and gibbet with its grisly cadaver
fell and rotted away and the gruesome events passed into local folklore. Then in 1938
archaeologists unearthed an iron-caged skull which revalidated the legend. It now
rests in the National Museum of Wales in Cardiff.

◀WELSHPOOL **DYLIFE TO MACHYNLLETH** [MAPS 25-31]

With the eerie creaking of a swinging gibbet in mind (see box above), starting at
over 1476ft/450m you'd be forgiven for
thinking it's a downhill glide all the way
to Machynlleth. But while it's another
great day on the trail, this is the

Distance	**15¼ miles (24.7km)**
Ascent	**2434ft (742m)**
Time	**7-8 hours**
WALKING TIME ONLY – ADD 20-30%	

Glyndŵr's Way so you'll need the usual time and a bit more resolve than you
might expect to reach your destination.

Provisions wise, farmyard taps are just about all there is – but hopefully you
planned for that yesterday and stocked up in Staylittle (see p122).

Pen y Crocbren (Map 25) Rejoining Glyndŵr's Way, you soon reach **Pen y
Crocbren** hill where you may need infrared assistance to detect the remains of
a Roman fortlet or signalling station left of the track and probably on the site of
an older Iron Age hill fort.

Glaslyn (Map 26) On a clear day the first hour or two evoke parts of the northern Pennines or Highlands so enjoy the airy heights as they briefly drop down
to the Clywedog river's trickling headwaters, before rising and rounding to the
rim of the Cambrian plateau where sits the mysterious Glaslyn lake, named like
its better known sibling below Snowdon summit, 40 miles (64km) to the north.

Around here it will take a keen and energetic walker to bound off southwards for our 12-mile (19.3km) loop via the 2467ft (752m) summit of
Pumlumon Fawr. If that fits your description **proceed to p173**, or alternatively return another day to tackle it with fresh legs.

Foel Fadian North of Glaslyn lake fork left to reach the **highest point** (Map 26; 1657ft/505m) of Glyndŵr's Way, below the hill of Foel Fadian (Map 27) on the brink of the western escarpment of the Cambrian mountains, offering a breathtaking vista. On the southern horizon the squat pyramid of Pumlumon Fawr observes your passing.

It's a short sharp descent on splintered rubble back to familiar farmlands and tree-lined lanes.

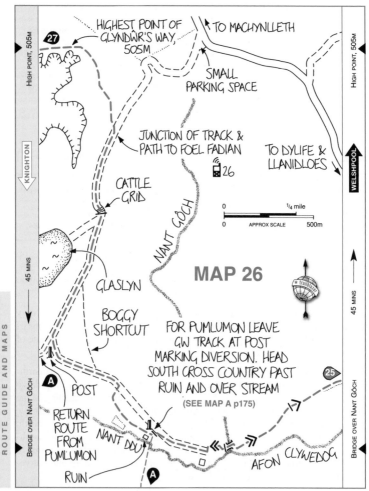

HIGH POINT, 505M

KNIGHTON

45 MINS

HIGHEST POINT OF GLYNDŴR'S WAY, 505M

TO MACHYNLLETH

SMALL PARKING SPACE

JUNCTION OF TRACK & PATH TO FOEL FADIAN
📱26

TO DYLIFE & LLANIDLOES

CATTLE GRID

NANT GOCH

GLASLYN

BOGGY SHORTCUT

MAP 26

0 — ¼ mile
0 — APPROX SCALE — 500m

FOR PUMLUMON LEAVE GW TRACK AT POST MARKING DIVERSION. HEAD SOUTH CROSS COUNTRY PAST RUIN AND OVER STREAM
(SEE MAP A p175)

POST

A

RETURN ROUTE FROM PUMLUMON

NANT DDU

RUIN

A

25

AFON CLYWEDOG

HIGH POINT, 505M

WELSHPOOL

45 MINS

BRIDGE OVER NANT GOCH

BRIDGE OVER NANT GOCH

ROUTE GUIDE AND MAPS

Cleiriau Isaf farm Pounding the backcountry asphalt towards Cleiriau Isaf farm (Map 28), you'll get a great view back towards Foel Fadian and the steep track you slithered down an hour or two ago. Spare a thought for anti-clockwise walkers heading for Dylife.

Talbontdrain (Map 29) You'll meet the road at the halfway point at Talbontdrain where, if you're having a hard day, you can bail out for Machynlleth (4-mile/6.4km road walk).

Rhiw Goch A short while after Talbontdrain, the trail rises steeply out of a forest corner onto Rhiw Goch with views north to the Tarrenau and Cader Idris. From this high point the site of the **Battle of Mynydd Hyddgen** (see p54 & p173) is just over 2 miles (3.2km) to the south. And there it can stay because you're turning north-westwards.

Bryn Mawr & Mynydd Bach Now you're following a ridge or high valley side past Bryn Mawr (Map 29) and Mynydd Bach (Map 30) which continues until you turn west above Machynlleth and wind your way down to the town. Alternatively, high above the town (Map 31), there's a path straight downhill that's less than a mile to Forge Road and the eastern end of Machynlleth.

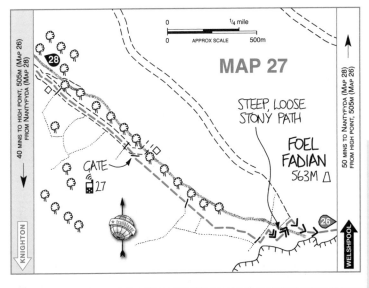

❏ **Walk side by side and on healthy grass** In other words where possible don't walk in single file or on worn areas in order to protect the fragile earth.

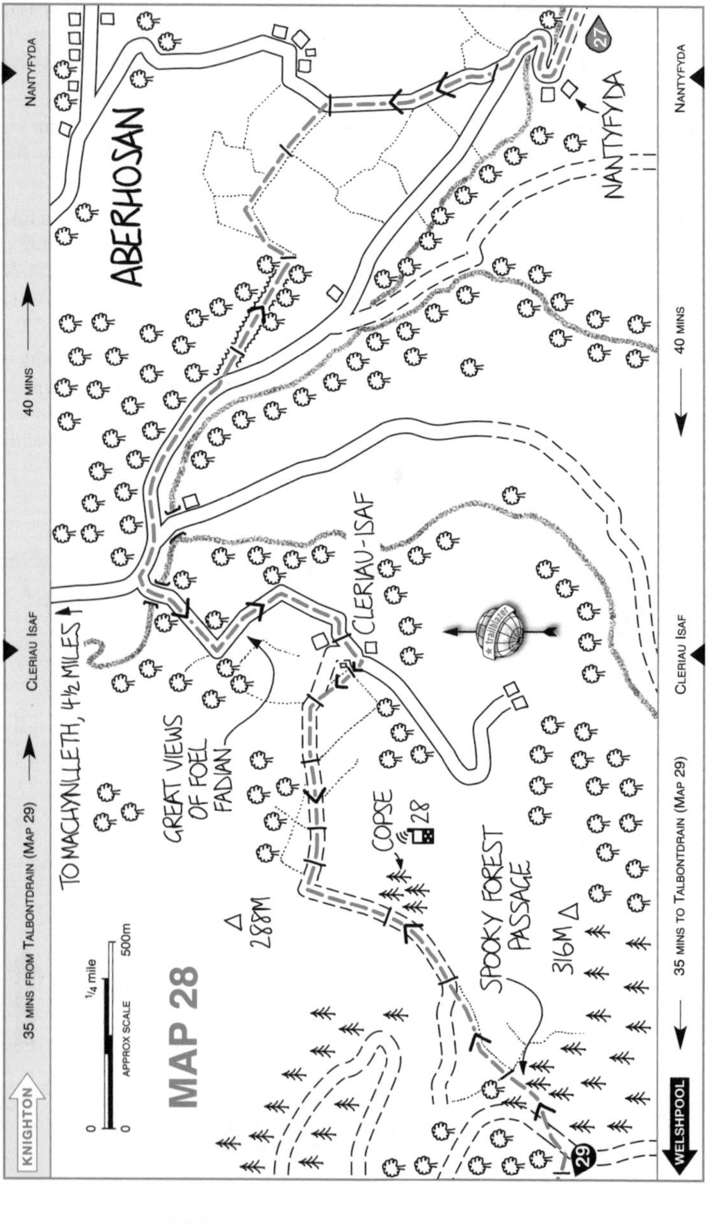

KNIGHTON

35 MINS FROM TALBONTDRAIN (MAP 29)

TO MACHYNLLETH, 4½ MILES

CLERIAU ISAF

40 MINS

NANTYFYDA

MAP 28

APPROX SCALE

0   ¼ mile

0   500m

GREAT VIEWS OF FOEL FADIAN

△ 288M

COPSE

28

SPOOKY FOREST PASSAGE

△ 316M

CLERIAU-ISAF

ABERHOSAN

NANTYFYDA

27

NANTYFYDA

40 MINS

CLERIAU ISAF

35 MINS TO TALBONTDRAIN (MAP 29)

WELSHPOOL

29

TO MACHYNLLETH,
3½ MILES

△366M

0   ¼ mile
0   APPROX SCALE   500m

30

BRYN
MAWR

28

FORD

LLWYN
GWYN

TALBONT-
DRAIN

RHIW
GOCH

CHRISTMAS
TREE

WOODEN
PEN

HIGH
POINT 29

MAP 29

MACHYNLLETH
[Map 31, p131 & map p135]

With its organic, wholefood cafés, shops selling lunar calendars, crystals and incense and dreadlocked residents on bicycles, Machynlleth is certainly not your typical Welsh market town. **The Guardian**

Marking the walk's **lowest elevation** at just 60ft/18m and less than 2 miles (3km) from the Irish Sea's tidal reach up the River Dyfi, **Machynlleth** ('Ma'huntleth'; ☐ visitmidwales.co.uk) or 'Mach' (pronounced 'Mac'), also marks your walk's putative halfway point. Whichever direction you're walking, Mach is ideally located to divide your walk in two or enjoy a day off. At this point you change direction back towards the English

borderlands: either 60 miles (96.4km) to Welshpool, or 74½ miles (120km) to Knighton, give or take.

Entering via a park, you'll pass Y Plas (Map 31), the former ancestral seat of the Marquesses of Londonderry and now a community centre with the **Owain Glyndŵr Monument** (see box p133) on the lawn opposite.

Rebel trekkers passing through Mach are required to make the pilgrimage to the site of Owain Glyndŵr's **Parliament House** (☐ canolfanowainglyndwr.org; Wed, Fri & Sat 10.30am-3.30pm; free) or *Senedd* in Welsh, right where the path joins the Maengwyn 'high' Street.

[cont'd on p132]

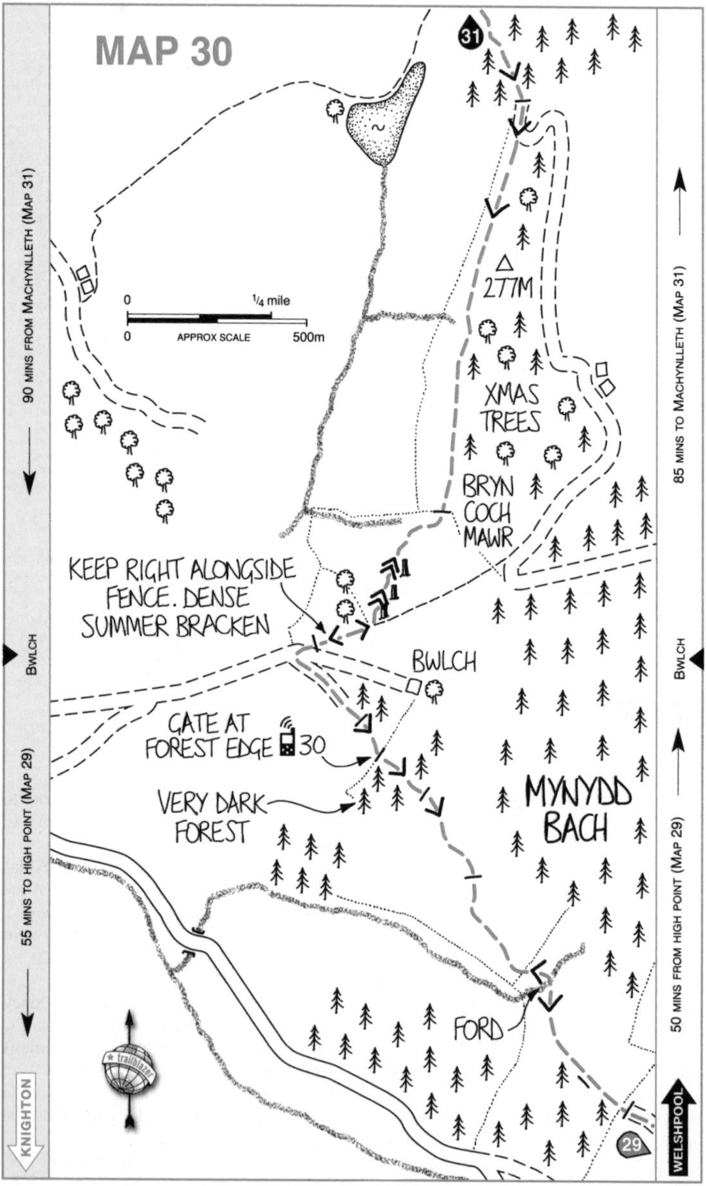

MAP 30

90 MINS FROM MACHYNLLETH (MAP 31)

85 MINS TO MACHYNLLETH (MAP 31)

0   ¼ mile
0   APPROX SCALE   500m

△ 277M

XMAS TREES

BRYN COCH MAWR

KEEP RIGHT ALONGSIDE FENCE. DENSE SUMMER BRACKEN

BWLCH

BWLCH

GATE AT FOREST EDGE ▢30

VERY DARK FOREST

MYNYDD BACH

55 MINS TO HIGH POINT (MAP 29)

50 MINS FROM HIGH POINT (MAP 29)

FORD

31

29

WELSHPOOL

KNIGHTON

ROUTE GUIDE AND MAPS

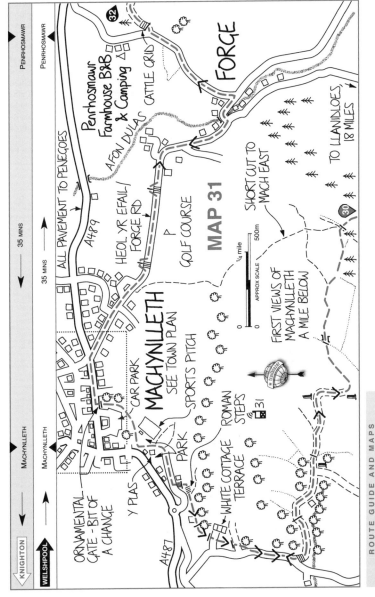

KNIGHTON ◀ | WELSHPOOL ▶ | MACHYNLLETH ▶ | MACHYNLLETH ▶ 35 MINS | 35 MINS | PENRHOSMAWR ◀ | PENRHOSMAWR ◀

32

FORGE

Penrhosmawr Farmhouse B&B & Camping △

AFON DULAS CATTLE GRID

ALL PAVEMENT TO PENEGOES

A489

HEOL YR EFAIL / FORGE RD

GOLF COURSE

MAP 31

TO LLANIDLOES, 18 MILES

SHORT CUT TO MACH EAST

¼ mile | 500m
APPROX SCALE
0 | 0

FIRST VIEWS OF MACHYNLLETH A MILE BELOW

30

MACHYNLLETH
SEE TOWN PLAN

CAR PARK

SPORTS PITCH

PARK

ROMAN STEPS

🎲 31

Y PLAS

A4487

ORNAMENTAL GATE - BIT OF A CHANCE

WHITE COTTAGE TERRACE

[Cont'd from p129] It was here in 1404 and four years into the rebellion that the first Welsh parliament (or perhaps just a gathering of barons) was held, and where Glyndŵr was officially crowned 'Prince of Wales', even if it's Llywelyn ap Gruffudd, buried at Abbeycwmhir, who's traditionally identified as the last native to carry that title. Striking though the distinctive dark slate building is, it was actually rebuilt early in the 20th century on mid-15th century foundations post-dating Owain Glyndŵr's time. As a result, what you see inside is something of a pastiche of a late-medieval hall. At the time of our visits several months apart, any former exhibits of Owain Glyndŵr and his deeds were no longer on full display, leaving a bookshop and a couple of artefacts in glass cases with frustrating QR codes to access the full story and which might as well be online (such as at 🖳 owain-glyndwr.wales).

Hopefully some sort of actual display in the style of the Offa's Dyke Centre in Knighton will return. Next door is the Owain Glyndŵr Centre, a community hall and a **café**.

Walking back to the dormant town clock (with its own Twitter account) and turning north towards the station takes you past the MOMA **art gallery** (🖳 moma .cymru; Tue-Fri 10am-4pm, Sat 10am-1pm; free). On the way, at 35 Maengwyn St a plaque commemorates the site of self-taught textile and fashion designer **Laura Ashley**'s first shop in the early 1960s, though by now most walkers will be intent on a Glyndŵr-like ransacking of the town's several supermarkets.

Transport
[See pp46-50] Considering what lies in either direction, Mach is an easier place to reach or leave than you might imagine. Up

---

🖳 'YOU'RE NOT IN WELSHPOOL NOW, BOYO!'
For half a century Machynlleth and the surrounding hills of Powys and Ceredigion have attracted individuals in search of alternative lifestyles who are commonly termed 'hippies'. You might detect this unmistakable vibe on arrival. That social phenomenon was one result of the widespread cultural upheavals of the Sixties, and included a reappraisal of capitalism, consumerism, pollution and humanity's very place in nature. With two catastrophic World Wars just a generation or two behind them, and the looming threat of a terminal nuclear conflagration, some sought a new way of living.

In west Wales this free-thinking, lotus-eating exodus has been partly attributed to the far-sighted establishment of the **Centre for Alternative Technology** (🖳 cat.org.uk) in 1972. Set in an old slate mine a couple of miles north of town, the Centre (along with the prescient attitudes of the then Prince of Wales), can be said to have presaged the whole environmental movement in Britain. It's still running today, if a little rough around the edges.

It wasn't just feckless drifters who were attracted to the area as somewhere to grow their pot in peace. Many talented and creative individuals (the majority from congested London and south-east England) saw a chance to express their skills and energy in a new locale, as Jez Danks' 2014 book *Towards the West, a Varied Crowd*, recalls. More conventional 'straights' also saw the appeal of dropping-out – 'downsizing' in contemporary parlance – to a simpler, healthier and more sustainable life away from the 'rat race', much as later became fashionable in southern France among the more bourgeois, and again as a result of the recent pandemic following the Work From Home revolution. All sought nothing more than *The Good Life* – as a popular 1970s BBC sitcom was titled – which, like all pioneering, was soon recognised as far from an easy life. Whether or not we notice or admit it, many of us have absorbed some of these once radical values, attitudes and beliefs over the passing decades.

❏ OWAIN GLYNDŴR MONUMENTS AND STATUES

As you walk past Y Plas towards your imminent rendezvous with Machynlleth's Parliament House, you'll notice the **Owain Glyndŵr Monument**, a 15-foot high hunk of polished and inscribed slate erected in 2000 when this walk gained National Trail status. Perhaps not coincidentally resembling the Llywelyn Monument near Builth, you can't help thinking that here in the so-called 'ancient capital of Wales' our hero deserves something more engaging. One example might have been the defiant figure put up in 2007 in **Corwen**, just 3 miles (4.8km) west of Glyndŵr's riverside estate of Glyndyfrdwy where his rebellion began (see p53). Here, caught in a rebel yell, an armoured Owain bestrides his rampant charger, sword aloft. It's enough to send a shiver down the spine of a humble English yeoman. This albeit commonplace equine arrangement replaced what was locally considered a somewhat comical dwarfish figure erected a few years earlier and which has since probably been smelted back into 2p coins.

Four miles (6.4km) west of Machynlleth you can admire another Glyndŵr statue in a small garden behind the former Roman outpost and ancient church of St Peter ad Vincula in the village of **Pennal**. It was here in 1406, that Glyndŵr's Pennal Letter to Charles VI of France was composed, outlining his vision for an independent Wales. Erected in 2004, the commissioning of the statue was supported by celebrities with Welsh connections, among them Led Zeppelin's Robert Plant who spent time nearby (see p136). A half-sized figure of Owain stands on a plinth, relaxed but vigilant, his sword on his shoulder and shield by his side. His tunic is encrusted in tattoo-like engravings of warring figures and the intertwining Celtic iconography for which Led Zeppelin had a fondness in their prime. The result resembles more of a proud but diminutive Middle Age chieftain with notes of Hobbit, than an actual medieval warrior-prince, while its scale unintentionally recalls the famous 'Stonehenge' scene from *Spinal Tap*.

Meanwhile, in Wales' current capital, the foyer in **Cardiff City Hall** boasts a decidedly quotidian life-size classical marble figure from the early 20th century, sword resting in one hand and what might well be the Pennal Letter in the other. In 2013 there was talk of Cardiff commissioning a new effigy of the Welsh nationalist hero whose stature grows year by year, but so far nothing seems to have come of it.

to a dozen **trains** a day serve the rail hub of Shrewsbury (75 minutes), via Welshpool.

Except Sunday, **buses** also leave from opposite the railway station with services including: the Lloyds Coaches No T2 between Aberystwyth and Bangor; the T12 to Wrexham; the T36 (if prebooked) and the 33/36 school/shopping service to Glantwymyn; the T37 (if prebooked) to Aberhosan; and in the other direction the X29 to Tywyn via Pennal.

Near the station you'll also find Mach Taxis (☎ 01654-702048; 🖳 machtaxis .com); other **taxi** operators in town include Peters Taxis (☎ 07546 486325; 🖳 peters taxi.co.uk).

Services

There are **ATMs** in the Nisa **supermarket** (daily 6am-10pm) near the station; and outside the big Co-op (Mon-Sat 7am-10pm, Sun 10am-4pm) at the east end of town – both good spots to pick up a **packed lunch** for the next day's walk. There's also an ATM by the clock tower. Given a charter in perpetuity in 1291 by the ever-accommodating Edward 1, Wednesday is **market day** which is bound to be unlike other provincial town gatherings.

The **post office** (8am-8pm) is in the Spar (daily 7am-11pm) just east of Parliament House. Rowlands **pharmacy** (Mon-Wed & Fri 9am-5.30pm, Thur 9am-

4.30pm, Sat 9am-12.30pm) is behind the clock tower, and **Machynlleth Health Centre** (☎ 01654-702224; Mon-Fri 8am-6.30pm) is behind the tyre garage near the corner of Forge Road past the Co-op, with a community **hospital** (no A&E) just over the road. A **laundrette** (Nigel's Laundrette; daily 8.30am-8pm) is at your service up New Street which is alongside the Spar. Nearby, disguised in an old school, The Store (**fb**; Mon-Fri 8.30am-5pm, Sat to 3.30pm) is the only place on the walk selling **butane gas** canisters.

There's **free wi-fi** and **internet computers** in the library (Mon 9.30am-1pm, Tue, Wed & Fri 9.30am-1pm & 2-5pm, Sat 10am-1pm) opposite Parliament House.

Where to stay

For all his valiant battles, Owain Glyndŵr didn't leave a great legacy of lodgings for overnighting pilgrims drawn to his ancient capital. Unless you hide-out in the hills like Butch Cassidy, the nearest tent **campsites** are a mile or two east of town, both on or close to the trail in **Penegoes** (see p137).

There's an inexpensive **bunkhouse**: *Toad Hall* (☎ 01654-700597; 1Tr/1D/1T/1S; ☃) in a converted barn attic behind the Texaco near the station (£26pp inc bedding).

Both a stone's throw from the clock tower, the two **pubs** with rooms include the *White Lion Hotel* (☎ 01654-703455; ▣ whitelionhotel.co.uk; 6D/3T/3Qd, most en suite) from £32.50pp (sgl occ £65) and the smart *Wynnstay* (☎ 01654-702941; ▣ wynnstay.wales; 1S/4D/3T/1Qd all en suite; ☃) with rooms from £52.50pp (sgl occ £70).

The only traditional **B&B** in town seems to be *Maenllwyd Guest House* (☎ 01654-702928; ▣ maenllwyd-guest-house .business.site; 4D/3T all en suite) from £42.50 (sgl occ from £60) just past the health centre.

Otherwise, a search on ▣ airbnb.co.uk will reveal a couple of rooms in private homes from £50.

Where to eat and drink

It's all right there along Heol Maengwyn or the clock tower road up to the station. The restaurant in the *White Lion Hotel* (see Where to stay; daily noon-9pm) has lunch options from £6.50 and main meals from £9.50, while the upmarket *Wynnstay* (**fb**; see Where to stay, Wed noon-2pm & Sun 12.30-2.30pm, daily 6.30-8.45pm) was described by The Guardian as 'a lovely, eccentric inn with good cooking and an 11-page wine list'! Try their very popular Sunday lunch (from £13.95). The cosy *Skinners Arms* (☎ 01654-703443; **fb**) is near the MOMA on Penrallt St and also serves food (Tue-Sat noon-7pm), Sun noon-2pm).

Besides the main street hotel/pub restaurants, choose from kebaberies like *Town Kebab House* (**fb**; Mon-Thur 3-10.30pm, Fri-Sun noon-11.30) at 49 Heol Maengwyn, which also does pizza and burgers; and fish & chips including the award-winning *Hennighans Fish & Chips* (▣ hennighans.co.uk, **fb**; Mon noon-2.30pm, Tue-Sat noon-8.30pm) which has two branches: the *Top Shop* (☎ 01654-702761) at 123 Maengwyn St and the *Bottom Chippy* (☎ 01654-700040) at Nos 44-46.

For freshly baked cakes and pastries in a historical setting head to tiny *Blasau Deli & Bakery* (**fb**; Mon-Fri 10am-5pm, Sat

---

❑ WHERE TO STAY: THE DETAILS
Unless specified, B&B-style accommodation is either en suite or has private facilities; ☞ means at least one room has a bath; ☃ signifies that dogs are welcome in at least one room but always by prior arrangement, an additional charge may also be payable (see also pp183-4); **fb** indicates a Facebook page which may have the most up-to-date opening times, especially for small or seasonal businesses.

Machynlleth

To railway station, 250m,
Toad Hall Bunkhouse, 150m,
Nisa (ATM), 150m &
Centre for Alternative Technology, 3 miles

0   50   100m

Community Hospital

Maenllwyd Guest House

Heol yr Eglus/Forge Rd

31

Health Centre

Hennighan's Top Shop

Maengwyn St A489

Co-op & ATM

Pendre Rd

Tregarth

Car park

Llynlloed Lane

Owain Glyndŵr's Parliament House

Plas Drive

31

Library

Bank Lane

New St

The Store

Launderette

Maengwyn Café

Toilets

Car park

Tarralit Rd

New St

Spar & Post Office

Maengwyn St A489

Hennighan's Bottom Chippy

Hoel Powys

Town Kebab House

Bank Lane

Maes Glas

MOMA Wales

Craig Fach

Skinners Arms

Tŷ Medi

Wynnstay

Bus stops

Penrallt St A487

Heol y Doll

St Peter's

Poplar Rd

Blasau Deli & Bakery @ Royal House

ATM

Clocktower

Pharmacy

White Lion

Pentrehedyn St A487

Bank St

ROUTE GUIDE AND MAPS

10am-2pm & 5-9pm), at the Royal House, a 16th century merchant's building in which King Charles I was hosted in 1643, or *Maengwyn Café* (☎ 01654-7021226, Tue, Wed, Fri & Sat, 8.30am-4.30pm) near Parliament House.

This is Machynlleth, the most **veggie**

and vegan friendly place for miles around, so take yourself to *Tŷ Medi* (🖳 ty-medi .co.uk, **fb**; Mon-Fri 9.30am-3.30pm, Sat 10am-3.30pm) opposite, where you can pick up a vegan sausage roll (£1.95) for the trail, or sit down for a full veggie or vegan breakfast for just £6.95.

KNIGHTON ▷ **MACHYNLLETH TO DYLIFE** [MAPS 31-25]

Note that there is **nowhere to buy food** on this stretch so stock up in Machynlleth before you leave, and even when you reach Dylife the sleeping and dining options are sparse and scattered, so plan carefully. With so much height to gain

Distance	**15¼ miles (24.7km)**
Ascent	**3799ft (1158m)**
Time	**8-9 hours**
WALKING TIME ONLY – ADD 20-30%	

today, the distance to Dylife could turn out to be a bit of a challenge. Starting close to sea level, out of town you'll be climbing pretty much non-stop for the first few miles, past **Mynydd Bach** (Map 30) and **Bryn Mawr** (Map 29). Then you bounce down through the **Hafren Forest's** outliers to the Afon Dulas river near **Aberhosan** (Map 28) at which point you get stuck into the full 1300-ft/400m and almost 3-mile/5km climb to the walk's **highest point** (Map 26; 1657ft/505m) below **Foel Fadian**. From this breezy bluff things ease off, for the most part, to the turn off above **Dylife** (Map 25), though that's unlikely to be the end of your day's walk depending on the location of your bed for the night.

[*Next route overview p124*]

❏ **BRON-YR-AUR: STAIRWAY TO BROKEN DREAMS**

For over half a century a humble 18th-century stone cottage just north of Machynlleth has been a site of pilgrimage for rock fans, young and old, much like the zebra crossing on London's Abbey Road or Jim Morrison's grave in Paris' Père Lachaise Cemetery. For it was at Bron-yr-Aur, surely, that Led Zeppelin, one of the greatest rock bands of all time, penned *Stairway to Heaven,* one of the greatest rock anthems ever?

At the time Bron-yr-Aur was a basic holiday cottage owned by the family of the band's lead vocalist, Robert Plant who'd visited regularly from the 1950s. Two decades later, after two hectic years of touring and hotel-room defenestrations, Plant and guitarist Jimmy Page retreated with their partners to this secluded bolthole in the Cambrian mountains to rest and write.

The legend goes that, lacking both electricity and running water, Bron-yr-Aur forced the hitherto high-energy rockers to adopt a softer, acoustic sound. Their remote hillside location only added to the ambience, a place where druids once performed esoteric rituals and wraith-like fairies gambolled playfully in 'the tree by the brook' where the duo stooped to fill their kettle each morning. Legions of rock fans followed, hoping to catch a bit of the anthem's magic.

Then, during a widely reported 2016 copyright trial brought by an American band, 'Spirit' over *Stairway's* famously alluring intro – a 'descending chromatic four-

MACHYNLLETH TO LLANBRYNMAIR [MAPS 31-37]

From Machynlleth to Llanbrynmair is a day composed of three successively higher climbs before the final descent into the Afon Twymyn valley where Llanbrynmair lies across the confluence of three rivers.

Distance	15½ miles (25km)
Ascent	3022ft (921m)
Time	7½ hours
WALKING TIME ONLY – ADD 20-30%	

Though you pass through a couple of villages in the morning, only **Glantwymyn** (Cemmaes Road) has a **shop** and even that has limited opening hours (see p142). It's a few minutes off the route and about four hours walk from Mach.

Today may hold the record for Glyndŵr's gates: expect around 70, though as mentioned elsewhere, in high summer they leave a few field gates open to mess with your rhythm. Plus, until they improve or repair the signage, this could also be the first day on the trail when you have to second-guess where the route might go across some bigger fields, unless you have a tracklog or have successfully mastered aligning our maps with a compass.

Penegoes Starting with a 40-minute spell of road walking, you cross a small hill and a farmyard and drop down into **Penegoes** (Map 32). If you're behind schedule the A489 directly east out of Machynlleth has a pavement all the way to Penegoes, saving maybe 20 minutes and not missing much.

PENEGOES [Map 32, p138]

Just a couple of miles east of Machynlleth in the tiny settlement of Penegoes is *Llwyn Lodgings* (☎ 01654-703733; 🖳 stayatllwyn .co.uk; 1D/1Tr en suite, 1Tr private facilities). This former 18th century inn has been reinvented as 'a home and lodgings for travellers, cyclists and walkers', with **rooms** from £30pp plus £7.50 for a continental breakfast. It has a fully equipped

chord progression' (to quote the judge) – lead guitarist Jimmy Page dropped a Zeppelin-sized bombshell. Sharing a writer's credit with Plant, he testified under oath that while the pair composed many tracks at Bron-yr-Aur while hunched around a cracking log fire, *Stairway* was not one of them. His plaintive guitar arpeggio soon joined by John Paul Jones' haunting recorder, redolent with prelapsarian yearnings, and all that followed, had been completed elsewhere and presented fully formed to the band at a recording studio in leafy Hampshire. This is a locality where 'Merlin' is more likely to evoke the hearty rasp of a 27-litre V12 Spitfire engine than a pointy-hatted piper prophesying a new dawn and perhaps, a once and future king.

Will that stay the parade of devotees convinced that all that glitters must be gold, as they tramp up the lane or along the adjacent Wales Coast Path to what today calls itself an 'off-grid micro farm'? Well, it makes you wonder... but probably not. Read the lyrics (perhaps for the first time) and it all fits together just too well; the pastoral imagery and ambiguous phrase 'all are one and one is all' combined with the arcane mysticism apocryphally ascribed to Owain Glyndŵr can easily be imagined here. Along with its visceral impact on your ears, that's said to be the secret behind *Stairway*'s timelessness; it can mean whatever you want it to mean. And so can the legend of the song's composition. The tune will come to you at last.

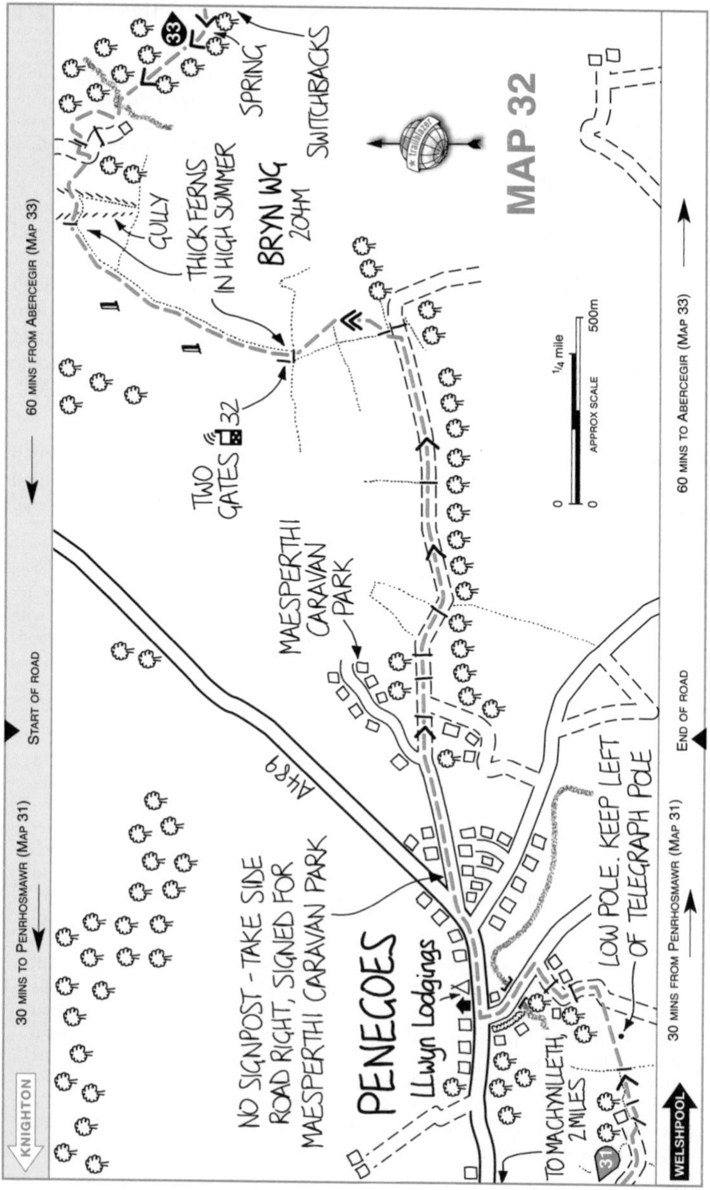
KNIGHTON
30 MINS TO PENRHOSMAWR (MAP 31)
START OF ROAD
60 MINS FROM ABERCEGIR (MAP 33)
NO SIGNPOST - TAKE SIDE ROAD RIGHT, SIGNED FOR MAESPERTHI CARAVAN PARK
PENEGOES
Llwyn Lodgings
A489
MAESPERTHI CARAVAN PARK
TWO GATES
32
THICK FERNS IN HIGH SUMMER
GULLY
BRYN WG 204M
SPRING
SWITCHBACKS
33
trailblazer
MAP 32
0
1/4 mile
0
500m
APPROX SCALE
TO MACHYNLLETH, 2 MILES
LOW POLE. KEEP LEFT OF TELEGRAPH POLE
31
WELSHPOOL
30 MINS FROM PENRHOSMAWR (MAP 31)
END OF ROAD
60 MINS TO ABERCEGIR (MAP 33)

shared kitchen and they can provide ingredients for self-catering walkers by prior arrangement. They also offer tent-only orchard **camping** (no wi-fi, £12.50pp) by the main road in summer, with a 'shower shed' and a communal cookhouse.

Up a side lane *Penrhosmawr Holidays* (Map 31; ☎ 01654-702257; 🖳 penrhos mawr.wixsite.com) has a range of accommodation: **B&B** (1D private facilities, from

£45pp), three **caravans** (sleep 4-6 from £20pp), one with hot tub, and a **campsite** (May-Sept; from £20 tent & 4 adults).

Some east-bound **buses** from Machynlleth also call in Penegoes, including the Lloyds Coaches No T12 to Welshpool and Wrexham; the T36 (pre-book) and the 33/36 school and shopping services to Glantwymyn; and the T37 (pre-book) to Aberhosan (see pp46-50 for more details).

Bryn Wg hill An unmarked turn-off in Penegoes leads to farm tracks, more gates and a short steep haul onto Bryn Wg hill, followed by a gradual descent with stirring views up the Dyfi or 'Dovey' valley and towards **Abercegir**.

Abercegir (Map 33) One of the prettier villages on the walk, though with no services. With a bit of forward planning, you could take advantage of Lloyds Coaches No T37 **bus** service (pre-booking essential) which calls in Abercegir en route between Machynlleth and Aberhosan twice a day on week days (see p48 for more details).

Cefn Coch (Map 33) Next up, a longer stretch around Cefn Coch hill will hopefully deliver more striking vistas up the valley to the north, before dropping into **Glantwymyn** (Cemmaes Road; see below); back on the busy A489/470.

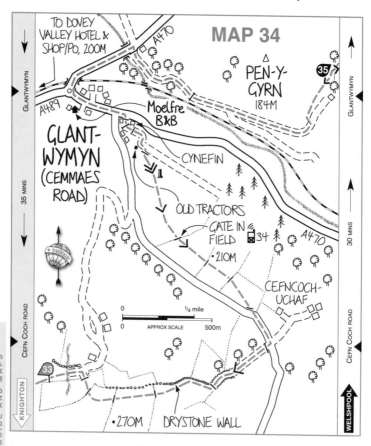

GLANTWYMYN (CEMMAES ROAD) [Map 34]

This village, named Cemmaes Road in English after a now disused railway station on the Cambrian line, has a couple of **B&B** options for the night and a useful shop.

By the roundabout *Moelfre B&B* (☎ 07498-720679, 🖳 moelfrebb.wixsite.com, **fb**; 1T/2D en suite) is at your service, with rooms and breakfast from £40pp. The *Dovey Valley Hotel* (off Map 34; ☎ 01650-511335; 🖳 doveyvalleyhotel.com, **fb**; 3D/

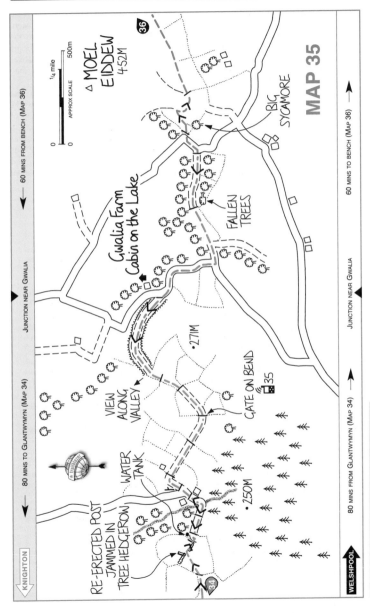

KNIGHTON

80 MINS TO GLANTWYMYN (MAP 34) →

← JUNCTION NEAR GWALIA

← 60 MINS FROM BENCH (MAP 36)

RE-ERECTED POST JAMMED IN TREE HEDGERON

WATER TANK

VIEW ALONG VALLEY

•271M

•250M

GATE ON BEND

Gwalia Farm
Cabin on the Lake

FALLEN TREES

△ MOEL EIDDEW 452M

36

BIG SYCAMORE

MAP 35

APPROX SCALE

0 — ¼ mile
0 — 500m

WELSHPOOL

80 MINS FROM GLANTWYMYN (MAP 34) →

JUNCTION NEAR GWALIA

60 MINS TO BENCH (MAP 36) →

ROUTE GUIDE AND MAPS

2T; ⓛ) is just down the road with rooms from £37.50pp (sgl occ from £65). Rates include a full Welsh breakfast, but note that they only serve **evening meals** from Thursday to Sunday. However, the *Villager Fryer* fish & chip van (☎ 07849-748374, pre-orders essential) calls at the hotel on Wednesdays (summer 5.30-8pm).

Alternatively, continue on for 2¼ miles/3.5km to *Gwalia Farm Cabin on the Lake* (Map 35; ☎ 01650-511377, 💻 gwalia farm.co.uk, **fb**; 1D; min 2 nights midweek) for a spot of luxury glamping and hot-tub wallowing (from £295).

Most Glyndŵrists will simply wonder if there's a need to make a lunchtime dash

for cold drinks and snacks at the basic **shop/post office** (☎ 01650-511422; Mon, Tue, Thur & Fri 9am-1pm), next to the Dovey Valley Hotel, or eat what they have in the woods just after crossing the River Twymyn which clockwise walkers may have last seen in Dylife gorge (p123).

Glantwymyn is on a couple of **bus** routes, including Lloyds Coaches No T12 which connects Machynlleth to Welshpool and Wrexham. Alternatively there's the T36 back to Machynlleth (pre-booking essential) or the 33/36 school/shopping bus which shuttles between Machynlleth and Dinas Mawddwy (see pp46-50 for more details).

❏ THE SONS OF GLYNDŴR

The 1970s wave of hirsute incomers (box p132) was paralleled by an acceleration in 'second home' ownership; affluent, mostly English city dwellers buying inexpensive rural properties which then stood empty most of the year, a rural scourge which survives today. As house prices inevitably rose, local resentment grew, especially in Ceredigion and around Machynlleth.

'Come home to a real fire' was a catchphrase which mocked a popular 1970s coal board slogan, as a spate of Welsh holiday homes were mysteriously torched. The arson was an orchestrated campaign attributed to a group called appropriately enough, Meibion Glyndŵr or the 'Sons of Glyndŵr', the most influential of the Welsh nationalists of that era. Between December 1979 (when four properties from Pembroke to the Llyn peninsula were set alight in one night) and the early 1990s, over 220 empty and mostly English-owned holiday homes or caravans were fire-bombed. Communiqués from Meibion Glyndŵr claiming responsibility were provocatively signed 'Rhys Gethin', one of Owain Glyndŵr's leading generals who led the decisive routing of the English at the Battle of Bryn Glas, south-west of Knighton in 1402.

In 2004 one Plaid Cymru (Welsh national party) MP suggested some of the attacks were the result of 'black flag' operations by MI5 or similar to discredit Welsh nationalism, a suggestion for which a colleague accused him of 'watching too many episodes of the *X Files*' (a popular 1990s TV drama investigating sometimes batty conspiracies). With the police and other agencies busy with the IRA and animal rights activists, the Meibion Glyndŵr were never caught or even identified and dispersed unseen into the Cambrian mists. It suggested a small and tight-knit group, although in 1993 21-year-old Sion Roberts was convicted of sending letter bombs to estate agents and Conservative politicians in England and Wales.

Today you'll find entire villages on or close to the Glyndŵr's Way without a single indigenous occupant, but whatever their origin, these people at least live here and make up the local economy, while the most obvious result of the post-war campaign for Welsh recognition and autonomy is the bilingual signage in public spaces, and of course the Senedd in Cardiff where the National Assembly for Wales was formed in 1998. Its creation followed a referendum whose result was even closer than the Brexit result of 2016.

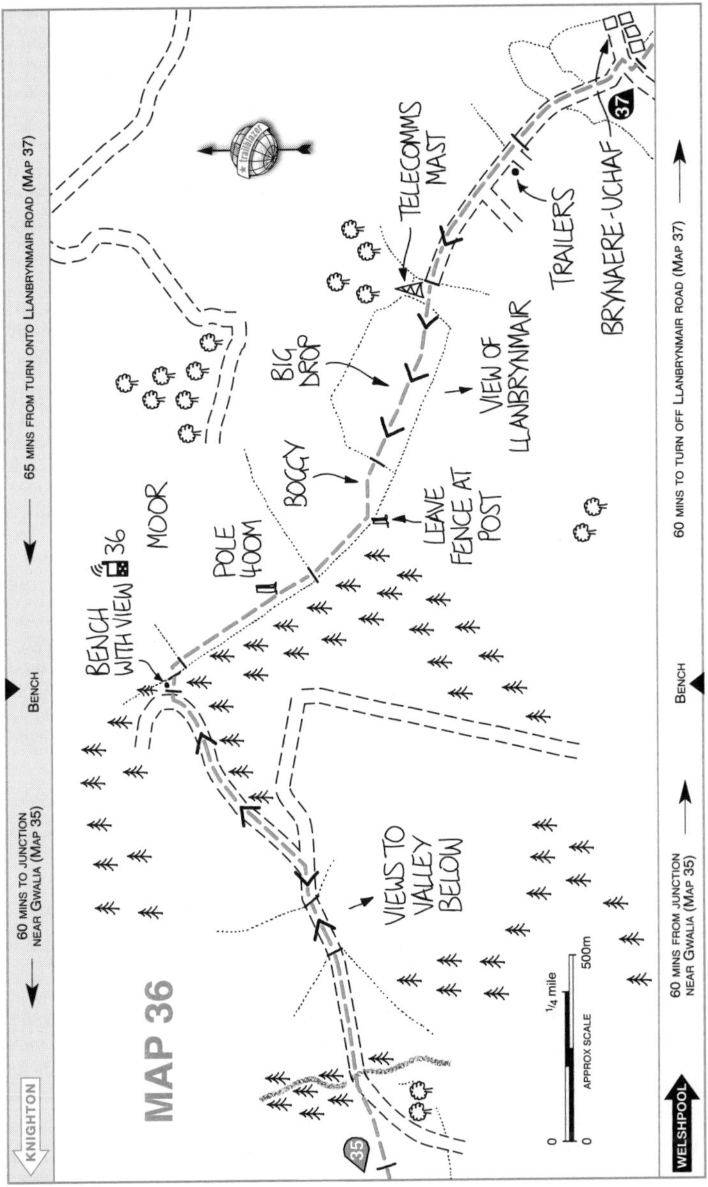

Map 36 143

MAP 36

KNIGHTON

BENCH

WELSHPOOL

60 MINS TO JUNCTION NEAR GWALIA (MAP 35)

65 MINS FROM TURN ONTO LLANBRYNMAIR ROAD (MAP 37)

60 MINS FROM JUNCTION NEAR GWALIA (MAP 35)

60 MINS TO TURN OFF LLANBRYNMAIR ROAD (MAP 37)

BENCH

BENCH WITH VIEW

MOOR

POLE 400M

BOGGY

BIG DROP

TELECOMMS MAST

LEAVE FENCE AT POST

VIEW OF LLANBRYNMAIR

TRAILERS

BRYNAERE-UCHAF

VIEWS TO VALLEY BELOW

¼ mile

500m

APPROX SCALE

ROUTE GUIDE AND MAPS

Moel Eiddew (Map 35) From this point there is just a brief stretch along mossy country lanes; the rest is all trail as you work your way across the southern flanks of Moel Eiddew. Climb gradually upwards and onwards past clear-felled forest overlooking the valley below to arrive at the walk's well-timed and best located **bench** (Map 36), a short distance before the day's 1312ft/400m **high point**. Soon you'll be standing like Ahab at Moel Eiddew's eastern prow overlooking the Afon Twymyn with views north to the Berwyns, before a toe-mashing drop past a telecom mast and around a couple of farms to the Llanbrynmair road. From here the 10-minute walk into Llanbrynmair will take you to a couple of accommodation options and an excellent shop and café.

LLANBRYNMAIR   [MAP 37]

You won't begrudge the 10-minute walk off route into the village, but be warned: according to local folklore, if you encounter a sinister frog or a toad, don't give the abominable amphibian a chance to count your teeth and they'll fall out! Wily wayfarers will appraise themselves of the many other supernatural entities lurking in the forests and thickets by leafing through the *Mabinogion*, a 12th-century compendium of ancient Celtic myths and legends.

In terms of **rooms**, the *Wynnstay Arms* (☎ 01650-521431; 🖳 wynnstayarmshotel .co.uk; 2T/2D/2Tr shared facilities; 🐾) may be overdue for a makeover but from £25pp must be one of the cheapest pub B&Bs in the land. They also serve a menu of pub classics every day in their **restaurant** (Tue-Sun noon-2pm, daily 7-8.30pm). Alternatively, hop over the road to

Wynnstay House B&B (☎ 01650-521201; 🖳 caffijojo.co.uk). They will do single nights in their two two-bedroom self-catering apartments at £45pp (sgl occ £80).

Crossing the road again, the *Caffi JoJo & Wynnstay Stores* (☎ 01650-521217; 🖳 caffijojo.co.uk; shop: Mon-Sat 8am-4pm & Sun 10am-3pm; café: Mon-Sat 9am-3pm & Sun 10am-3pm) is worth a visit just to see how good things can be in a Welsh village shop, as you tuck into a freshly cooked breakfast (from £6.50) made from locally sourced ingredients, then load up with snacks for the coming day.

If you've left your phone charger in Machynlleth, half-a-dozen No T12 **buses** (Lloyds Coaches) a day take just 20 minutes to cover what took you all day. In the other direction buses go all the way to Welshpool and Wrexham (see p48 for more details).

KNIGHTON ▷ **LLANBRYNMAIR TO MACHYNLLETH**   [MAPS 37-31]

With a full Welsh breakfast inside you, start the day with the stiff 750ft/228m climb up onto **Moel Eiddew** (Maps 36 & 35) with views to make it all worthwhile, followed by a gradual descent to the A470 at **Glantwymyn** (Map 34, see

Distance	15½ miles (25km)
Ascent	2700ft (823m)
Time	7-8 hours
WALKING TIME ONLY – ADD 20-30%	

p140) and the **shop** (limited opening hours). It's a shorter, steep haul onto the pastures and drystone walls of **Cefn Coch** (Map 33) which brings you into **Abercegir** village (no services) and great views up the Dyfi valley. From here it's one final hop up onto the fells to reach **Penegoes** (Map 32) and the back way into **Machynlleth**, which marks both the lowest altitude and the westernmost point of your walk.

[Next route overview p136]

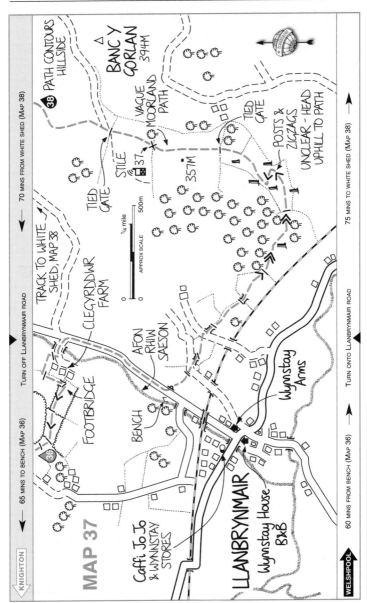

MAP 37

KNIGHTON

BANC Y GORLAN 394M

38 PATH CONTOURS HILLSIDE

VAGUE MOORLAND PATH

TIED GATE

POSTS & ZIGZAGS

UNCLEAR – HEAD UPHILL TO PATH

STILE

37

357M

TIED GATE

70 MINS FROM WHITE SHED (MAP 38)

75 MINS TO WHITE SHED (MAP 38)

TRACK TO WHITE SHED, MAP 38

CLEGYRDDWR FARM

AFON RHIW SAESON

TURN OFF LLANBRYNMAIR ROAD

FOOTBRIDGE

BENCH

36

65 MINS TO BENCH (MAP 36)

¼ mile
500m
0
0
APPROX SCALE

Caffi Jo Jo & Wynnstay Stores

LLANBRYNMAIR

Wynnstay House B&B

Wynnstay Arms

TURN ONTO LLANBRYNMAIR ROAD

60 MINS FROM BENCH (MAP 36)

WELSHPOOL

ROUTE GUIDE AND MAPS

WELSHPOOL LLANBRYNMAIR TO LAKE VYRNWY   MAPS 37-45

Are you ready for the **10 hours or more** it might take to tramp to **Lake Vyrnwy**, plus a bit further to your lodgings? Maybe not, so break the stage accordingly, while factoring in the following day's not insubstantial 14¼-miler (22.9km) on to Meifod.

Distance	**18¾ miles (30.3km)**
Ascent	**3061ft (933m)**
Time	**10 hours**
WALKING TIME ONLY – ADD 20-30%	

This will be your last stage in the Cambrian wilds, crossing just one main road all day but with a useful **shop** in Llangadfan (see p150).

Cerrig y Tan (Map 38) From Llanbrynmair reclaim the heights with the now familiar effort, bringing you on to Cerrig y Tan, revisiting fabulous views towards Cader Idris, before ambling along a forestry track which ends at sometimes boggy moorlands around **Eithin Llŵyn** hill (Map 39).

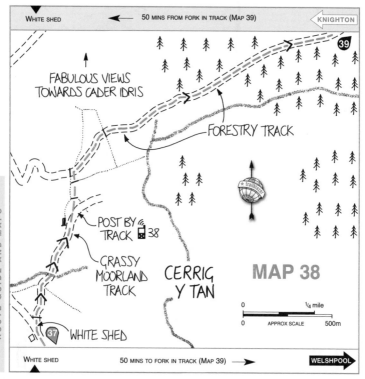

WHITE SHED ← 50 MINS FROM FORK IN TRACK (MAP 39)   KNIGHTON ▷

FABULOUS VIEWS TOWARDS CADER IDRIS

FORESTRY TRACK

39

★ Trailblazer

POST BY TRACK 📱 38

GRASSY MOORLAND TRACK

CERRIG Y TAN

MAP 38

0   ¼ mile
0   APPROX SCALE   500m

37 WHITE SHED

WHITE SHED   50 MINS TO FORK IN TRACK (MAP 39) →   WELSHPOOL ▷

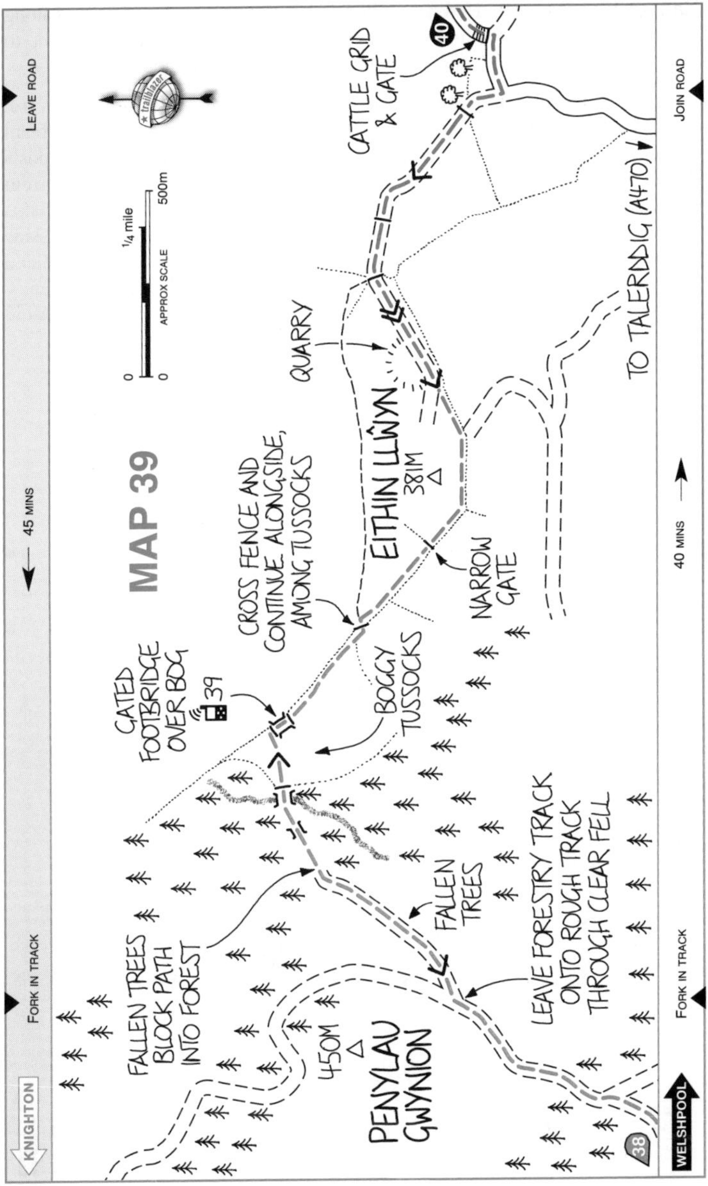
MAP 39
KNIGHTON
← 45 MINS
40 MINS →
WELSHPOOL
FORK IN TRACK
LEAVE ROAD
FORK IN TRACK
JOIN ROAD
38
40
APPROX SCALE
0
0
1/4 mile
500m
trailblazer
FALLEN TREES BLOCK PATH INTO FOREST
450M
PENYLAU GWYNION
FALLEN TREES
LEAVE FORESTRY TRACK ONTO ROUGH TRACK THROUGH CLEAR FELL
GATED FOOTBRIDGE OVER BOG
39
BOGGY TUSSOCKS
CROSS FENCE AND CONTINUE ALONGSIDE, AMONG TUSSOCKS
EITHIN LLŴYN
381M
NARROW GATE
QUARRY
TO TALERDDIG (A470)
CATTLE GRID & GATE

Nant yr Eira (Map 40) Here you follow a deserted country lane winding along the tranquil valley of Nant yr Eira past the **seasonal chapel** adjacent to Neinthirion homestead. If this isn't an AONB, it certainly should be.

Pen Coed moorland (Map 41) After passing through Dolwen farm yard, tracks lead you up onto the **Pen Coed** moorland, home to a troupe of **feral ponies**. Without a tracklog, expect to blunder a bit as the knee-high posts buried in thick summer bracken aren't always easy to spot and the current National Trail tracklog briefly follows a parallel, non-waymarked route that is incorrectly aligned on OS maps. As it is, they soon converge on the far side of the common where more field paths, incongruously pristine woodland boardwalks complete with dog stiles, and then more quiet lanes with a generous serving of gates bring you into **Llangadfan** (see p150) on the A458 Welshpool road.

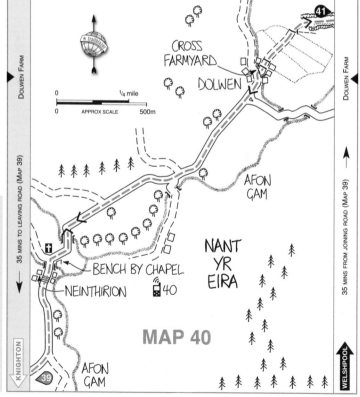

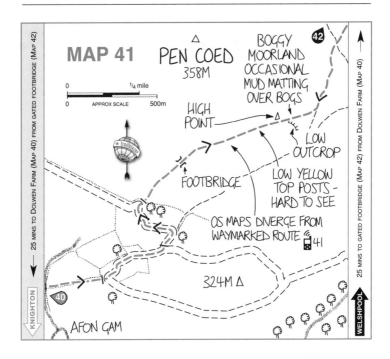

MAP 41   PEN COED 358M

BOGGY MOORLAND OCCASIONAL MUD MATTING OVER BOGS

0   ¼ mile

0   APPROX SCALE   500m

HIGH POINT

LOW OUTCROP

FOOTBRIDGE

LOW YELLOW TOP POSTS – HARD TO SEE

OS MAPS DIVERGE FROM WAYMARKED ROUTE 41

324M △

AFON GAM

25 MINS TO DOLWEN FARM (MAP 40) FROM GATED FOOTBRIDGE (MAP 42)

25 MINS TO GATED FOOTBRIDGE (MAP 42) FROM DOLWEN FARM (MAP 40)

KNIGHTON

WELSHPOOL

❏ DYFI VALLEY BIOSPHERE RESERVE (BIOSFFER DYFI)

Many consider the Dyfi river ('Dovey' to the English) and its valley to be one of Wales' most beautiful. For clockwise walkers, on a good day you're sure to be impressed as you inch around Cefn Coch (Map 33) towards Glantwymyn. Little wonder then that as you hit the old Roman road above Dylife (Map 25), and then turn off into the forest at Penylau Gwynion a couple of days later (Map 39), you've wandered across 800 square kilometres of UNESCO-accredited biosphere. One of only seven in Britain (others include the South Downs and Isle of Wight as well as more likely candidates on Scotland's Atlantic Coast and North Devon), biospheres are 'managed ecosystems where man lives in harmony with the natural environment'. Coastal dunes near the Dyfi river's estuary downstream of Machynlleth, are part of what render this landscape special.

In 2022 the biosphere, which includes offshore segments, received a boost when the mythical Cantre'r Gwaelod, a lost 'Welsh Atlantis' mentioned in the 13th-century *Black Book of Carmarthen*, was thought to have been located. Close studies of the 14th-century *Gough Map (Bodleian Map)*, one of the earliest accurate maps of the British Isles, showed that the Ceredigion Bay coastline may have been up to eight miles further out to sea, exposing long submerged islands in the mouth of the Dyfi estuary.

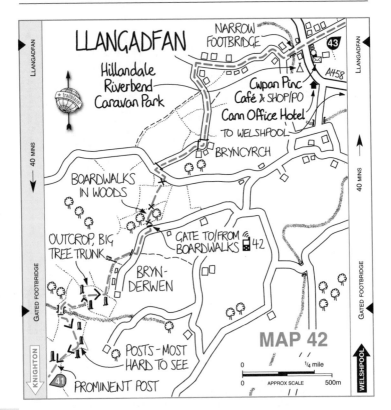

LLANGADFAN [MAP 42]

This village is blessed with *Cwpan Pinc*, an all-day **shop/PO** (☎ 01938 820633, **fb**; Mon-Fri 8.30am–5pm, Sat 8.30am-4pm, Sun 9am-3pm) and **café** (summer daily 8.30am-4pm, hot food 9am-2pm; winter takeaway only Tue & Wed) just as you're flagging. The café occasionally does Saturday night takeaways in the summer, such as burger and chips or chilli and rice (contact them for details).

If you've had enough for the day, there's a **campsite**, *Hillandale Riverbend Caravan Park* (☎ 01938-820356; 🖳 hillandale.co.uk/our-parks/riverbend-caravan-park; from £19 per 2-person tent) on the

banks of the sedate River Banwy, a shallow tributary of the River Severn.

Alternatively, for a proper bed there's **B&B** at the *Cann Office Hotel* (☎ 01938-820202; 🖳 cannoffice.com; **fb**; 1S/2D/2T/1Qd, all en suite; ☛; (L) just down the road. With rooms from £47.50pp (sgl occ £80), the 14th-century pub's curious name is an anglicised *Cae'n y Ffos*, meaning 'fortified field'. They serve **food** every day (Mon-Fri 12.30-10pm, Sat & Sun from noon) made from locally sourced ingredients, including light lunches, afternoon teas and pub classic evening meals (from £11.50) with their popular carvery (£14.50) on Sundays.

You may wonder why the Glyndŵr's Way takes a northward turn towards Lake Vyrnwy? And in doing so, why doesn't it pass by Glyndŵr's ancestral home in Sycharth (see p52), another 11 miles/17.6km to the north-east ? One tenuous explanation to the former may be the rebellion's first setback at the Battle of Vyrnwy, 'near Welshpool' against the English Earl Burnell in late September 1400 and less than a fortnight into the campaign. Unlike the rebellion's other battle sites, no location is apparent but it must have happened somewhere close to the Vyrnwy river and Meifod is the closest the river ever gets to Welshpool.

As for Sycharth, that's a bit out of the way and fell outside the Powys boundary when the walk was founded in the mid-1970s (see colour map at the end of the book).

Dyfnant Forest (Maps 43 & 44) If you've more in the tank (or you've woken up in Llangadfan and it's tomorrow already), ahead lies a scramble across farm fields and maybe the trail's last vestiges of ageing stiles before another long forestry track leads through the Dyfnant Forest.

By and by you emerge from the trees and pass the sinister ranks of holiday cabins in **Ddol Cownwy** (Map 45) where a turn leads to a gritty ascent up one last hill before dropping and turning to reveal the glittering expanse of **Lake Vyrnwy** and the late-Victorian slate-block dam wall below.

By the mid-19th century the link was being made between unclean drinking water and virulent diseases like typhoid and cholera which ravaged the slums of industrial cities like Liverpool, Manchester and Birmingham. Liverpool needed clean water which the nearby Lake District could not supply in adequate volume and so the upper Vyrnwy valley was selected as optimal location for a huge reservoir and dam.

By 1888 the village of Llanwddyn had been summarily demolished and rebuilt below the UK's first large stone dam. Today water flows along a 68-mile (109km) aqueduct to Liverpool at up to 50 million gallons a day and on the rare occasions the reservoir is full, water spills down the dam face rather than via tunnels; an impressive sight. Nearly 70 years after the Vyrnwy dam had been completed, Liverpool Corporation sought this time to flood the village of Capel Celyn, 15 miles (24km) north-west of Llanwddyn in the Tryweryn valley. While the Tryweryn dam did open in 1963, this time the local outcry was far less muted and feelings remain strong today. That same year three men were jailed for bombing the dam's transformers, a hitherto unheard of act of eco-sabotage which recalls Edward Abbey's 1975 novel *The Monkey Wrench Gang*, describing similar dam-busting actions in Utah's Grand Canyon.

The resistance to the Tryweryn dam was a watershed moment for **Welsh nationalism**, seeing membership of Plaid Cymru double and its emergence as a viable political force. A new sense of national pride was born as well as a revival of the Welsh language once spoken in Capel Celyn, despite being proscribed since Tudor times. No big dams for English cities have been built in Wales since the Clywedog (see p117) in 1967, devolution came in 1998 and in October 2005 Liverpool City Council issued a public apology 'for any insensitivity by our predecessor Council'.

ROUTE GUIDE AND MAPS

Lake Vrnwy (Map 45; 🖥 lake-vyrnwy.com) Popular with leisure seekers and bird spotters, you may emerge a little dazed at the western edge of **Llanwddyn** (see p156) just as the last of the day-trippers are heading home. Although there is still an expanse of car parks, the tourist and adjacent RSPB visitors' centres fell victims to the pandemic. A **bird hide** survives – watch out for the

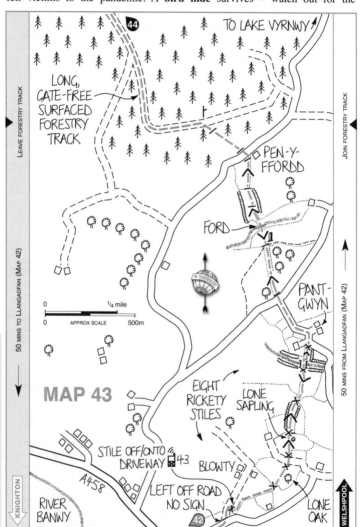

LONG, GATE-FREE SURFACED FORESTRY TRACK

TO LAKE VYRNWY

PEN-Y-FFORDD

FORD

PANT-GWYN

EIGHT RICKETY STILES

LONE SAPLING

MAP 43

STILE OFF/ONTO DRIVEWAY 🖥 43

BLOWTY

LEFT OFF ROAD NO SIGN

A458

RIVER BANWY

LONE OAK

0   ¼ mile
0   APPROX SCALE   500m

LEAVE FORESTRY TRACK

JOIN FORESTRY TRACK

50 MINS TO LLANGADFAN (MAP 42)

50 MINS FROM LLANGADFAN (MAP 42)

ROUTE GUIDE AND MAPS

KNIGHTON

WELSHPOOL

goosander, a saw-billed duck which nests in trees – but the **café**, *Artisans* (☎ 01691-870317; 🖳 **fb**; 10am-4.30pm) looked a bit depleted. Formerly a sawmill, you can **hire bikes** here for the 11-mile (17.7km) lap of the reservoir, where you may find **kayak, canoe or paddle board** rental too (☎ 01691-870615; 🖳 bethaniaadventure.co.uk). Just don't get sucked into the dam intake!

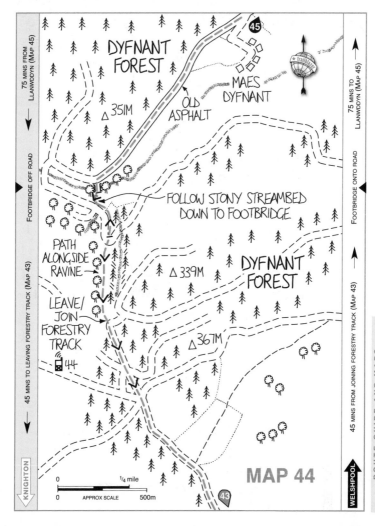

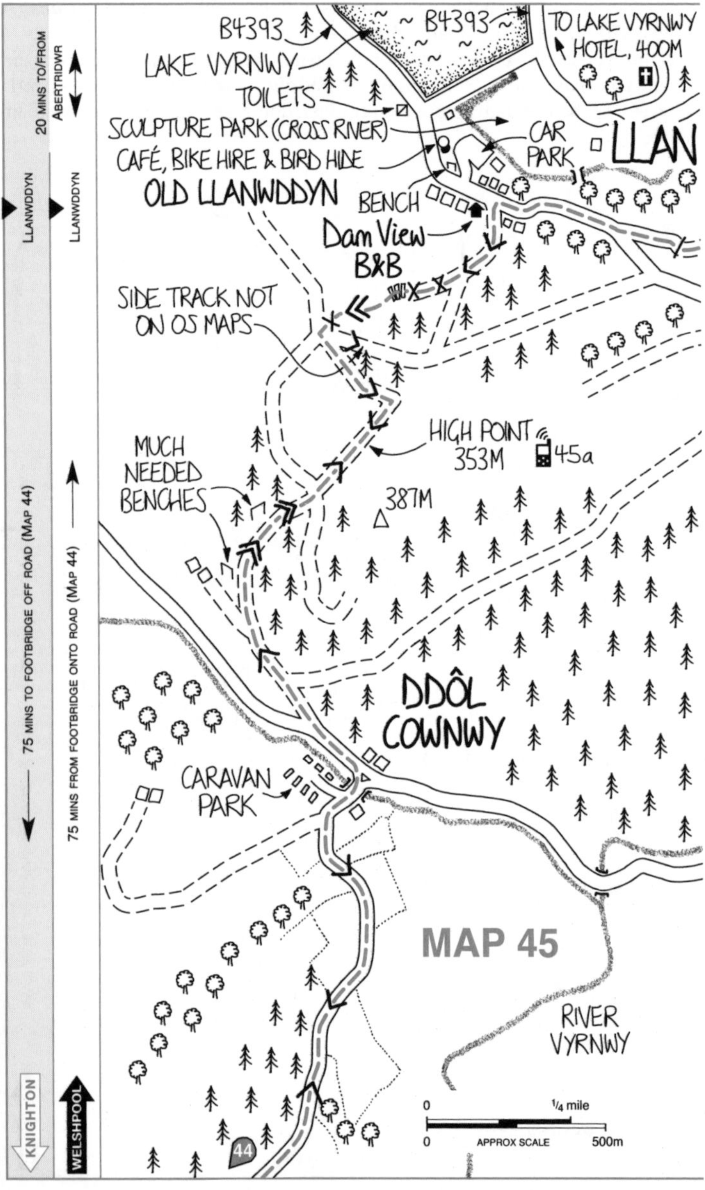

B4393
~ B4393 ~
TO LAKE VYRNWY
HOTEL, 400M

LAKE VYRNWY
TOILETS
SCULPTURE PARK (CROSS RIVER)
CAFÉ, BIKE HIRE & BIRD HIDE
OLD LLANWDDYN

CAR PARK
LLAN

BENCH
Dam View B&B

SIDE TRACK NOT ON OS MAPS

HIGH POINT 353M
45a

MUCH NEEDED BENCHES

387M

DDÔL COWNWY

CARAVAN PARK

MAP 45

RIVER VYRNWY

0   1/4 mile
0   APPROX SCALE   500m

44

20 MINS TO/FROM ABERTRIDWR

LLANWDDYN

LLANWDDYN

75 MINS TO FOOTBRIDGE OFF ROAD (MAP 44)

75 MINS FROM FOOTBRIDGE ONTO ROAD (MAP 44)

ROUTE GUIDE AND MAPS

KNIGHTON

WELSHPOOL

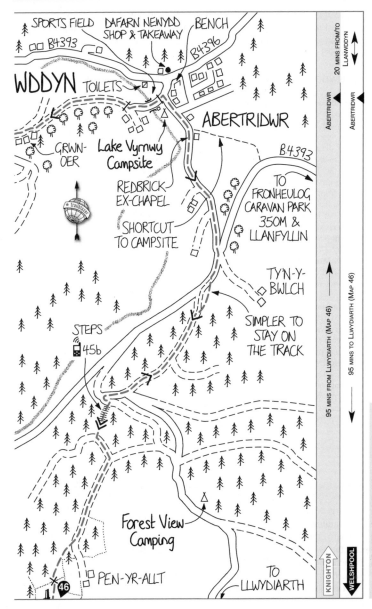

SPORTS FIELD
DAFARN NEWYDD SHOP & TAKEAWAY
BENCH
B4393
B4396
WDDYN
TOILETS
ABERTRIDWR
GRWN-OER
Lake Vyrnwy Campsite
REDBRICK-EX-CHAPEL
B4393
TO FRONHEULOG CARAVAN PARK 350M & LLANFYLLIN
SHORTCUT TO CAMPSITE
TY'N-Y-BWLCH
trailblazer
SIMPLER TO STAY ON THE TRACK
STEPS
45b
Forest View Camping
PEN-YR-ALLT
46
TO LLWYDIARTH

20 MINS FROM/TO LLANWDDYN

ABERTRIDWR

ABERTRIDWR

95 MINS FROM LLWYDIARTH (MAP 46)

95 MINS TO LLWYDIARTH (MAP 46)

KNIGHTON

WELSHPOOL

ROUTE GUIDE AND MAPS

As it is, if you've come through from Llanbrynmair in one go, you're probably lacking the energy to even spare a wander through the **Sculpture Trail** accessed over a footbridge below the dam wall and which might better be described as an arboretum with carvings.

LLANWDDYN & ABERTRIDWR
[Map 45, pp154-5]

After the original **Llandwddyn** was submerged by the reservoir in the 1880s, with the new **St Wddyn's church** perched alone on the opposite side of the valley, the relocation deprived new Llanwddyn of an organic village centre. In the hot summer of 2022, the foundations of old Llanwddyn rose again from the drying mud as water levels dropped to a fifty-year low.

On the east side of the river the newer settlement is signed Llanwddyn but known as **Abertridwr**. It has the all-important **village shop** and **take-away**, *Dafarn Newydd* (☎ 01691-870211; 🖳 dafarnnewyddstores .wales; Mon-Sat 8am-6.30pm; Sun 9am-6.30pm) at a three-way junction, with good value hot **food** on offer such as breakfast sandwiches, fish & chips or pizza.

Campers are spoilt for choice around here, at least in the summer. Wily wild campers will already be scouting out their spot (note the handy **public toilets** near the shop, and on the other side of the dam, near the café by the former visitors' centres), though there may be semi-formal riverside camping at *Lake Vyrnwy Campsite* (🖳 lakevyrnwycampsite.co.uk; see website for open dates; from £8pp; 🐾) just down from the shop for a few weeks in mid-summer.

They have portaloos and a washing up area on site, but no showers.

If not, a little off-trail and 20 minutes from the shop (via an uphill footpath shortcut just before the redbrick former chapel; see Map 45), *Fronheulog Caravan Park* (☎ 01691-870362; 🖳 fronheulogcaravan park.co.uk; adults only; 🐾) offers tent space for £5pp but again has no showers, so have a rinse in the river or public toilets. *Fronheulog* is Welsh for 'sunny bank'.

Meanwhile 1¾ miles (2.8km) south of the shop and also a little off route, at *Forest View* (☎ 07948-243116; 🖳 edensnook.co .uk) camping costs £15pp. There are showers as well as a 'barn lounge', a cosy cooking cabin and they serve **breakfasts** too (8-11am); from £2 for a bacon sandwich or £10 for the full Welsh, including tea or coffee.

You need to pin down **rooms** in advance at Lake Vyrnwy, possibly timing a visit to avoid a summer weekend. The only surviving **B&B** is *Dam View Cottage* right on the trail as you come off the hill and dating from the dam's construction (☎ 07400-229982; 🖳 damviewcottagewales.com; 1D/2T or D all en suite; Ⓛ) with rooms from £50pp (sgl occ £100) and they can provide evening meals by prior arrangement. That leaves the upmarket Victorian-era *Lake Vyrnwy Hotel & Spa* (☎ 01691-

KNIGHTON▷ **LAKE VYRNWY TO LLANBRYNMAIR**   [MAPS 45-37]

It's a long day from the reservoir to Llanbrynmair (unless you opt to spread it across two days) and it's also your first full day in the wilds of the Cambrian mountains across pasture, moorland and forest. Luckily, this is one of the stages

Distance	**18¾ miles (30.3km)**
Ascent	**2694ft (821m)**
Time	**10-11 hours**
WALKING TIME ONLY – ADD 20-30%	

on the Glyndŵr's Way where a handy village **shop** and **café** pops up around lunchtime. **Llangadfan** (Map 43) is just 7½ miles (11.9km) in, leaving a full afternoon to cover the remaining 11¼ miles (18.3km) across the hills and forests down to Llanbrynmair.   [*Next route overview p144*]

870692; ⌨ lakevyrnwy.com; **fb**; 🐾), a 10-minute walk north of the dam with over 50 rooms from £60pp. The bar is open to all every day (Mon-Thur 5-11pm, Fri from 4pm, Sat & Sun from noon); bookings are recommended for the **restaurant** (lunch noon-3pm, afternoon tea noon-5pm, dinner 6-9pm) with tapas (from £6) served all day in addition to separate lunch and evening menus offering dishes such as slow roasted pork belly (£22).

You'll also find some hidden riverside cabins on ⌨ airbnb.co.uk a mile south of the shop, but for *a single night* at Lake Vyrnwy that seems to be your lot within walking range. It's worth knowing that *Tan y Craig B&B* in **Meifod** (see p164) will pick you up here (or in Llwydiarth, see Map 46) and drop you back next day for a small fee, enabling a two-night stay in Meifod.

The only **bus** service is the Qube Dial-a-Ride T82 from outside the Abertridwr shop on Wednesday morning at 8.25am to Oswestry (pre-booking essential). Don't be late! (See p48 for more details).

◀WELSHPOOL LAKE VYRNWY TO MEIFOD　　　　**[MAPS 45-50]**

Fully recovered from yesterday's long haul, today it's back to your average mileage from around Abertridwr to Meifod and with a couple of useful village **shops** en route.

Distance	**14¼ miles (22.9km)**
Ascent	**1775ft (541m)**
Time	**6-7 hours**
WALKING TIME ONLY – ADD 20-30%	

Yr alt Boeth forest After climbing a helpful staircase up into the Yr alt Boeth forest, as you emerge on a hill near **Pen yr allt** (Map 45) you might gaze eastwards down the Vyrnwy valley and have a fleetingly sad epiphany: the hardscrabble farmyards, windswept Cambrian moorlands and brooding forests are behind you now. Ahead lies a gradual re-entry to the neatly trimmed English borderlands you may have left a little over a week ago.

Llywdiarth (Map 46) Soon you drop into the pretty village of Llywdiarth (also known as Pont Llogel) with a welcome **shop/PO** (☎ 01938-820208; Mon-Fri 9am-1pm & 2-5.30pm except Wed pm, Sat 9am-noon) right on the trail, selling a few basic groceries.

Allt Dolanog hill (Map 47) The character of the walk now changes as you follow the north bank of the **Vyrnwy river** flowing from the dam's sluices. A path leads all the way to Dolanog, but in less than a mile you flit off across fields and farm tracks before crossing a road for a very pleasant hike over the fence-free expanse of Allt Dolanog hill; a fitting location for an ancient hill fort (although there is no longer anything much to see on the ground).

Dolanog (Map 47) Entering the village, the fine bronze sculpture of an open book by a log bench will catch your eye. It commemorates **Ann Griffiths** (1776-1805); you'll have noticed the plaque near Dolwar Fach farm (Map 47) where she was born. A zealous Calvinist convert, she was Wales' foremost religious poet whose words were later reworked into stirring hymns. One **bus** a week calls here: Owen's Travelmaster No 76A runs on Monday mornings only from Dolanog (at the telephone box near the church) via Pontrobert and Meifod to Welshpool (see p48 for details).

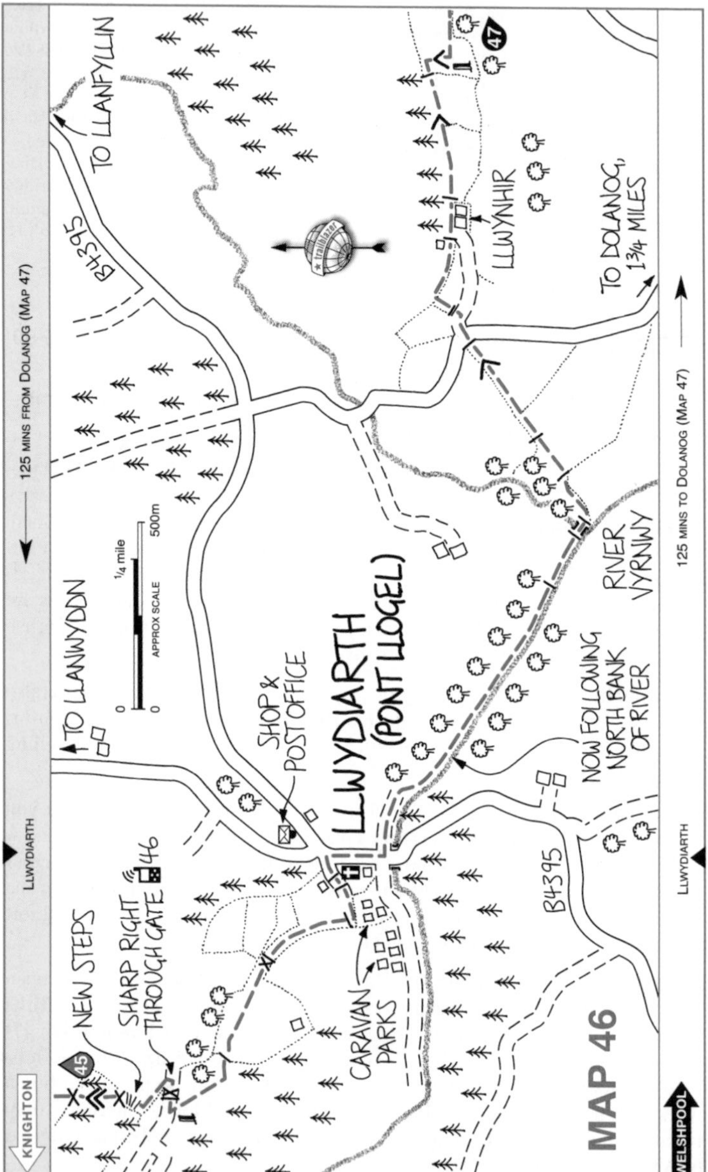

MAP 46

125 MINS FROM DOLANOG (MAP 47)

125 MINS TO DOLANOG (MAP 47)

TO LLANFYLLIN

B4395

TO LLANWYDDN

KNIGHTON

LLWYDIARTH

NEW STEPS

SHARP RIGHT THROUGH GATE 46

45

SHOP & POST OFFICE

¼ mile

500m

0

0

APPROX SCALE

LLWYDIARTH (PONT LLOGEL)

CARAVAN PARKS

NOW FOLLOWING NORTH BANK OF RIVER

RIVER VYRNWY

B4395

LLWYNHIR

47

TO DOLANOG, 1¾ MILES

WELSHPOOL

LLWYDIARTH

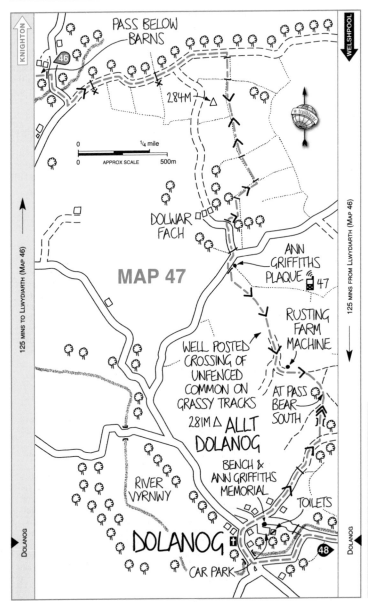

PASS BELOW BARNS

46

284M

¼ mile

0

0   500m

APPROX SCALE

trailblazer

DOLWAR FACH

ANN GRIFFITHS PLAQUE 47

MAP 47

125 MINS TO LLWYDIARTH (MAP 46)

125 MINS FROM LLWYDIARTH (MAP 46)

RUSTING FARM MACHINE

WELL POSTED CROSSING OF UNFENCED COMMON ON GRASSY TRACKS

AT PASS BEAR SOUTH

281M △ ALLT DOLANOG

BENCH & ANN GRIFFITHS MEMORIAL

RIVER VYRNWY

TOILETS

48

DOLANOG

DOLANOG

DOLANOG

CAR PARK

Pontrobert (Map 49) In Dolanog you cross to the south side of the Vyrnwy and walk right alongside it for a while before rising up the valley side and crossing the river again as you enter Pontrobert. The village was named after the thoughtful chap who first spanned the River Vyrnwy here in 1670, though the current bridge dates from the 1830s. Just by the bridge is the handy village **shop/PO** (☎ 01938-500230; Mon-Fri 8am-1pm; Sat 8am-noon) and down the road you'll pass the ***Royal Oak*** pub (Mon-Sat 5pm-11pm, Sun noon-11pm, drinks only).

If you happen to be here on a Monday morning you might coincide with Pontrobert's once-a-week **bus** service. Owen's Travelmaster No 76A calls here en route between Dolanog and Welshpool (see p48 for details).

Dyffryn Hill (Map 50) From Pontrobert the Glyndŵr's Way navigates more hedgerows, fields and country lanes, ending with a final circling of Dyffryn Hill to enter **Meifod**, back on the Vyrnwy river.

❏ **DOLOBRAN FRIENDS MEETING HOUSE**   (MAP 49, p162]

Tramping your merry way out of Pontrobert, chewing on a straw and pondering what wonders Meifod might behold, an ill-timed blink and you'll miss the brick cottage of the Dolobran Friends Meeting House or Quaker 'chapel' hidden among the trees. Built in 1701 (some say forty years earlier), it's thought to be the first such place in Wales, commissioned by the well-to-do Lloyd family who resided in nearby Dolobran Hall. At the time non-conformists like the Religious Society of Friends (better known as Quakers – originally a term of ridicule) were heavily persecuted by Restoration-era Anglicans under Charles II. But probably due to their proven entrepreneurial acumen over the following century, Quakers remain the best known of the many Protestant sects which rose up during the English Civil War, when the former Stuart monarchy's stranglehold on religious belief was loosened.

Rejecting the entrenched hierarchies of church and state, and believing all people were equal under God, initially Quakers had no ordained clergy and many early preachers were women. Quaker founder George Fox once said '*God who made the world did not dwell in temples made with hands*' and so the typical interior of a Meeting House is not unlike a mosque, a plain room with no lavish altar or other ritual trappings and where Friends might still sit in wordless contemplation, known as 'waiting-' or 'silent worship'.

The enterprising Dolobran Lloyds (a name adopted in the 15th century after their estate of Llwydiarth, aka: Pont Llogel) eventually moved to then Quaker-friendly Birmingham. Some went on to found the eponymous bank which survives today – Barclays and Friends Provident being other Quaker-founded financial institutions. In America, the state of Pennsylvania was founded by William Penn, a prominent English Quaker and close friend of George Fox. He was supported by Charles, one of the Dolobran Lloyds, who served as Pennsylvania's Deputy-Governor and later, President. Other American Quakers were heavily involved in the founding of the abolition movement and the subsequent Underground Railroad.

Today most Quakers are of the evangelical persuasion who engage in 'programmed worship' and espouse biblical infallibility. A tiny proportion identify as non-theist Quakers, who might be called Humanists.

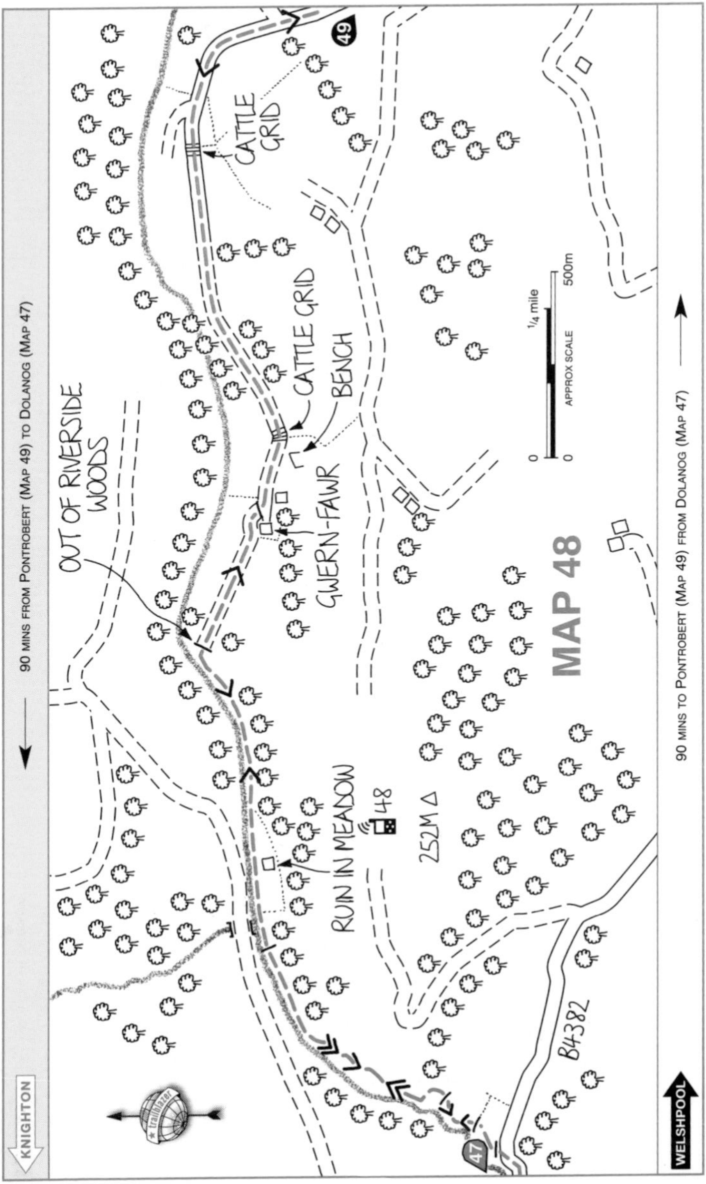
90 MINS FROM PONTROBERT (MAP 49) TO DOLANOG (MAP 47)
KNIGHTON
trailblazer
OUT OF RIVERSIDE WOODS
CATTLE GRID
CATTLE GRID
BENCH
GWERN-FAWR
RUIN IN MEADOW
48
252M
MAP 48
49
47
B4382
0
0
APPROX SCALE
1/4 mile
500m
WELSHPOOL
90 MINS TO PONTROBERT (MAP 49) FROM DOLANOG (MAP 47)

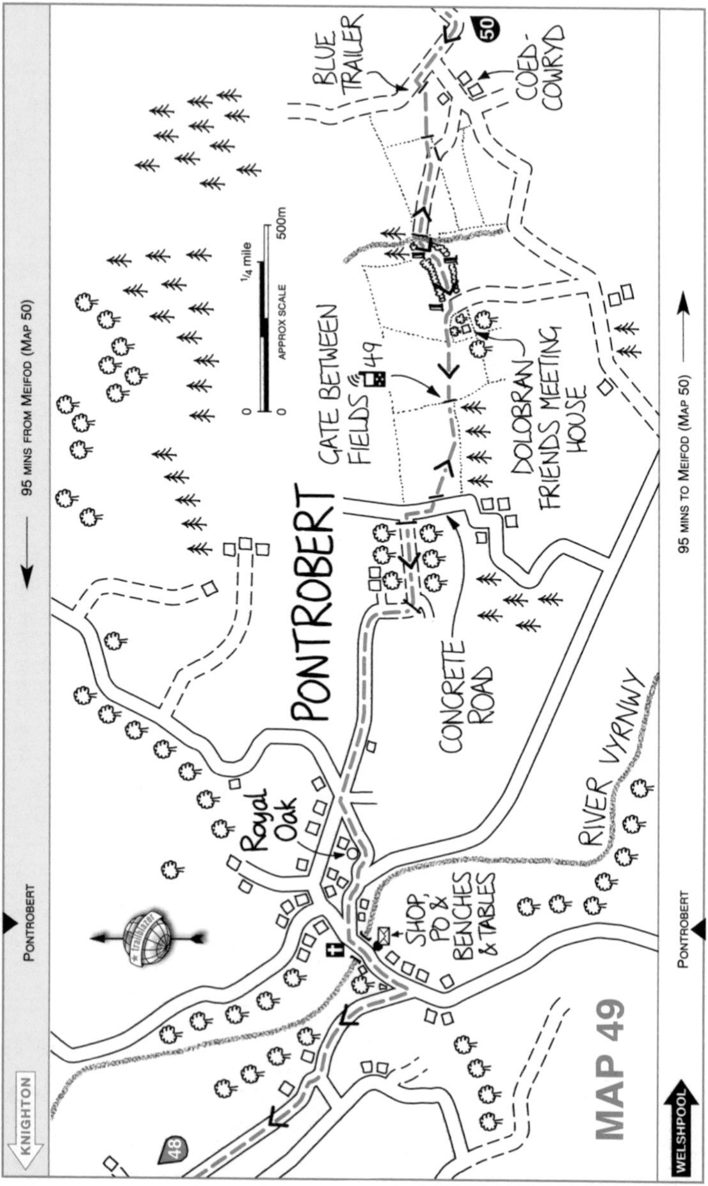

MAP 49

KNIGHTON

PONTROBERT

95 MINS FROM MEIFOD (MAP 50)

95 MINS TO MEIFOD (MAP 50)

WELSHPOOL

PONTROBERT

PONTROBERT

BLUE TRAILER

COED-COWRYD

50

GATE BETWEEN FIELDS

49

DOLOBRAN FRIENDS MEETING HOUSE

¼ mile

500m

APPROX SCALE

0

0

CONCRETE ROAD

Royal Oak

SHOP, PO & BENCHES & TABLES

RIVER VYRNWY

48

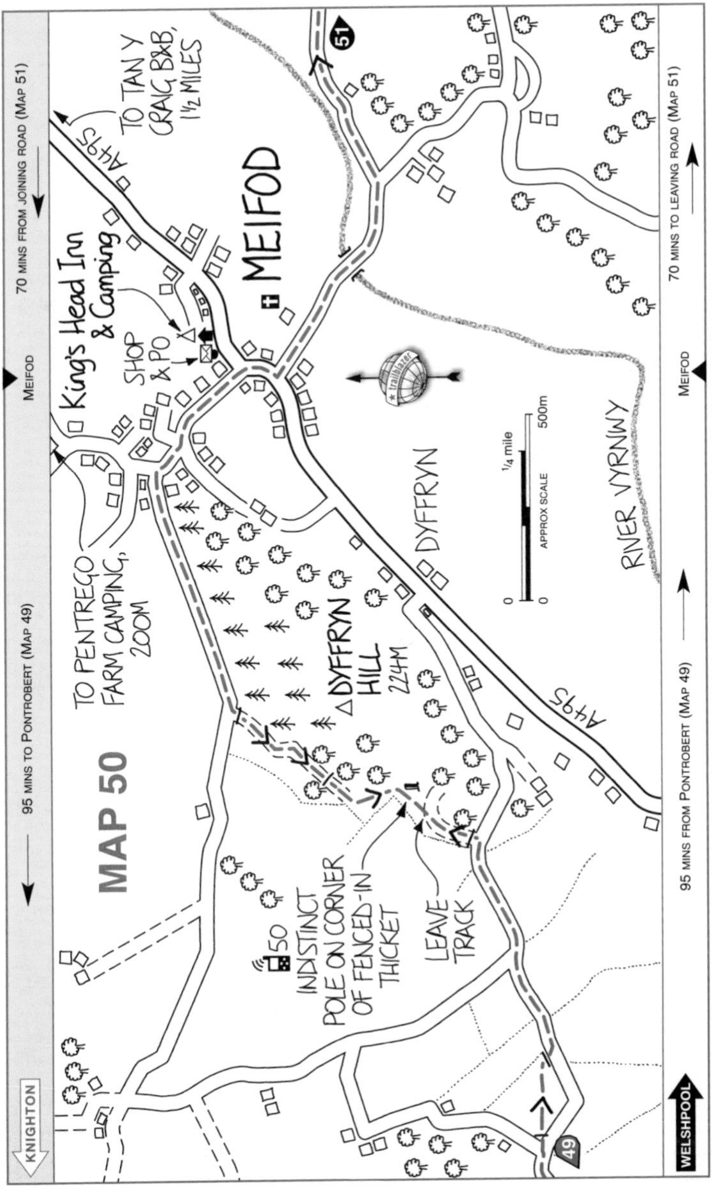

MAP 50

95 MINS TO PONTROBERT (MAP 49)

70 MINS FROM JOINING ROAD (MAP 51)

TO TAN Y CRAIG B&B, 1½ MILES

51

MEIFOD

A495

King's Head Inn & Camping

SHOP & PO

TO PENTRECO FARM CAMPING, 200M

MEIFOD

DYFFRYN

△ DYFFRYN HILL 224M

☐ 50

INDISTINCT POLE ON CORNER OF FENCED-IN THICKET

LEAVE TRACK

KNIGHTON

¼ mile

500m

0

APPROX SCALE

0

RIVER VYRNWY

A495

MEIFOD

70 MINS TO LEAVING ROAD (MAP 51)

95 MINS FROM PONTROBERT (MAP 49)

WELSHPOOL

49

MEIFOD   [MAP 50, p163]

Set on a spacious green opposite the main street, there's been a Christian place of worship on the site of the current 12th-century **St Tysilio and St Mary** cathedral church (🖥 coflein.gov.uk/en/site/163220) for nearly 1500 years, in other words as old as Christianity in Wales. Inside, in one corner you'll find an ancient carved Celtic cross, looking a little neglected.

A couple of miles down the A495, near the confluence of the rivers Vyrnwy and Banwy, is the site of **Mathrafal Castle** (🖥 castlewales.com/mathrafl.html). From the 9th to the 13th century this was the original capital of the (then united) Kingdom of Powys and seat of its princes from whom Owain Glyndŵr was descended. Today, like Sycharth and Glyndyfrdwy, only a mound survives.

But in truth, the **Meifod Post Office & Stores** (☎ 01938-500286; **fb**; Mon-Sat 7am-7pm) is what you really want to see and has longer than average hours, serving as a newsagent, general store and off-licence as well as a post office.

Next door is the **Kings Head Inn** (☎ 01938-500867; **fb**; 1T/5D/2Qd all en suite; 🐕) with **rooms** at £60pp (sgl occ £120) or you can **camp** on the sports field round the back for £12pp and use the ablution blocks as well as the pub's spacious covered ter-race. They also serve food every day (Thur-Mon noon-8.45pm, Tue & Wed 5-8.45pm) with pub classic mains from £14, regular specials and occasional summer barbecues.

The only other camping option is in a field at **Pentrego Farm** (☎ 01938-500353) half a mile north of the village centre for around £5pp.

Half an hour's walk north-east of town along the A495 to Oswestry, at the ivy-clad **Tan y Graig** (off Map 50; ☎ 07817-669946; 🖥 tanygraig.co.uk; 1T/1D en suite; Ⓛ) **B&B** costs from £50pp (sgl £70, sgl occ £90). Both rooms also have sofa beds so could sleep three. They can provide evening **meals** by prior arrangement and will collect you from and return you to Meifod, as well as Lake Vyrnwy or Llwydiard/Pont Llogel for a small charge, enabling you to spend two nights here.

Otherwise, 🖥 airbnb.co.uk shows up a room or two from around £40 if you're quick.

Along this stage Owen's Travelmaster **bus** No 76A runs on Monday mornings only to connect Dolanog, Pontrobert and Meifod with Welshpool. But once in Meifod, Tanat Valley Coaches No 76/76B has up to four buses daily (except Sunday) to Welshpool if you've run out of puff or time on the last leg (see pp46-50 for more details).

KNIGHTON **MEIFOD TO LAKE VYRNWY**   **[MAPS 50-45]**

After yesterday's warm up, today's more typical distance leads you gradually into the Cambrian mountains which feed some of the run-off into Lake Vyrnwy. Criss-crossing fields and country lanes, you pass through the quiet villages of **Pontrobert** (shop; see p160), Dolanog and **Llwydiarth/Pont Llogel** (shop/PO; see p157),

Distance	14¼ miles (22.9km)
Ascent	2241ft (683m)
Time	**6-7 hours**
	WALKING TIME ONLY
	SEE P83 – ADD 20-30%

Along the way you'll find yourself walking alongside and cross-crossing the **River Vyrnwy**, then from Dolanog a steep climb or two brings you up into outliers of the Dyfnant forest before arriving at the river's end right at the Lake Vyrnwy dam wall near **Abertridwr**. Unless you're camping, lodging options are lean here so plan well ahead.   *[Next route overview p156]*

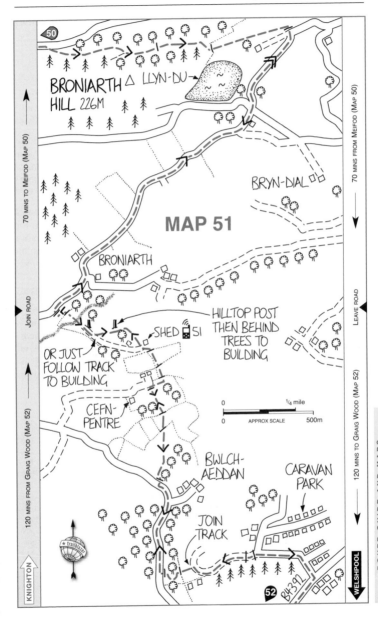

◀WELSHPOOL MEIFOD TO WELSHPOOL [MAPS 50-54]

You might fancy a lie-in before the comparatively modest final stretch to Welshpool, but it may not end up the easy day suggested by the mileage. The Glyndŵr's Way finds a way to meander from field to field and hill to hill with no

Distance	11¼ miles (18.2km)
Ascent	1880ft (573m)
Time	5-6 hours
WALKING TIME ONLY – ADD 20-30%	

villages or services along the way, so stock up in Meifod before you set off.

Broniarth Hill (Map 51) After crossing the Vyrnwy, the day starts with a climb up Broniarth Hill before switching back along a country lane and your penultimate views westwards to the now distant Cambrians. Twenty miles (32km) to the west-north-west the twin humps of the near 3000-foot (905m) Aran Fawddawy might catch your eye.

Figyn Wood & Y Golfa hill (Map 52) Thereafter, field follows gate follows copse follows gate. After an unfairly brutal haul up through **Figyn Wood**, for most Glyndŵrists the day's well earned highlight will be a defiant clamber up to the 1119ft/341m trig point atop **Y Golfa hill** set, coincidentally it seems, on the edge of a golf course. Looking back west one last time and with a sonorous hoot of the Welshpool-Llanfair Light Railway far below, this feels like the climax of your Glyndŵr's adventure, even if it's still a straightforward 90 minutes down to **Welshpool**.

The end/start of Glyndŵr's Way The official **terminus of Glyndŵr's Way** is a small green space called **Pont Howell Park** alongside the 200-year-old Montgomery Canal at the south end of the main high street. Once here, all that remains is to get someone to snap a commemorative photo of you by the polished granite obelisk inscribed with the trusty NT acorn and 'Llwybr Glyndŵr's Way'. Well done you!

WELSHPOOL (Y TRALLWNG)
[MAP 54, p170]

The border town gained the 'Welsh-' prefix to distinguish it from the like-named Poole in Dorset and, you may be pleased to see, is a fair bit livelier than Knighton, just two days walk to the south. Over the canal from Pont Howell Park the **Y Lanfa Powysland Museum** (🖳 en.powys.gov.uk; open Mon-Wed, Fri & Sat from 9.30am, closes Mon 6.30pm, Tue & Fri 5pm; Wed & Sat 1pm; free) is displayed across the first floor above the library in a restored canal-side warehouse. If you have a couple of hours before catching a train, expand your regional knowledge by investigating some well laid out exhibits on regional archaeology, history and geology as well as the origins of the Welsh hat. There's bound to be something here of interest and there's also **free internet** downstairs on a full-sized keyboard and screen.

Other points of interest include the site of a motte and bailey castle dating from the Norman era; now a bowling green. It's said that at one point in Wales' medieval past, you were never more than 12 miles from a castle of some sort. And just off Broad St is the old **cockpit**, a finely restored red-brick building that takes its name from the days when cock-fighting was how Welshpoolians spent their free time and money.

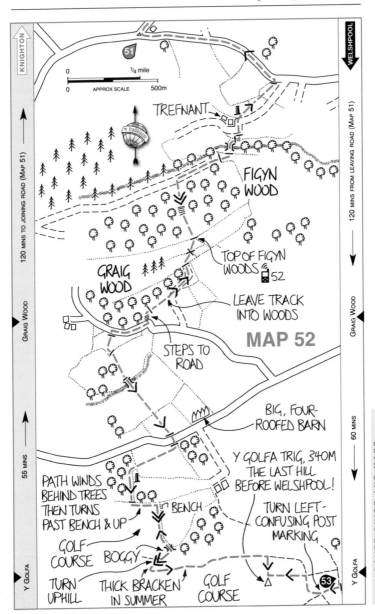

KNIGHTON

0 ¼ mile
APPROX SCALE
0 500m

WELSHPOOL

TREFNANT

FIGYN WOOD

120 MINS TO JOINING ROAD (MAP 51)

120 MINS FROM LEAVING ROAD (MAP 51)

GRAIG WOOD

TOP OF FIGYN WOODS 52

LEAVE TRACK INTO WOODS

GRAIG WOOD

MAP 52

STEPS TO ROAD

BIG, FOUR-ROOFED BARN

60 MINS

Y GOLFA TRIG, 340M
THE LAST HILL BEFORE WELSHPOOL!

55 MINS

PATH WINDS BEHIND TREES THEN TURNS PAST BENCH & UP

BENCH

TURN LEFT—CONFUSING POST MARKING

GOLF COURSE BOGGY

Y GOLFA

TURN UPHILL

THICK BRACKEN IN SUMMER

GOLF COURSE

53

Y GOLFA

ROUTE GUIDE AND MAPS

With some of that to spare yourself, consider a visit to **Powis Castle & Garden** (see box below).

Transport

[See pp46-50] With an early start out of Meifod, it's easy to catch a **train** to Shrewsbury (one stop; 22 mins; up to 5 daily) for connections to Birmingham, Manchester, South Wales (via Knighton) or back to Aberystwyth, via Machynlleth.

National Express' NX409 **coach** service will take you all the way to London (6 hours).

Celtic Travel's No X75 **bus** serves Llanidloes or Shrewsbury, and Lloyds Coaches' No T12 also stops here up to seven times a day between Machynlleth and Wrexham.

For a **taxi** call Wright Taxis ☎ 01938-552531 or Amber Cabs ☎ 01938-556611.

Services

The **Tourist Information Centre** (☎ 01938 552043; Tue-Sun 9.30am- 4.30pm; 💻 welshpooltowncouncil.gov.uk/services/tour ist-office) is by a small park on Church St where you can **buy train tickets** (the station is unmanned) as well as maps and guidebooks for Glyndŵr's Way. They can help with accommodation too.

There are no longer any banks in Welshpool so for an **ATM** head to one of the big **supermarkets**: there's a Tesco (Smithfield Rd; Mon-Sat 6am-midnight, Sun 10am-4pm) near the station; and a Morrison's (Berriew St; Mon-Sat 7am-9pm, Sun 10am-4pm) behind the museum. For groceries there's also Aldi (Mon-Sat 8am-10pm, Sun 10am-4pm) on Mill Lane, along with a couple of convenience stores on Broad St, including Premier (Mon-Fri 6am-8pm, Sat & Sun 7am-8pm) which also houses the **post office**.

There's a **launderette** next to the neo-classical former town hall on the High St. If you're setting off on the walk and have forgotten some item of **camping gear**, see what Alexander's (☎ 01938-552329; 💻 al exandersofwelshpool.co.uk; Mon-Sat 8am-5.30pm) at 29 Broad Street can do for you.

Where to stay

Coming into town, in an effort to confuse centuries of marauders the main street's name switches from Raven- to Mount- to High- then Broad Street and finally Severn Street in less than a mile. There isn't a huge range of lodging options here so take a peak on 💻 airbnb.co.uk too.

At 49 Mount St you'll pass *The Stone House* B&B (☎ 01938-691039; **fb**; 1D/1Tr both en suite) with rooms from £40pp (sgl occ £60).

❏ **POWIS CASTLE & GARDEN**   [off Map 54, p170]
💻 *nationaltrust.org.uk/powis-castle-and-garden; garden daily 10am-5pm, castle noon-4pm; £15)*

Less than a mile south-west of town, medieval Powis Castle looms dramatically over an Italianate garden. A hill fort since the Dark Ages, it later became a seat of the princes of Powys but was sacked in the early weeks of Glyndŵr's rebellion.

Today's castle is notable for housing the Clive Collection, treasures amassed by the controversial 18th-century figure, **Robert Clive** ('of India'), a Shropshire lad who, after a lucrative spell leading campaigns with the rapacious East India Company (EIC), ended up the richest self-made man in Europe. He bought himself a seat as an MP but in 1774, disgraced by parliamentary revelations of the EIC's conduct in India, and battling opium addiction, depression and other health issues, Clive took his own life aged just 49. A decade later, his oldest son Edward, who also served in India, married into the local Herbert family who occupied Powis castle at that time. Access to the Clive family's vast fortune helped fund the castle's heavy restoration in the Edwardian era.

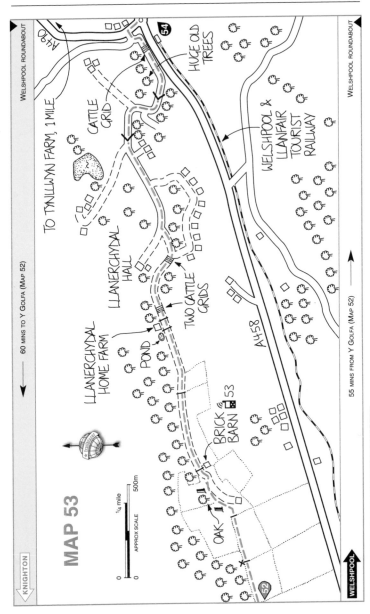

← 60 MINS TO Y GOLFA (MAP 52)

WELSHPOOL ROUNDABOUT

WELSHPOOL ROUNDABOUT

A490

54

TO TYNLLWYN FARM, 1 MILE

CATTLE GRID

HUGE OLD TREES

WELSHPOOL & LLANFAIR TOURIST RAILWAY

LLANERCHYDAL HALL

LLANERCHYDAL HOME FARM

POND

TWO CATTLE GRIDS

A458

MAP 53

¼ mile

APPROX SCALE

0   500m

BRICK BARN 53

OAK

WELSHPOOL

52

55 MINS FROM Y GOLFA (MAP 52)

ROUTE GUIDE AND MAPS

Welshpool MAP 54

Where to stay
3 Stone House B&B
11 Westwood Park Hotel
13 Royal Oak Hotel

Where to eat and drink
1 Raven Inn
2 Golden Bamboo
4 Andrew's Fish Bar
5 Tuck Box
6 Costa
7 Greggs
8 Coco
9 Baba Ali's
10 The Cornstore
12 Bay Tree Vintage Tea Room
13 Royal Oak Hotel
14 Silver Fish
15 Spice:UK
16 Spice Fusion
17 Welshpool Kebab House

WELSHPOOL ROUNDABOUT

15 MINS →

START OF GLYNDŴR'S WAY

END OF GLYNDŴR'S WAY

To Tynllwyn Farm B&B
(1 mile, 25mins, see text

Guilsfield Rd A490

A458

Brook St

Mount St

High St

Powells Lane

Bus stops

Car parks

Hall St

Broad St

Launderette

Old Town Hall

St Mary's

Boots

Mollie's Sweet Shop

Post Office

Alexanders

Cockpit

Church St

Red Bank

Salop Rd A458

Hospital

Aldi

Montgomery Canal

Mill Lane

Motte & bailey castle

Tow path to/from Buttington
Bridge on Offa's Dyke Path,
1.3 miles, 35mins &
Green Dragon Inn Camping,
1.7 miles, 45mins

B4381

A483

Railway station

Footbridge

Smithfield Rd

Tesco & ATM

Police station

Towpath

End/start of Glyndŵr's Way

Severn St

Tourist Info

Pharmacy Car park

Toilets

Y Lanfa Powysland Museum

Berriew St

Morrisons & ATM

Toilets

Car park

Deer Park

To Powis Castle

Park Lane

Gates to Powis Castle & Garden

0 100 200m

← 15 MINS

To Powis Castle

At the town centre crossroads is the upmarket **Royal Oak Hotel** (☎ 01938-552217; 🖥 royaloakwelshpool.co.uk; 4D/2T/1S/1Tr; ➴) with rooms from £66pp (sgl occ £116).

Five minutes walk from the centre is the **Westwood Park Hotel** (☎ 01938 553474; 🖥 westwoodparkhotel.co.uk; 2D/2T en suite, 3T shared bathroom; 🐾) on Salop Road, with rooms from £30-35pp (sgl occ £60). They can also arrange luggage transfer for walkers. Although they don't serve food (other than breakfast for guests), they will provide plates and cutlery for you to eat your own takeaway or snack food in their dining room.

Before you walk into town, a mile north of the Raven Square roundabout leads to **Tynllwyn Farm B&B** (off Map 54; ☎ 01938-553175; 🖥 tynllwynfarm.co.uk; 3D/2T all en suite) from £45pp (sgl occ £60). Evening meals are available by prior arrangement and they can also do luggage transfer. Call in advance for a pick-up as the short walk along the narrow A490 looks a bit dicey.

Your nearest **campsite** is the **Green Dragon Inn** (off Map 54; ☎ 01938-553076; **fb**) in **Buttington**, 2 miles (3.2km) north-east of town between the A458 and a railway line and close to Offa's Dyke. It's £19 per tent, and they also have camping **pods** (sleeps 2, from £50) and a bell tent (1D, £80, bedding not provided). They serve **food** every day (noon-9pm).

Where to eat and drink

While Welshpool may not be blessed with the finest eateries known to humanity, you do have a pretty good spread of the usuals short of a live Mongolian barbecue.

Just by the old town hall on Broad St there's a **Costa** (Mon-Sat 8am-5.30pm, Sun 8am-4.30pm) while early birds will gather at **Greggs** (Mon-Sat 6.30am-6pm, Sun 7.30am-5pm) nearby, or the **Coco Coffee House** (☎ 01938 552366; **fb**; Mon-Sat 7.30am-5pm, Sun 8am-4pm) over the road, with food including vegan options, to takeaway or eat in. Otherwise, grab a sandwich from the **Tuck Box** (**fb**; 8am-2.30pm) round the corner, or see what's just come

out of the oven at **The Little Welsh Bakery** (01938-552616; 🖥 thelittlewelshbakery.co .uk; **fb**; Mon-Sat 8.30am-4pm) at 39 Broad St. If you've come from Knighton you may have already sampled their wares at their sister shop in Llanidloes all those days ago.

On Church St **The Cornstore** (☎ 01938-554614; **fb**; Thur-Sat noon-2.30pm & 5:30-10pm; Sun noon-3.30pm) restaurant seems a better-than-average joint, with a great range of home-cooked lunch and dinner options. Nearby another popular spot is the **Bay Tree Vintage Tearoom** (☎ 01938-555456; **fb**; Mon-Thur 9am-5pm, Fri & Sat 9am-midnight) for indulgent cakes by day and burgers, steaks and cocktails on weekend evenings.

The **Royal Oak Hotel** (see Where to stay; **fb**) has a good restaurant with seasonal mains such as pan fried fillet of seabass (£20.95) and also does bar meals (daily noon-9pm) and afternoon teas (2-6pm, booking essential).

There are several other **pubs** along the main road all the way to the **Raven Inn** (☎ 01938-553101; 🖥 theraveninn.net; **fb**; 🐾; food daily noon-9.30pm) where they take 'dog-friendly' to another level with a menu of 'Dog's Dinners' especially for your four-legged companion! Humans can choose from a good selection of pub classics from £14.50.

You'd hope Robert Clive would be thrilled to learn Welshpool has two Indian restaurants: **Spice:UK** (☎ 01938 553431; 🖥 spice-uk.com; Sun-Thur 5-10.30pm. Fri & Sat 5-11.30pm) at 13 Berriew St, and **Spice Fusion** (☎ 01938 556669; Sun-Thur 5-11.30pm, Fri & Sat 5pm-1am) at 29 Severn St, both of which also do takeaway.

Next door the **Welshpool Kebab House** (☎ 01938-556215; 🖥 welshpool kebab.com; Mon-Thur 3-10.30pm, Fri noon-10.50pm, Sat 2.30-11pm, Sun 2.15-10.30pm) also serves pizzas and burgers.

For fish & chips it's **Silver Fish** (☎ 01938-553107; **fb**; Mon-Sat 11.30am-9pm) at 6 Berriew St or **Andrew's Fish Bar** (☎ 01938-522635; **fb**; Mon-Sat 11.30am-2.30pm & 4.30-9pm) at 32 High St.

You'll get Chinese food to go from **The Golden Bamboo** (☎ 01938-553570;

Wed-Mon 5-11pm) at 46 Mount St.

And finally, walkers of a certain age will find themselves drooling over the sugary delights inside *Mollie's Sweet Shop* opposite the Royal Oak; it's the sort of guilty pleasure you only find in provincial towns and includes those long-forgotten Pez dispensers.

Starting from Welshpool

Start here if you're walking Glyndŵr's Way from Welshpool to Knighton. Look for the Knighton direction arrow symbol with shaded overview text (as below) and follow the timings text with this symbol on one edge of each map, working back through the book. The shaded route summaries below describe the trail between significant places and are written for walking the path anti-clockwise (from north to south). For map profiles see the overview maps at the end of the book. For an overview of this information see the Village & town facilities table on pp32-3 and the Itineraries on pp34-7.

KNIGHTON>

KNIGHTON> WELSHPOOL TO MEIFOD   [MAPS 54-50]

It's a relatively short start to your big adventure, with a gradual ascent out of Welshpool to **Y Golfa hill** where you can excitedly scan what lies ahead. From here onwards you'll have a chance to get used to the trail's meanderings through Craig Wood and **Figyn Wood**, across the

Distance	11¼ miles (18.2km)
Ascent	1903ft (580m)
Time	5-6 hours
	WALKING TIME ONLY
	SEE P83 – ADD 20-30%

hills and fields, along backroads and through woods before alighting in **Meifod** on the River Vyrnwy. Better days lie ahead.

Note that there are **no villages, shops or services** on this stage so stock up in Welshpool before you set off.

[*Next route overview p164*]

APPENDIX A: THE PUMLUMON (PLYNLIMON) FAWR HORSESHOE

THE PUMLUMON FAWR HORSESHOE   [Maps A-E, pp175-9]

Distance	**12 miles (19.3km)**
Ascent	**2087ft (636m)**
Time	**7-8 hours**
WALKING TIME ONLY – ADD 20-30%	

It's unclear how the original there-and-back excursion to the 2467ft (752m) summit of **Pumlumon Fawr** became attached to the Glyndŵr's Way. It seems Richard Sale's pre-National Trail 1992 guidebook (see p45) was the first to blithely throw out the suggestion in a couple of lines. A 1999 report on the imminent National Trail considered adding a circular route to the site of the **Battle of Mynydd Hyddgen** (off Map D) where in 1401 Glyndŵr's army beat off a much larger force of English settlers and Flemish mercenaries, all of which helped bolster his campaign's Goliath-slaying reputation.

Whatever its origins, we've developed that idea into a satisfying **12 mile (19.3km) horseshoe circuit** with the clockwise return leg passing close to the undefined site of the battle. The tougher and initially pathless outbound section traverses **Open Access Land** (see p75) to the sources of the **River Severn** (Afon Hafron) and the **River Wye** – Wales' best-known rivers.

Navigation and terrain

Both ends of the horseshoe connect with the Glyndŵr's Way less than half a mile apart east of **Glaslyn** (Map 26). Distance-wise, the loop adds a mile over the backtracking option, but it's worth repeating that, until you reach the Severn's source (after 4 miles/6km), the eastern leg (outbound for clockwise walkers) traverses **barely walkable**, knee-high tussocks of heather and grass as well clumps of rushes concealing saturated sphagnum **bogs**. This is terrain which even lowly sheep are smart enough to avoid, while navigation is largely along fence lines. Apart from the summit cairn mounds, the only **waymarks** of any kind are a pair of white-topped posts near Pen Pumlumon Arwystli (see below). The western (return) leg is entirely unwaymarked but the unbroken paths and their forks are mostly clearer. Note that rights of way as shown on OS maps may not represent a navigable path on the ground.

For your walking pleasure we've published an edited **tracklog** on 🖥 wiki locs.org, search: 'Pumlumon Glyndŵr's Horseshoe'.

Planning

This is a **challenging** walk. Unless you're engaged in some sort of SAS selection march, this is not a route to tackle with anything more than a **small day-pack** and a forecast of **fine weather**. If it was closer to a town things would be easier, but starting and ending as it does in the middle of nowhere, we advise thinking carefully before breaking the hitherto steady rhythm of an uninterrupted Glyndŵr's traverse to grapple with this moorland outing.

On top of this you need to factor in that either end of our horseshoe is an hour's walk from the nearest lodgings at Dylife (see p124) so this excursion may end up covering more like **18 miles** (29km; 9-10hrs), door-to-door.

Ways to reduce that additional distance might be to arrange a pick-up from the **small roadside parking area** (Map 26, p126) by a gate on the Dylife road, less than a mile north of Glaslyn, or to **camp** two nights around Glaslyn, with **three days of provisions** to cover the 40+ miles between Llanidloes and Machynlleth via Pumlumon. (The shop in Staylittle may ease the task).

Which direction?

The route description below is based on a **clockwise** direction of travel, starting from the eastern end. Although, as already mentioned, this offers a challenging start in terms of terrain, things improve as you go on.

If you opt for a technically-easier (anti-clockwise) excursion from Glaslyn via our western leg, be warned that you'll find the deceptively level approach ends suddenly on the shores of **Llyn Llygad Rheidol** (Map D) tucked below Pumlumon Fawr's north face. At this point the path shoots up some 850ft (250m) in a mile.

Route description (clockwise)

Leave the Glywdwr's Way at the **pole** (Map A) marking the start of the short (and pointless) diversion off the jeep track leading west to Glaslyn. Hack south across the springy scrub, across a gully by a **mine ruin** and make your way southwards with effort, aiming for the west side of the valley, where a **narrow sheep trail** eases your southbound progress for a few hundred metres.

Breaking the horizon to the south-east is a conspicuously isolated plantation resembling a huge hangar. You're heading just right of it, so leave the sheep trail as it curves right round the south side of **Banc Bugeilyn**. Head south across country, dodging boggy rushes towards a **lone, rotund Christmas tree** (Norwegian spruce) on the south side of the saddle/watershed. There is a low fence to the east and another up ahead to the south. From the tree stagger uphill and cross the southern fence (the only such manoeuvre on this walk). Without walking aids you can ease the struggle by veering left to the unbarbed fence (as they all are up here) and use it as a handrail.

Things relent as you reach an unnamed high point (Map B; 1772ft/540m) at a **junction of fences**. Turn south-west with the fence still on your left, later turning south to reach the summit of **Carnfachbugeilyn** with a huge cairn mound built up into a 'crater'.

Continue south-west alongside a fence and where it takes a sharp turn to the south, you'll soon cross a **stile** where the enviably well-paved **Severn Way** starts at a nearby cairn with an '1865' boundary marker overlooking a couple of peaty pools. This is the **source of the Severn**, at 220 miles (354km) Britain's longest river, though the official marker post, where an actual stream sometimes forms, is over the stile and 300m back down towards the Hafren Forest. Terrain-wise, the tougher part of this circuit is now over; from this point until you leave Llyn Llygad Rheidol, grassy paths are both easy to follow and to walk on. Carry on south with a fence now on your right, over a saddle and up.

Where the fence turns a corner, a basic **stile** (Map C) sees your trail continue across an unfenced expanse past a lone **white-topped post** and a sparse spruce plantation to the east. Another white-topped pole marks a **right fork** within sight of three huge, rock-pile cairn shelters at the summit of **Pen Pumlumon Arwystli**. The trail continues south-west then west, down to a

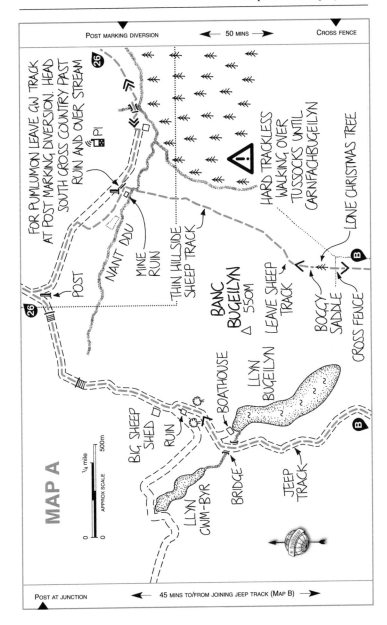

MAP A

APPROX SCALE

¼ mile

500m

POST AT JUNCTION

45 MINS TO/FROM JOINING JEEP TRACK (MAP B)

POST MARKING DIVERSION

50 MINS

CROSS FENCE

FOR PUMLUMON LEAVE CWJ TRACK AT POST MARKING DIVERSION. HEAD SOUTH CROSS COUNTRY PAST RUIN AND OVER STREAM

P!

26

POST

26

NANT DDU

MINE RUIN

THIN HILLSIDE SHEEP TRACK

HARD TRACKLESS WALKING OVER TUSSOCKS UNTIL CARNFACHBUGEILYN

LONE CHRISTMAS TREE

BANC BUGEILYN △ 550M

LEAVE SHEEP TRACK

BOGGY SADDLE

B

CROSS FENCE

BIG SHEEP SHED

RUIN

BOATHOUSE

LLYN BUGEILYN

LLYN CWM-BYR

BRIDGE

JEEP TRACK

B

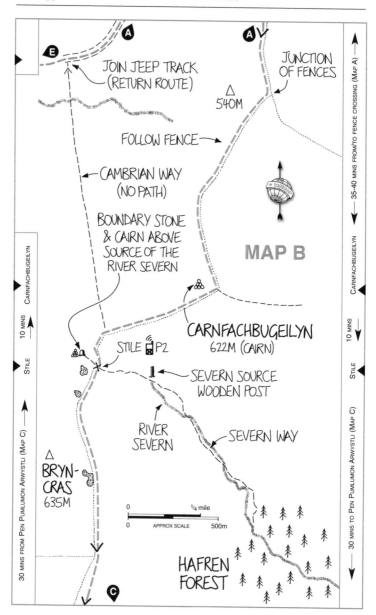

A

E

JOIN JEEP TRACK
(RETURN ROUTE)

A

JUNCTION
OF FENCES

△ 540M

FOLLOW FENCE →

CAMBRIAN WAY
(NO PATH)

BOUNDARY STONE
& CAIRN ABOVE
SOURCE OF THE
RIVER SEVERN

MAP B

CARNFACHBUGEILYN
622M (CAIRN)

STILE 📱 P2

SEVERN SOURCE
WOODEN POST

RIVER
SEVERN

SEVERN WAY

△ BRYN-
CRAS
635M

0   ¼ mile
0   APPROX SCALE   500m

HAFREN
FOREST

CARNFACHBUGEILYN   10 MINS   STILE   30 MINS FROM PEN PUMLUMON ARWYSTLI (MAP C)

35-40 MINS FROM/TO FENCE CROSSING (MAP A)   CARNFACHBUGEILYN   10 MINS   STILE   30 MINS TO PEN PUMLUMON ARWYSTLI (MAP C)

C

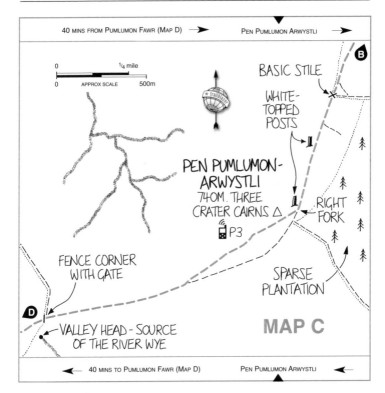

40 MINS FROM PUMLUMON FAWR (MAP D) →   PEN PUMLUMON ARWYSTLI →

B

BASIC STILE

WHITE-
TOPPED
POSTS

PEN PUMLUMON-
ARWYSTLI
740M. THREE
CRATER CAIRNS △
📱 P3

RIGHT
FORK

FENCE CORNER
WITH GATE

SPARSE
PLANTATION

MAP C

D

VALLEY HEAD - SOURCE
OF THE RIVER WYE

0 ... ¼ mile
0 ... APPROX SCALE ... 500m

← 40 MINS TO PUMLUMON FAWR (MAP D)   PEN PUMLUMON ARWYSTLI ←

saddle and up to another fence corner with a gate. At 2316ft (706m) you're now overlooking a valley head and the **start of the River Wye** (Afon Gwy) which flows for 132 miles (212km) south-east via Llangurig, Hay and Chepstow to the Bristol Channel.

Up ahead a small cairn and maybe a small pool marks **Pen Pumlumon Llygad-bychan** (Map D), also know as 'Plynlimon East Top'. From here a clear path leads down to another saddle marked by a **big, white-topped cairn** then climbs beside a fence up to **Pumlumon Fawr**. Suddenly you're at the trig point set among more cairn mounds. Looking north you might make out Cader Idris and the Aran summits. To the south are the Brecons and below you to the west, the vast Nant y Moch reservoir, already the second of four barrages damming the short-lived Afon Rheidol.

Your route back to Glaslyn now passes Pumlumon's northern cairn where a **clear grassy path** drops steeply to a small saddle right below Pumlumon Fach. It forks right to drop again to meet the access track at the small reservoir of **Llyn Llygad Rheidol**. Cross the barrage wall and turn north-west once you've located the thin trail paralleling the Nant y Llyn stream. You may lose

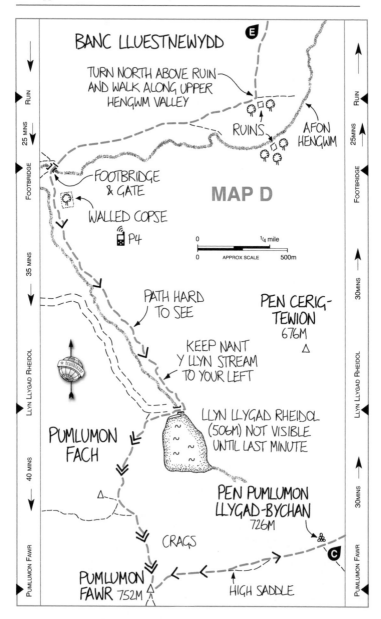

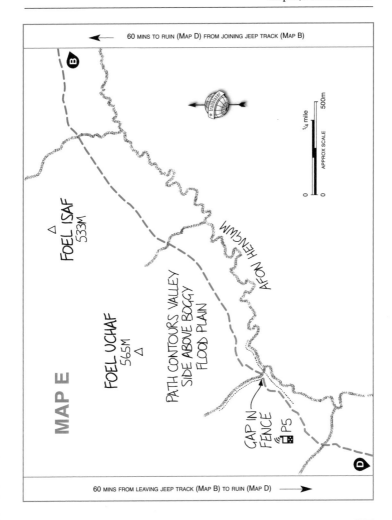

the path occasionally but the stream on the left is your guide. Below, eventually you'll spy a **small walled copse** and beyond it, a **gated footbridge** over the Afon Hengwm crossing back into Powys, just before it meets the Afon Hyddgen. You'll have hopefully spotted a path running east across the lower slopes of Banc Lluestnewydd, hopping over a few boggy patches along the way. Near a **crumbling ruin** alongside a wind-bent ash tree, turn north-east into the upper **Hengwm valley**.

At the head of the valley (Map E), OS maps unhelpfully indicate a 'path' cutting over a 1706ft (520m) spur leading over to **Llyn Bugeilyn**. This may be a right of way but any trail is long lost in more foot-trapping tussocks where waist-deep pits lie hidden in the rushes. Better to carry on as you were, contouring round the east side of the spur where you'll meet a **jeep track** (Map B) and rejoin the northbound Cambrian Way which leads to the **bridge** (Map A) over the stream linking Llyn Bugeilyn and Llyn Cwm-byr. You can now switch back to autopilot. Nearby is a boathouse and up ahead you'll pass a stone ruin close to a huge corrugated iron sheep shed. Follow the track uphill to **rejoin Glyndŵr's Way** south of Glaslyn.

APPENDIX B – CYCLING THE WAY

If you're a keen cyclist or even a mountain biker, there'll be many occasions on the Glyndŵr's Way where you might wish you were gliding along on a bike, not least when foot-pounding the deserted **country lanes** which make up over a quarter (36 miles/58km) of the walk. At other times you'll be living out your Steve McQueen fantasies, bombing across lush grassy fields, but without the Nazis on your tail. The National Trails Glyndŵr's map page even recommends a few token cycling sections, but there are many more. Including the backroads, around **80%** of this National Trail is rideable.

Legally, cycling is not permitted on **footpaths** (yellow arrow roundel with a black footprint graphic), but the walk switches constantly between footpaths (short dashes on OS maps; about 40km in total) and blue-roundeled **bridleways** (longer dashes on OS maps) as well as rare **byways** (red roundel) along which you can also ride. So on Stage 1 you can legally pedal from Llangunllo nearly all the way to Felindre; a fabulous ride across Beacon Hill common (see Maps 4-7) that can be done in less than four hours. Stage 2 is rideable nearly all the way to Abbeycwmhir – another great day in and out of the saddle. It's the same on Stages 3, 5, 6 and 7 which are between 75–100% rideable. Stages 4, 8 and 9 are 65% rideable, and where they're not you can push or find another way round. Highlighting the rideable sections on the *A-Z Glyndŵr's Way* OS map booklet (see p43) is a particularly easy way of visualising what's possible and is a good back-up map anyway.

The sections you ought not ride or want to avoid (chiefly the **stile-heavy** eastern approach to Abbeycwmhir, see Map 13, or the first two miles north of Llangadfan, see Map 43) are easily avoided on deserted backroads. Finding other country lanes or byways all adds to the fun. Just remember, smoothly asphalted lanes can be as **hilly** as the trail, and cycling means episodes of high exertion followed by rest, versus the walker's largely steady all-day march.

❏ GLYNDŴR'S WAY BY BIKE

	Distance Km	Legally cyclable	Footpath Km	Tarmac Km
Knighton–Felindre	25	85% nearly all from Llangunllo	3.5	3
Felindre–Abbeycwmhir	25	95% bar end at Abbeycwmhir	0.5	8.5
Abbeycwmhir–Llanidloes	25	75% tiring gullies	5.5	9.8
Llanidloes–Dylife	21	65% deserted footpaths	8	5.4
Dylife–Machynlleth	25	100%	0	3.5
Machynlleth–Llanbrynmair	25	80% Peneloes to high bench	4	5
Llanbrynmair–Lake Vyrnwy	30	85% moors and forest tracks	4.5	7.3
Lake Vyrnwy–Meifod	23	65% riverside, deserted FP	8	7.7
Meifod–Welshpool	18	65% deserted footpaths	6	7.5
Totals			**40**	**57.7**

Note: all figures estimated. GW 18% footpath, 27% tarmac (82% cyclable)

There'll be times when, even if you could ride up in the lowest gear, the energy expended will be much greater than simply hopping off and pushing.

A couple of descents, like westbound off Foel Fadian (see Map 27), are initially **too steep** and loose to ride safely on a loaded bike, certainly alone. Anyway, at times it's more relaxing to walk along, pushing the bike and enjoy the scenery. Realistically, the hundreds of **gates** will slow you right down, so consistently covering two walking stages in one day – about 30 miles – will be on the limit unless you're very fit. And because of those gates, we found sprung **dropper seat posts** are very much not just another MTB gimmick.

Hills notwithstanding, much will depend on the proportion of easily rideable tracks and asphalted lanes on a given day (elevation gains are broadly similar). In dry conditions the tracks and trails are never rough enough to warrant full suspension (fat tyres help of course), but in high summer patches of impenetrable bracken will be an effort to ride through, and forests of tall, dense thistles will pound your knuckles and shins.

We've cycled Glyndŵr's Way on both a conventional hardtail MTB as well as a top-of-the-range full suspension e-MTB. For more, follow the link from the Glyndŵr's page on 🖳 trailblazer-guides.com or see our video review on 🖳 youtube.com (search eBikepacking Glyndwr's Way).

APPENDIX C – GLOSSARY OF WELSH WORDS

aber	river mouth	*dinas*	hill-fortress, city	*mynach*	monk
afon	river	*disgwylfa*	viewpoint,	*mynydd*	mountain
allt	steep hillside		lookout	*nant*	brook
bach	little	*dol, dolau*	meadow	*newydd*	new
betws	church	*ffin*	boundary	*pandy*	fulling mill
blaen	head, source	*ffridd*	lower part of hill	*pen*	head, top
bran	crow	*ffynnon*	spring	*pentre*	village
bryn	hillside	*gwaun*	moorland, pasture	*plas*	hall, mansion
bwlch	pass	*hafod*	summer dwelling	*pont*	bridge
cae	field	*hen*	old	*porth*	gateway
caer	fortress	*hendre*	winter dwelling	*pwll*	pool
carreg	stone, rock	*heol*	road or street	*rhos*	moorland
castell	castle	*isaf*	lower	*rhyd*	ford
cefn	ridge	*llan*	enclosure, church	*tref*	homestead, hamlet
celli	grove, copse	*llanerch*	glade	*twyn*	hillock
clawdd	dyke, bank, hedge	*llech*	slab, stone	*ty*	house
coch	red	*llwyd*	grey or brown	*tyddyn*	smallholding
coed	wood	*maes*	field	*uchaf*	higher, upper
cwm	valley	*mawr*	great	*ynys*	island
cwrt	court	*moel*	bare hill	*ystrad*	vale, valley

APPENDIX D – TAKING A DOG

TAKING A DOG ALONG THE WAY

Many are the rewards that await those prepared to make the extra effort required to bring their best friend along the trail. You shouldn't underestimate the amount of work involved, though. Indeed, just about every decision you make will be influenced by the fact that you've got a dog: how you plan to travel to the start of the trail, where you're going to stay, how far you're going to walk each day, where you're going to rest and where you're going to eat in the evening etc.

If you're also sure your dog can cope with (and, just as importantly, will enjoy) walking 10 miles or more a day for several days in a row, you need to start preparing accordingly. Extra thought also needs to go into your itinerary. The best starting point is to study the village and town facilities table on pp32-3 (and the advice on pp30-1), and plan where to stop and where to buy food.

Looking after your dog

To begin with, you need to make sure that your own dog is fully **inoculated** against the usual doggy illnesses, and also up to date with regard to **worm pills** (eg Drontal) and **flea preventatives** such as Frontline – they are, after all, following in the pawprints of many a dog before them, some of whom may well have left fleas or other parasites on the trail that now lie in wait for their next meal to arrive. **Pet insurance** is also a very good idea; if you've already got insurance, do check that it will cover a trip such as this.

On the subject of looking after your dog's health, perhaps the most important implement you can take with you is the **plastic tick remover**, available from vets for a couple of quid. These removers, while fiddly, help you to remove the tick safely (ie without leaving its head behind buried under the dog's skin).

Being in unfamiliar territory also makes it more likely that you and your dog could become separated. For this reason, make sure your dog has a **tag with your contact details on it** (a mobile phone number would be best if you are carrying one with you); you could also consider having it **microchipped** for further security.

When to keep your dog on a lead

● **On mountain tops** It's a sad fact that, every year, a few dogs lose their lives falling over the edge of steep slopes.

● **When crossing farmland**, particularly in the lambing season (around May) when your dog can scare the sheep, causing them to lose their young. Farmers are allowed by law to shoot at and kill any dogs that they consider are worrying their sheep. During lambing, most farmers would prefer it if you didn't bring your dog at all. The exception is if your dog is being attacked by cows. A couple of years ago there were three deaths in the UK caused by walkers being trampled as they tried to rescue their dogs from the attentions of cattle. The advice in this instance is to let go of the lead, head speedily to a position of safety (usually the other side of the field gate or stile) and call your dog to you.

● **Around ground-nesting birds** It's important to keep your dog under control when crossing an area where certain species of birds nest on the ground. Most dogs love foraging around in the woods but make sure you have permission to do so; some woods are used as 'nurseries' for game birds and dogs are only allowed through them if they are on a lead.

What to pack

You've probably already got a good idea of what to bring to keep your dog alive and happy, but the following is a checklist:

● **Food/water bowl** Foldable cloth bowls are popular with walkers, being light and take up little room in the rucksack. You can get also get a water-bottle-and-bowl combination, where the bottle folds into a 'trough' from which the dog can drink.

● **Lead and collar** An extendable one is probably preferable for this sort of trip. Make sure both lead and collar are in good condition – you don't want either to snap on the trail, or you may end up carrying your dog through sheep fields until a replacement can be found.

● **Medication** You'll know if you need to bring any lotions or potions.

● **Tick remover** See p183.

● **Bedding** A simple blanket may suffice, or you can opt for something more elaborate if you aren't carrying your own luggage.

● **Poo bags** Essential.

● **Hygiene wipes** For cleaning your dog after it's rolled in stuff.

● **A favourite toy** Helps prevent your dog from pining for the entire walk.

● **Food/water** Remember to bring treats as well as regular food to keep up the mutt's morale. That said, if your dog is anything like mine the chances are they'll spend most of the walk dining on rabbit droppings and sheep poo anyway.

● **Corkscrew stake** Available from camping or pet shops, this will help you to keep your dog secure in one place while you set up camp/doze.

● **Raingear** It can rain!

● **Old towels** For drying your dog.

When it comes to packing, I always leave an exterior pocket of my rucksack empty so I can put used poo bags in there (for deposit at the first bin we come to). I always like to keep all the dog's kit together and separate from the other luggage (usually inside a plastic bag inside my rucksack). I have also seen several dogs sporting their own 'doggy rucksack', so they can carry their own food, water, poo etc – which certainly reduces the burden on their owner!

Cleaning up after your dog

It is extremely important that dog owners behave in a responsible way when walking the path. Dog excrement should be cleaned up. In towns, villages and fields where animals graze or which will be cut for silage, hay etc, you need to pick up and bag the excrement.

Staying with your dog

In this guide we have used the symbol 🐕 to denote where a hotel, pub or B&B welcomes dogs. However, this always needs to be arranged in advance and some places may charge extra. Before you turn up always double check whether the place where you would like to stay accepts dogs and whether there is space for them; many places have only one or two rooms suitable for people with dogs.

When it comes to eating, most landlords allow dogs in at least a section of their pubs, though few restaurants do. Make sure you always ask first and ensure your dog doesn't run around the pub but is secured to your table or a radiator.

Henry Stedman

APPENDIX E: GPS & WHAT3WORDS WAYPOINT REFERENCES

Each waypoint below was taken on the route at the reference number marked on the map as below. **GPS references** are given below. **What3words references** that correspond to these waypoints are also shown here and may be particularly useful in an emergency (see p20). Gpx files for waypoints can be downloaded from 🖳 trailblazer-guides.com.

WPT	OS GRID REF	WHAT3WORDS	DESCRIPTION
01	52.34423, -3.07595	///leaves.diner.iterative	Turn west up Ebrandy hill
02	52.33563, -3.12453	///broad.gossiping.trespass	Footbridge over brook
03	52.33357, -3.14638	///tipping.vibrating.proven	Leave lane down into woods
04	52.36526, -3.18842	///premiums.trips.niece	Beacon Hill crossroads
05	52.37301, -3.20564	///mess.bogus.dockers	Turn left onto moorland path
06	52.38252, -3.23262	///petition.recur.torn	Turn north
07	52.41079, -3.22245	///club.monorail.prestige	Turn off track, head north
08	52.42308, -3.25428	///wiring.seemingly.squeaking	Rhuvid farmyard
08b	52.42112, -3.29425	///sunk.chum.spoons	Cross track by trailer, head uphill
9	52.40512, -3.29260	///darkest.square.licks	Join road by sheep pen
10	52.39399, -3.32902	///ember.elect.rests	Llanbadarn shop
11	52.38567, -3.35785	///tailed.tangent.transmit	Footbridge over bog, head uphill
12	52.36311, -3.34552	///hiked.swim.trophy	Leave road through gate up into woods
13	52.33112, -3.36431	///heartburn.strength.arose	Leave lane over stile
13b	52.33449, -3.39858	///results.effort.croaking	Cross track in woods
14	52.34338, -3.40649	///shine.flush.braked	Turn left for Esgair farms
15	52.36422, -3.42895	///proudest.punters.verse	Footbridge before woods
16	52.38596, -3.45921	///gobbling.fats.withdrew	Leave road onto forestry track
17	52.41622, -3.45912	///quail.pasta.shorter	Left then right by quarry
18	52.42723, -3.46438	///constants.drawn.corn	Gate at top of field
19	52.44244, -3.50570	///compacts.lightbulb.nipped	Join Gorn Road
20	52.45254, -3.54275	///dressing.crate.elbowing	Path behind houses
21	52.47202, -3.54843	///difficult.punch.wording	Leave access track up into trees
22	52.47046, -3.60955	///thrashed.dose.refuse	Join road above reservoir
23	52.48096, -3.64005	///loaders.eventful.motored	Footbridge with gate
24	52.50935, -3.66092	///combining.relocated.premiums	Gate and down across field
25	52.52731, -3.67590	///hits.flamenco.moral	Track down to Dylife
26	52.53804, -3.72276	///installs.besotted.announced	Leave track for path to Foel Fadian
27	52.54580, -3.74620	///cheaply.compelled.mankind	Gate
28	52.55430, -3.78887	///pulse.tram.stocky	Copse
29	52.54032, -3.81206	///isolated.dusty.munch	Top of steep climb
30	52.56000, -3.83908	///fragments.pokers.disgraced	Gate after forest
31	52.58668, -3.85631	///confronts.dices.bangle	Roman Steps
32	52.59685, -3.78572	///momentous.summaries.lunging	Two gates
33	52.60104, -3.76816	///waking.places.backup	Gate off driveway
34	52.61823, -3.73202	///unpacked.tint.because	Gate in fields
35	52.62635, -3.70444	///toward.pats.margin	Leave fence line, go uphill
36	52.63422, -3.65352	///reserves.deeds.knots	Bench with a view

WPT	OS GRID REF	WHAT3WORDS	DESCRIPTION
37	52.61635, -3.60499	///refer.trickling.lawfully	Stile
38	52.62865, -3.59946	///minute.rules.paraded	At post leave track
39	52.64662, -3.56207	///executive.stuck.enlighten	Gated footbridge over bog
40	52.64749, -3.53268	///twinkling.plea.object	Bench by chapel
41	52.66555, -3.49696	///frown.chosen.intestine	OS maps diverge from way-marked route
42	52.67819, -3.47657	///paces.scuba.gossip	Gate to woodland boardwalks
43	52.68904, -3.45850	///exact.majors.fishery	Gate off driveway
44	52.72115, -3.47718	///physics.ironic.usages	Leave track down path
45	52.75328, -3.46174	///wharfs.pots.reefs	High point
45b	52.74530, -3.43948	///interlude.routine.mastering	Steps up to woods
46	52.73296, -3.44404	///pampering.other.horns	After new steps: right, gate sharp left
47	52.71723, -3.38599	///efficient.combines.storyline	Ann Griffiths plaque
48	52.71089, -3.36507	///escalated.unto.fattest	Ruin in meadow
49	52.70251, -3.30093	///cassettes.remarking.mysteries	Gate between fields
50	52.70636, -3.27015	///impulse.irrigate.kindest	Indistinct post
51	52.69497, -3.23488	///broadens.tall.arranged	Shed
52	52.67127, -3.21588	///head.crab.submitted	Top of Figyn Woods
53	52.65761, -3.19344	///streetcar.cutaway.grudges	Brick barn

Pumlumon Fawr Horseshoe side trip

P1	*52.52341, -3.71894*	*///eventful.flashing.predict*	*Leave GW at fork*
P2	*52.49481, -3.73972*	*///lance.racetrack.outreach*	*Stile by Severn source*
P3	*52.47484, -3.74600*	*///tucked.lushly.doctors*	*Crater cairns Arwystli*
P4	*52.48630, -3.79081*	*///tamed.universally.reinvest*	*Walled copse*
P5	*52.49941, -3.76722*	*///difficult.neatly.narrating*	*Gap in fence*

INDEX

Map key

♠	Where to stay	⊞	Library/bookstore	● Other
○	Where to eat and drink	@	Internet	CP Car park
Λ	Campsite	⊤	Museum/gallery	🚍 Bus station/stop
⊠	Post Office	✝	Church/cathedral	═☐═ Rail line & station
£	Bank/ATM	⊤	Public telephone	▢ Park
ⓘ	Tourist Information	☒	Public toilet	📱082 GPS waypoint
		□	Building	

Glyndŵr's Way	Gate	Water
Other path	Stile	Trees/forest
4 x 4 track	Kissing gate	Trig point △
Road	Bridge	Guide post
Steps	Hedge	Car park CP
Slope/steep slope	Fence	Map continuation ❺ ❽ (black = clockwise red = anti-clockwise)

Symbols used in text

⬮ Bathtub in at least one room   Ⓛ packed lunch available if requested in advance

fb indicates a Facebook page   🐕 Dogs allowed subject to prior arrangement

Direction indicators on map side bars

 Walking clockwise from Knighton to Welshpool

 Walking anti-clockwise from Welshpool to Knighton

 Route to Welshpool continues on Map 5

 Route to Knighton continues on Map 8

We've applied to destinations which are closer to home Trailblazer's proven formula for publishing definitive practical route guides for adventurous travellers. Britain's network of long-distance trails enables the walker to explore some of the finest landscapes in the country's best walking areas. These are guides that are user-friendly, practical, informative and environmentally sensitive.

'The same attention to detail that distinguishes its other guides has been brought to bear here'.

THE SUNDAY TIMES

● **Unique mapping features** In many walking guidebooks the reader has to read a route description then try to relate it to the map. Our guides are much easier to use because walking directions, tricky junctions, places to stay and eat, points of interest and walking times are all written onto the maps themselves in the places to which they apply. With their uncluttered clarity, these are not general-purpose maps but fully edited maps drawn by walkers for walkers.

● **Largest-scale walking maps** At a scale of just under 1:20,000 (8cm or 3¹/₈ inches to one mile) the maps in these guides are bigger than even the most detailed British walking maps currently available in the shops.

● **Not just a trail guide – includes where to stay, where to eat and public transport** Our guidebooks cover the complete walking experience, not just the route. Accommodation options for all budgets are provided (pubs, hotels, B&Bs, campsites, bunkhouses, hostels) as well as places to eat. Detailed public transport information for all access points to each trail means that there are itineraries for all walkers, for hiking the entire route as well as for day or weekend walks.

Cleveland Way *Henry Stedman*, 1st edn, ISBN 978-1-905864-91-1, 240pp, 98 maps

Coast to Coast *Henry Stedman*, 10th edn, ISBN 978-1-912716-25-8, 268pp, 109 maps

Cornwall Coast Path (SW Coast Path Pt 2) *Stedman & Newton*, 7th edn, ISBN 978-1-912716-26-5, 352pp, 142 maps

Cotswold Way *Tricia & Bob Hayne*, 5th edn, ISBN 978-1-912716-41-8, 204pp, 53 maps

Dales Way *Henry Stedman*, 2nd edn, ISBN 978-1-912716-30-2, 192pp, 50 maps

Dorset & South Devon (SW Coast Path Pt 3) *Stedman & Newton*, 3rd edn, ISBN 978-1-912716-34-0, 340pp, 97 maps

Exmoor & North Devon (SW Coast Path Pt I) *Stedman & Newton*, 3rd edn, ISBN 978-1-9912716-24-1, 224pp, 68 maps

Glyndŵr's Way *Chris Scott*, 1st edn, ISBN 978-1-912716-32-6, 220pp, 70 maps

Great Glen Way *Jim Manthorpe*, 2nd edn, ISBN 978-1-912716-10-4, 184pp, 50 maps

Hadrian's Wall Path *Henry Stedman*, 7th edn, ISBN 978-1-912716-37-1, 250pp, 60 maps

London LOOP *Henry Stedman*, 1st edn, ISBN 978-1-912716-21-0, 236pp, 60 maps

Norfolk Coast Path & Peddars Way *Alexander Stewart*, 2nd edn, ISBN 978-1-912716-39-5, 224pp, 75 maps

North Downs Way *Henry Stedman*, 2nd edn, ISBN 978-1-905864-90-4, 240pp, 98 maps

Offa's Dyke Path *Keith Carter*, 6th edn, ISBN 978-1-912716-42-5, 268pp, 98 maps

Pembrokeshire Coast Path *Jim Manthorpe*, 6th edn, 978-1-912716-13-5, 236pp, 96 maps

Pennine Way *Stuart Greig*, 6th edn, ISBN 978-1-912716-33-3, 272pp, 138 maps

The Ridgeway *Nick Hill*, 5th edn, ISBN 978-1-912716-20-3, 208pp, 53 maps

South Downs Way *Jim Manthorpe*, 8th edn, ISBN 978-1-912716-47-0, 204pp, 60 maps

Thames Path *Joel Newton*, 3rd edn, ISBN 978-1-912716-27-2, 256pp, 99 maps

West Highland Way *Charlie Loram*, 8th edn, ISBN 978-1-912716-29-6, 224pp, 60 maps

'The Trailblazer series stands head, shoulders, waist and ankles above the rest. They are particularly strong on mapping ...'
THE SUNDAY TIMES

TRAILBLAZER TITLE LIST

Adventure Cycle-Touring Handbook
Adventure Motorcycling Handbook
Australia by Rail
Cleveland Way (British Walking Guide)
Coast to Coast (British Walking Guide)
Cornwall Coast Path (British Walking Guide)
Cotswold Way (British Walking Guide)
The Cyclist's Anthology
Dales Way (British Walking Guide)
Dorset & Sth Devon Coast Path (British Walking Gde)
Exmoor & Nth Devon Coast Path (British Walking Gde)
Glyndŵr's Way (British Walking Guide)
Great Glen Way (British Walking Guide)
Hadrian's Wall Path (British Walking Guide)
Himalaya by Bike – a route and planning guide
Iceland Hiking – with Reykjavik City Guide
Inca Trail, Cusco & Machu Picchu
Japan by Rail
Kilimanjaro – the trekking guide (includes Mt Meru)
London Loop (British Walking Guide)
London to Walsingham Camino
Madeira Walks – 37 selected day walks
Moroccan Atlas – The Trekking Guide
Morocco Overland (4x4/motorcycle/mountainbike)
Nepal Trekking & The Great Himalaya Trail
Norfolk Coast Path & Peddars Way (British Walking Gde)
North Downs Way (British Walking Guide)
Offa's Dyke Path (British Walking Guide)
Overlanders' Handbook – worldwide driving guide
Pembrokeshire Coast Path (British Walking Guide)
Pennine Way (British Walking Guide)
Peru's Cordilleras Blanca & Huayhuash – Hiking/Biking
Pilgrim Pathways: 1-2 day walks on Britain's sacred ways
The Railway Anthology
The Ridgeway (British Walking Guide)
Scottish Highlands – Hillwalking Guide
The Silk Roads – a route and planning guide
Sinai – the trekking guide
South Downs Way (British Walking Guide)
Thames Path (British Walking Guide)
Tour du Mont Blanc
Trans-Canada Rail Guide
Trans-Siberian Handbook
Trekking in the Everest Region
The Walker's Anthology
The Walker's Anthology – further tales
West Highland Way (British Walking Guide)

For more information about Trailblazer and our
expanding range of guides, for guidebook updates or
for credit card mail order sales visit our website:

trailblazer-guides.com

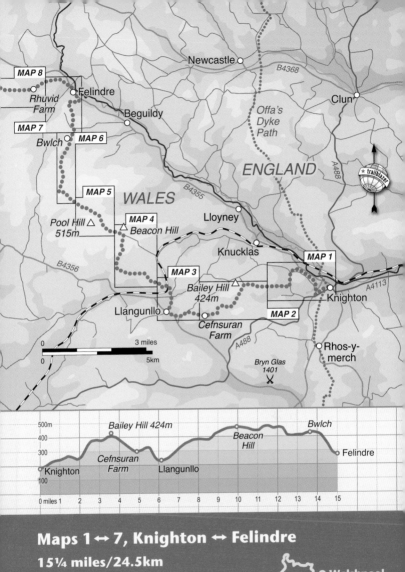

MAP 8
Rhuvid Farm
Felindre
MAP 7
Beguildy
Newcastle
B4368
Clun
Offa's Dyke Path
ENGLAND
Bwlch
MAP 6
A488
WALES
B4355
MAP 5
Lloyney
Pool Hill △ 515m
MAP 4
Beacon Hill
Knucklas
MAP 1
B4356
MAP 3
Bailey Hill 424m △
Knighton
A4113
Llangunllo
Cefnsuran Farm
MAP 2
A488
Rhos-y-merch
3 miles
5km
Bryn Glas 1401

500m
400
Bailey Hill 424m
Cefnsuran Farm
Beacon Hill
Bwlch
300
Felindre
Knighton
Llangunllo
100
0 miles 1 2 3 4 5 6 7 8 9 10 11 12 13 14 15

Maps 1 ↔ 7, Knighton ↔ Felindre

15¼ miles/24.5km

◁ WELSHPOOL **8hrs**

KNIGHTON ▷ **8hrs**

Note: Add 20-30% to these times for stops

Welshpool

Felindre
Knighton

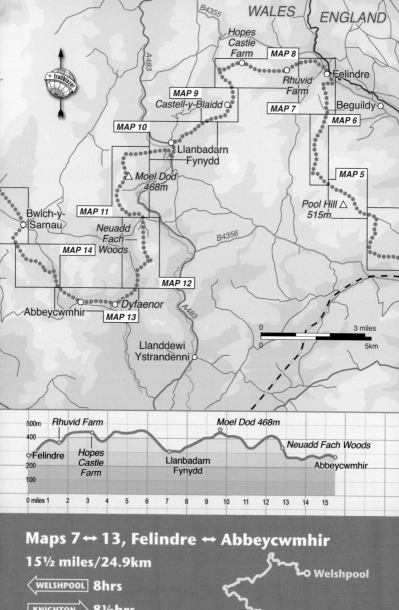

WALES   ENGLAND

B4355

Hopes Castle Farm

MAP 8

Rhuvid Farm

Felindre

MAP 9

Castell-y-Blaidd

MAP 7

Beguildy

MAP 10

MAP 6

Llanbadarn Fynydd

△ *Moel Dod 468m*

MAP 5

Pool Hill △ *515m*

Bwlch-y-Sarnau

MAP 11

Neuadd Fach Woods

MAP 14

B4356

MAP 12

Abbeycwmhir

Dyfaenor

MAP 13

A483

Llanddewi Ystrandenni

0 _____ 3 miles

0 _____ 5km

Elevation profile

500m		*Rhuvid Farm*							*Moel Dod 468m*			

400

Felindre

Hopes Castle Farm

300

Neuadd Fach Woods

Llanbadarn Fynydd

Abbeycwmhir

200

100

0 miles 1   2   3   4   5   6   7   8   9   10   11   12   13   14   15

Maps 7 ↔ 13, Felindre ↔ Abbeycwmhir

15½ miles/24.9km

◁ WELSHPOOL **8hrs**

KNIGHTON ▷ **8½hrs**

Note: Add 20-30% to these times for stops

○ **Welshpool**

Abbeycwmhir ○

○ **Felindre**

○ **Knighton**

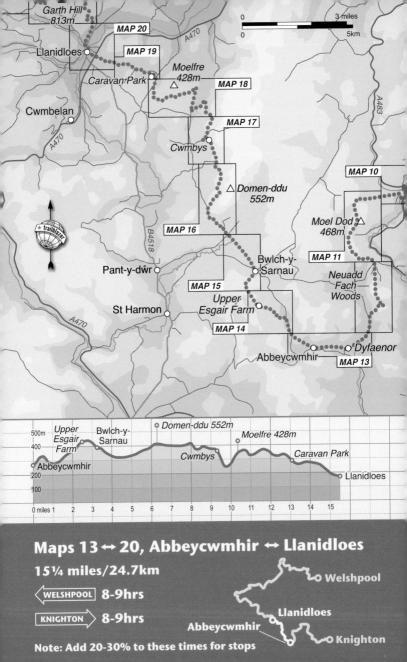

Maps 13 ↔ 20, Abbeycwmhir ↔ Llanidloes

15¼ miles/24.7km

WELSHPOOL 8-9hrs

KNIGHTON 8-9hrs

Note: Add 20-30% to these times for stops

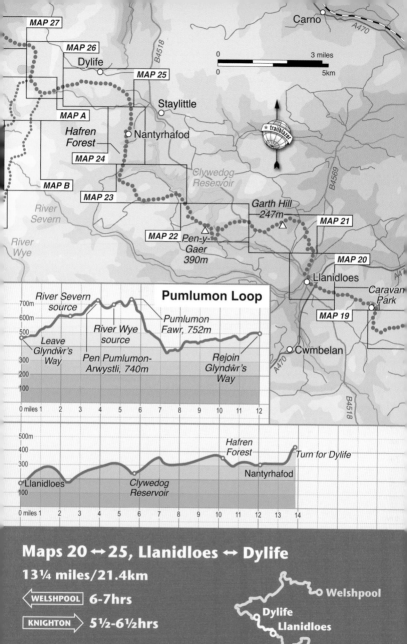

Pumlumon Loop

(elevation profile)

River Severn source
River Wye source
Pumlumon Fawr, 752m
Leave Glyndŵr's Way
Pen Pumlumon-Arwystli, 740m
Rejoin Glyndŵr's Way

700m
600m
500m
300m
200m
100m

0 miles 1 2 3 4 5 6 7 8 9 10 11 12

(second elevation profile)

Hafren Forest
Turn for Dylife
Nantyrhafod
Clywedog Reservoir
Llanidloes

500m
400m
300m
200m
100m

0 miles 1 2 3 4 5 6 7 8 9 10 11 12 13 14

Maps 20 ↔ 25, Llanidloes ↔ Dylife

13¼ miles/21.4km

WELSHPOOL 6-7hrs

KNIGHTON 5½-6½hrs

Note: Add 20-30% to these times for stops

(inset location map)
Welshpool
Dylife
Llanidloes
Knighton

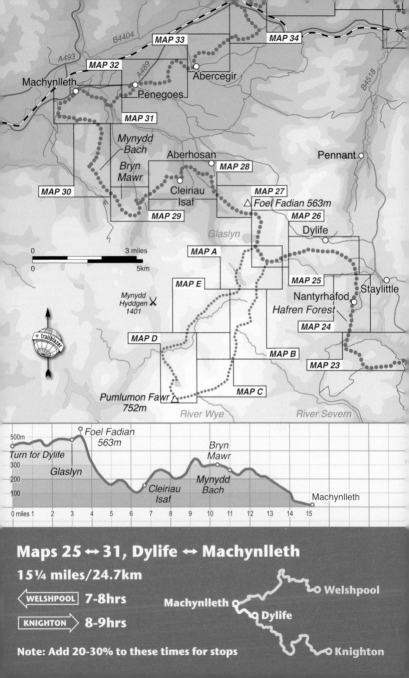

MAP 33
MAP 34

B4404

A493

A489

MAP 32

B4518

Machynlleth

Abercegir

MAP 31

Penegoes

Mynydd Bach

Aberhosan

MAP 28

Pennant

Bryn Mawr

MAP 30

Cleiriau Isaf

MAP 27

△ *Foel Fadian 563m*

MAP 29

MAP 26

Glaslyn

Dylife

0   3 miles
0   5km

MAP A

MAP 25

Mynydd Hyddgen 1401

MAP E

Staylittle

Nantyrhafod

Hafren Forest

★ trailblazer

MAP D

MAP 24

MAP B

MAP C

MAP 23

Pumlumon Fawr 752m △

River Wye

River Severn

500m — *Foel Fadian 563m*

Turn for Dylife

Glaslyn

300

200

100

Cleiriau Isaf

Bryn Mawr

Mynydd Bach

Machynlleth

0 miles 1   2   3   4   5   6   7   8   9   10   11   12   13   14   15

Maps 25 ↔ 31, Dylife ↔ Machynlleth

15¼ miles/24.7km

⟨WELSHPOOL **7-8hrs**

KNIGHTON⟩ **8-9hrs**

Welshpool

Machynlleth ○

○ Dylife

○ Knighton

Note: Add 20-30% to these times for stops

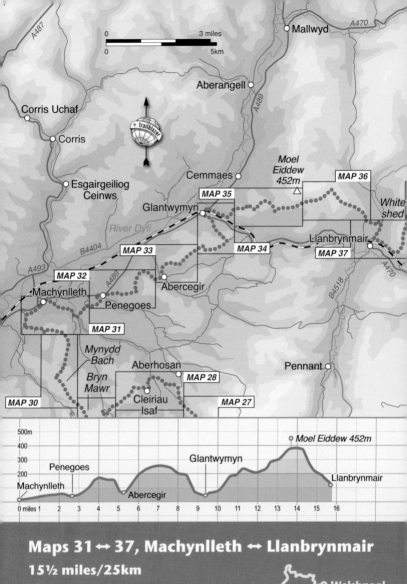

Corris Uchaf

Corris

Esgairgeiliog
Ceinws

Mallwyd

A470

Aberangell

A489

Cemmaes

Moel
Eiddew
452m △

MAP 36

White
shed

MAP 35

Glantwymyn

River Dyfi

B4404

MAP 33

MAP 34

Llanbrynmair

MAP 37

B4518

A470

MAP 32

A489

Abercegir

Machynlleth

Penegoes

MAP 31

Mynydd
Bach

Bryn
Mawr

Aberhosan

MAP 28

Cleiriau
Isaf

Pennant

A493

MAP 30

MAP 27

0   3 miles
0   5km

★ trailblazer

Elevation profile

500m
400
300
200

Moel Eiddew 452m

Penegoes

Glantwymyn

Machynlleth

Abercegir

Llanbrynmair

0 miles 1   2   3   4   5   6   7   8   9   10   11   12   13   14   15   16

Maps 31 ↔ 37, Machynlleth ↔ Llanbrynmair

15½ miles/25km

WELSHPOOL 7½hrs

KNIGHTON 7-8hrs

Welshpool

Machynlleth

Llanbrynmair

Knighton

Note: Add 20-30% to these times for stops

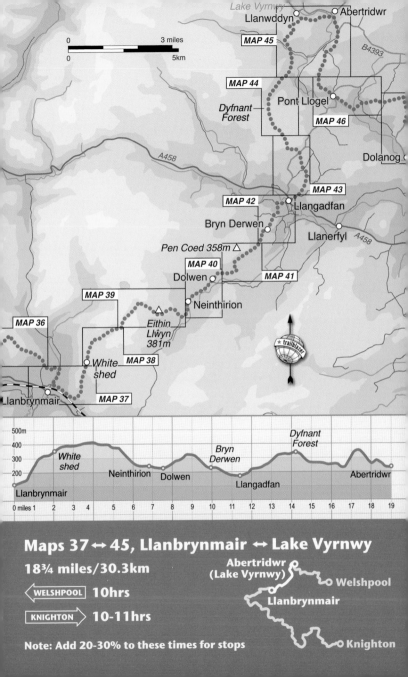

MAP 45

Lake Vyrnwy
Llanwddyn
Abertridwr

B4393

MAP 44

Dyfnant
Forest

Pont Llogel

MAP 46

Dolanog

A458

MAP 43

MAP 42

Llangadfan

Bryn Derwen

Llanerfyl

A458

Pen Coed 358m △

MAP 40

MAP 41

Dolwen

MAP 39

Neinthirion

MAP 36

△
Eithin
Llŵyn
381m

MAP 38

White
shed

MAP 37

Llanbrynmair

0 miles   3 miles
0   5km

★ trailblazer

500m
400
300
200

White
shed

Bryn
Derwen

Dyfnant
Forest

Neinthirion
Dolwen
Llangadfan
Abertridwr

Llanbrynmair

0 miles 1   2   3   4   5   6   7   8   9   10   11   12   13   14   15   16   17   18   19

Maps 37 ↔ 45, Llanbrynmair ↔ Lake Vyrnwy

18¾ miles/30.3km

Abertridwr
(Lake Vyrnwy)   Welshpool

Llanbrynmair

← WELSHPOOL **10hrs**

KNIGHTON → **10-11hrs**   Knighton

Note: Add 20-30% to these times for stops

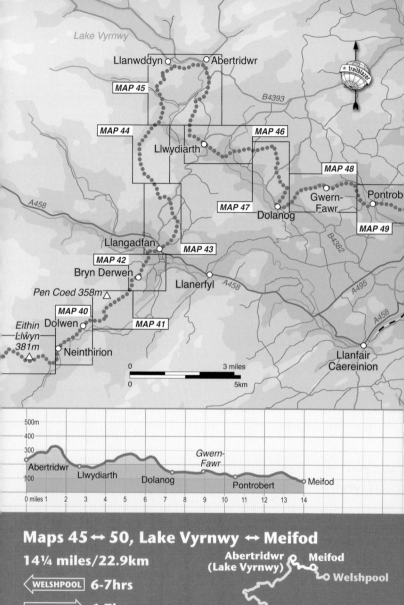

Lake Vyrnwy

Llanwddyn Abertridwr

MAP 45

B4393

MAP 44

Llwydiarth

MAP 46

MAP 48

A458

MAP 47

Gwern-
Fawr

Pontrob

Dolanog

MAP 49

B4382

Llangadfan

MAP 43

MAP 42

Bryn Derwen

Llanerfyl

A458

A495

Pen Coed 358m

MAP 40

Dolwen

MAP 41

A458

Eithin
Llŵyn
381m

Neinthirion

Llanfair
Caereinion

0 ——— 3 miles

0 ——— 5km

500m
400
300
200
100

Abertridwr

Llwydiarth

Dolanog

Gwern-
Fawr

Pontrobert

Meifod

0 miles 1   2   3   4   5   6   7   8   9   10   11   12   13   14

Maps 45 ↔ 50, Lake Vyrnwy ↔ Meifod

14¼ miles/22.9km

Abertridwr
(Lake Vyrnwy)   Meifod

◁ WELSHPOOL   6-7hrs
          Welshpool

KNIGHTON ▷   6-7hrs

Note: Add 20-30% to these times for stops

Knighton

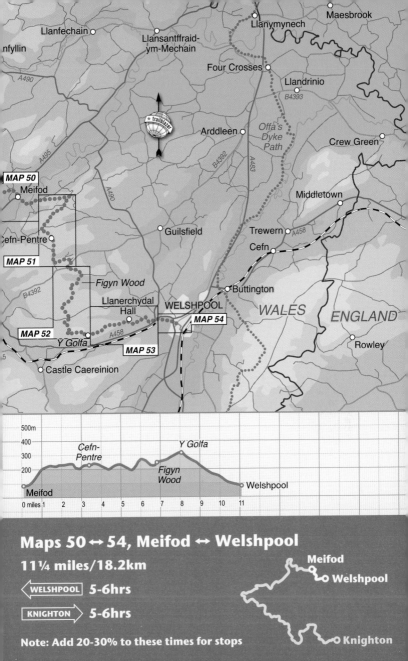

Maps 50 ↔ 54, Meifod ↔ Welshpool

11¼ miles/18.2km

◄ WELSHPOOL 5-6hrs

KNIGHTON ► 5-6hrs

Note: Add 20-30% to these times for stops

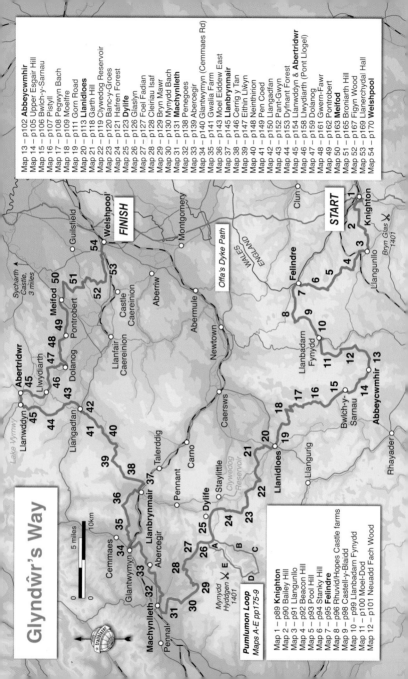

Glyndŵr's Way

START

Knighton

FINISH

Welshpool

Offa's Dyke Path